Metaprogramming in C#

Automate your .NET development and simplify overcomplicated code

Einar Ingebrigtsen

BIRMINGHAM—MUMBAI

Metaprogramming in C#

Copyright © 2023 Packt Publishing

Associate Group Product Manager: Kunal Sawant

Publishing Product Manager: Akash Sharma

Content Development Editor: Rosal Colaco

Technical Editor: Maran Fernandes

Copy Editor: Safis Editing

Project Coordinator: Deeksha Thakkar

Proofreader: Safis Editing

Indexer: Manju Arasan

Production Designer: Shyam Sundar Korumilli

Business Development Executive: Debadrita Chatterjee

Developer Relations Marketing Executives: Rayyan Khan and Sonia Chauhan

First published: June 2023

Production reference: 1090623

Published by Packt Publishing Ltd.
Livery Place
35 Livery Street
Birmingham
B3 2PB, UK.

ISBN 978-1-83763-542-9

www.packtpub.com

Contributors

About the author

Einar Ingebrigtsen works as chief architect at Aksio InsurTech, a company focusing on building insurance and pension solutions. His heart is in architecture and improving the lives of developers and he loves to create solutions that make other developers more productive and help in delivering great products to end users. Einar has been developing software professionally since 1994 and has done so in everything from games on different platforms to broadcast TV software, to telecom software, to line of business software within multiple different verticals. Of all of his experiences, he has fallen in love with a specific flavor of architecture, mindset, and approach – namely, event sourcing. Most of his time at work (and spare time) is devoted to building out a platform that has the goal of democratizing event sourcing called Cratis (`https://cratis.io`).

I want to thank everyone who has been patient with me while writing this book, especially my wife, Anne Grethe, and my two kids, Mia and Herman. It has taken up a lot of my spare time to get this done. I also want to thank everyone at Packt who has been part of the project, giving me pointers and guidance throughout the process. It's been absolutely invaluable.

About the reviewer

Marius Iulian Mihailescu is an associate lecturer at Spiru Haret University and co-founder/chief research officer at Dapyx Solution, Bucharest, Romania. His work is focused on applied/theoretical cryptography and information security, dealing with the identification process of threats and vulnerabilities using artificial intelligence and machine learning. He is currently also working as an IT project manager at the Institute for Computers, Romania, where he is responsible for the development process of several projects.

His research interests are extended to areas such as computer vision, biometrics, machine learning, artificial intelligence, and deep learning. The goal of his research is focused on understanding the real requirements of complex systems (cloud computing, big data, IoT, etc.) and their applications in different domains (such as computer forensics, behavioral psychology, and financial derivatives), and to provide real and practical solutions for guaranteeing the **Confidentiality, Integrity, and Availability (CIA)** of the processes.

Marius completed his Ph.D. studies in computer science on improving the security techniques for guaranteeing the confidentiality and integrity of the biometrics data at the Faculty of Mathematics and Computer Science at the University of Bucharest, Romania. During this time, he was also a part-time research associate for the **ATHOS** (short for, **Automated System of Authentication through Biometric Signature**) project from S.C. Softwin S.R.L., where he worked on improving the load balancing mechanisms in a parallel computing system.

Table of Contents

Preface   xi

Part 1: Why Metaprogramming?

1

How Can Metaprogramming Benefit You?   3

Reasoning about your code	3	Maintaining software	8
Developer concerns	4	Generating code	8
Automation	5	Compile time safety	10
Metaprogramming	5	**Summary**	**11**
Removing manual structure and process	7		

2

Metaprogramming Concepts   13

Technical requirements	**13**	Creating custom attributes	19
Implicit – using what is already there	**14**	**Domain-specific languages**	**21**
Leveraging the power of reflection	15	Gherkin – technical sample	22
Explicit – additional adornment of code	**18**	**Summary**	**24**

3

Demystifying through Existing Real-World Examples   25

Technical requirements	**25**	Prerequisites for your system	26

ASP.NET controllers	26	ASP.NET validation	30
Custom HTTP Get handler	27	Automatically hooking up model state handling	33
Controller	29	Summary	35

Part 2: Leveraging the Runtime

4

Reasoning about Types Using Reflection — 39

Technical requirements	39	Business app	45
Assembly discovery in the running process	40	Discovering types	46
Assembly	40	Back to business	47
		Domain concepts	49
Leveraging library metadata to get project referenced assemblies	41	Cross-cutting concerns	51
		Open/closed principle applied	53
Reusable fundamentals	42	Summary	54

5

Leveraging Attributes — 55

Technical requirements	55	Finding types with specific attributes	60
What is an attribute and how can it be applied?	55	Personal Identifiable Information (PII)	60
		Generic attributes	64
Limiting attribute usage	57	Summary	66
Sealing your attribute class	59		

6

Dynamic Proxy Generation — 67

Technical requirements	67	Virtual members and overrides	74
An introduction to IL and Reflection.Emit	67	Implementing an interface	75
		NotifyObjectWeaver class	77
Creating a dynamic assembly and module	68	Summary	88

7

Reasoning about Expressions   89

Technical requirements	89	Traversing an expression tree	95
What are expressions?	90	Using expressions as descriptors of members on types	98
Expression	92		
Lambda expression	94	Summary	101

8

Building and Executing Expressions   103

Technical requirements	103	Creating a query engine	106
Creating your own expressions	104	A MongoDB-like database	107
Creating expressions as delegates and executing them	105	Building a simple query engine	108
		Summary	115

9

Taking Advantage of the Dynamic Language Runtime   117

Technical requirements	117	Reasoning about a dynamic type	121
Understanding the DLR	118	Creating DynamicObject and providing metadata	124
The CLR at a glance	118		
The DLR building blocks	119	Building a JSON schema type	125
Call sites and binders	121	Summary	133

Part 3: Increasing Productivity, Consistency, and Quality

10

Convention over Configuration   137

Technical requirements	137	Inversion of control and its role	138

Refactoring the code   143   Further refactoring   150

Automatic ServiceCollection   Composing   154

registrations by convention   149   Summary   158

11

Applying the Open-Closed Principle   161

Technical requirements   162   Practical use case   167

Encapsulating type discovery   163   Helping the developer   170

Encapsulating the discovery of   Supporting properties   172

instances   165   Using the GDPR infrastructure   174

Hooking up with the service collection   166   Adding more providers   178

                                                   Summary   180

12

Go Beyond Inheritance   181

Technical requirements   181   Using the infrastructure   194

Method signature conventions   181   Summary   198

Infrastructure   185

13

Applying Cross-Cutting Concerns   199

Technical requirements   199   CommandResult   203

What are cross-cutting concerns?   200   Authorization based on metadata or

Leveraging the ASP.NET pipeline   201   structure   212

Building consistent result objects   201   Summary   223

14

Aspect-Oriented Programming   225

Technical requirements   225   What is AOP?   225

Aspects   226
Pointcuts   226
Join points   227

Logging   228
Creating a logging sample   229
Adding the Microsoft logger   230

Interceptors   232

Trying out the interceptor   235

Mixins   238
Mixing it up   239

Authorization   245
Using pointcuts   246

Summary   252

Part 4: Compiler Magic Using Roslyn

15

Roslyn Compiler Extensions   255

Technical requirements   255
How to set up a project and its
moving parts   255
What can they do?   256
Setting it up   257
Adding common rules   259

Common project settings   261

How to package your extension for
reuse   263
Common package properties   264
Analyzer   265

Summary   267

16

Generating Code   269

Technical requirements   270
Generating additional code for the
Roslyn compiler   270
ASTs   270
Application metrics   271
Improving the developer experience   275

(Ab)using the compiler to generate

not just C# code   288
Building the generator   289

Improving the developer experience   294
Debugging   294
Optimization   295

Summary   295

17

Static Code Analysis   297

Technical requirements	298	Trying out the analyzer	305
What is static code analysis?	298	How to write a code fix for an analyzer	307
How to write an analyzer	299	How to write automated tests	310
Fleshing out an analyzer	299	Analyzer tests	311
Handling the syntax nodes	302	Code fix tests	313
Release tracking	303	Summary	315

18

Caveats and Final Words   317

Performance implications	317	When to use what	319
Hidden magic – handle with care	318	Summary	320

Index   321

Other Books You May Enjoy   330

Preface

"Always code as if the guy who ends up maintaining your code will be a violent psychopath who knows where you live."

– Martin Golding

In the world of software, there are so many things that can go wrong and often do go wrong. We're a relatively young industry that is in an ever-changing state. Things haven't settled and innovation happens at lightning speed. It's not like carpentry, which has had a few thousand years of experience of what works and what doesn't. In software, we're still inventing the tools and reinventing them as we go. The business benefit and the possibility to increase productivity for our end users sets the expectations high and in an increasingly competitive market, time to market is of the essence.

At the level we write our software today, we have a huge potential to leverage the metadata surrounding our own code to ensure the quality and maintainability of the software we write. This is where the metaprogramming journey starts.

Metaprogramming can be really fun to work with, but it represents true opportunities for developers and businesses to set themselves apart. Things that metaprogramming can do for you include the following:

- Improve the maintainability of your code

- Automate tedious tasks

- Let developers focus more on your business and not the plumbing

- Help you stay more compliant

- Reduce risk related to security

There are technical reasons to dive into metaprogramming, as with any other technique, but I think there is true value to be discovered in leveraging it to help you and your team become more productive and, at the end of the day, deliver more business-critical features that are easier to change and maintain over the years.

Who this book is for

The book is for any C# developer who is curious about metaprogramming and what it could do for you. More specifically, the following personas are the target audience:

- Developers who are familiar with C# and .NET as a runtime looking to expand their horizons and learn in more depth about the .NET runtime and compiler capabilities

- Software architects familiar with C# and .NET and looking for inspiration on how to improve their architecture

- CTOs or development managers with either a developer background or who understand software development and want inspiration to potentially grease the wheels of the developer organization

What this book covers

Chapter 1, How Can Metaprogramming Benefit You?, dives into what metaprogramming is and how it can improve developers' day-to-day work. It gives some concrete basic examples to explain its capabilities.

Chapter 2, Metaprogramming Concepts, provides explanations of the differences between implicit and explicit metadata through concrete examples. In addition, it gives an insight into how the .NET runtime works.

Chapter 3, Demystifying through Existing Real-World Examples, shows how Microsoft, as an example, leverages metaprogramming and how you probably already use it.

Chapter 4, Reasoning about Types Using Reflection, provides an overview of how powerful the .NET runtime reflection is and how its implicit metadata can be leveraged.

Chapter 5, Leveraging Attributes, introduces leveraging C# attributes as an explicit metaprogramming technique and how it can be used, giving real-world applicable examples.

Chapter 6, Dynamic Proxy Generation, introduces code that generates code, at runtime. A powerful concept that can really boost your developers' productivity if used wisely.

Chapter 7, Reasoning about Expressions, provides an introduction to C# and .NET expression trees, how they represent a different aspect of metadata, and how they can be reasoned about and unpacked in your code.

Chapter 8, Building and Executing Expressions, provides an introduction to how you can build your own expressions at runtime and how these can be executed – an alternative technique to generating code.

Chapter 9, Taking Advantage of the Dynamic Language Runtime, covers what the Dynamic Language Runtime is and how it can be used to dynamically generate code – yet another alternative for your code is to create code.

Chapter 10, Convention over Configuration, unravels the superpower of conventions – code that repeats the patterns you probably already have, enabling your developers to become more productive and your code base to become more consistent.

Chapter 11, Applying the Open-Closed Principle, provides a dive into how you can create code bases that are open to extension but closed for modification – a powerful principle for maintainable software, using metaprogramming as an angle into it.

Chapter 12, Go Beyond Inheritance, provides another level on top of regular conventions, giving developers an opportunity to not just be limited by what the programming language offers, aiming for readability and maintainability.

Chapter 13, Applying Cross-Cutting Concerns, unlocks the concept of applying code consistently across an entire code base without having to revert to manual recipes.

Chapter 14, Aspect-Oriented Programming, provides details on the formalization of aspect-oriented programming and how this can help you provide cross-cutting concerns as a more formal technique.

Chapter 15, Roslyn Compiler Extensions, details the basics of what the .NET compiler SDK offers and how to get started with it, serving as the basis for the following chapters.

Chapter 16, Generating Code, provides an introduction to how you can generate code using code at the compiler level before you enter runtime – yet another great way to improve your developers' productivity and provide consistency in your code base.

Chapter 17, Static Code Analysis, provides an introduction to how you can build your own rules that perform analysis on any code being added to your project, helping you create consistent, uniform, and more maintainable code.

Chapter 18, Caveats and Final Words, looks into what the book has covered, what benefits there are, and what caveats there are. As with anything, you have to strike the right balance and know what to use when.

To get the most out of this book

Software/hardware covered in the book	Operating system requirements
C# using .NET 7	Windows, macOS, or Linux
Postman	Windows, macOS, or Linux
MongoDB	Windows, macOS, or Linux

If you are using the digital version of this book, we advise you to type the code yourself or access the code from the book's GitHub repository (a link is available in the next section). Doing so will help you avoid any potential errors related to the copying and pasting of code.

Download the example code files

You can download the example code files for this book from GitHub at `https://github.com/PacktPublishing/Metaprogramming-in-C-Sharp`. If there's an update to the code, it will be updated in the GitHub repository.

We also have other code bundles from our rich catalog of books and videos available at `https://github.com/PacktPublishing/`. Check them out!

Download the color images

We also provide a PDF file that has color images of the screenshots and diagrams used in this book. You can download it here: `https://packt.link/nZUlx`.

Conventions used

There are a number of text conventions used throughout this book.

`Code in text`: Indicates code words in text, database table names, folder names, filenames, file extensions, pathnames, dummy URLs, user input, and Twitter handles. Here is an example: "The provider looks for `ConfidentialAttribute` to decide whether it can provide."

A block of code is set as follows:

```
namespace Fundamentals.Compliance;
public interface ICanProvideComplianceMetadataForType
{
  bool CanProvide(Type type);
  ComplianceMetadata Provide(Type type);
}
```

Any command-line input or output is written as follows:

```
Checking type for compliance rules: Chapter11.Patient
Property: FirstName - Employment records
Property: LastName - Employment records
Property: SocialSecurityNumber - Uniquely identifies the employee
Property JournalEntries is a collection of type Chapter11.JournalEntry
with type level metadata
```

Bold: Indicates a new term, an important word, or words that you see onscreen. For instance, words in menus or dialog boxes appear in **bold**. Here is an example: "Then select **JSON** in the **Body** tab, add an empty JSON document, and click **Send**."

> **Tips or important notes**
> Appear like this.

Get in touch

Feedback from our readers is always welcome.

General feedback: If you have questions about any aspect of this book, email us at `customercare@packtpub.com` and mention the book title in the subject of your message.

Errata: Although we have taken every care to ensure the accuracy of our content, mistakes do happen. If you have found a mistake in this book, we would be grateful if you would report this to us. Please visit `www.packtpub.com/support/errata` and fill in the form.

Piracy: If you come across any illegal copies of our works in any form on the internet, we would be grateful if you would provide us with the location address or website name. Please contact us at copyright@packt.com with a link to the material.

If you are interested in becoming an author: If there is a topic that you have expertise in and you are interested in either writing or contributing to a book, please visit authors.packtpub.com.

Share Your Thoughts

Once you've read *Metaprogramming in C#*, we'd love to hear your thoughts! Scan the QR code below to go straight to the Amazon review page for this book and share your feedback.

https://packt.link/r/1-837-63542-0

Your review is important to us and the tech community and will help us make sure we're delivering excellent quality content.

Download a free PDF copy of this book

Thanks for purchasing this book!

Do you like to read on the go but are unable to carry your print books everywhere? Is your eBook purchase not compatible with the device of your choice?

Don't worry, now with every Packt book you get a DRM-free PDF version of that book at no cost.

Read anywhere, any place, on any device. Search, copy, and paste code from your favorite technical books directly into your application.

The perks don't stop there, you can get exclusive access to discounts, newsletters, and great free content in your inbox daily

Follow these simple steps to get the benefits:

1. Scan the QR code or visit the link below

https://packt.link/free-ebook/9781837635429

2. Submit your proof of purchase
3. That's it! We'll send your free PDF and other benefits to your email directly

Part 1:
Why Metaprogramming?

In this part, you will get an introduction to what metaprogramming is, its benefits, and ideas of how you can leverage it through real-world examples. You'll also see how you are most likely already using it, directly or indirectly, and how to get some quick wins and early benefits.

This part has the following chapters:

- *Chapter 1, How Can Metaprogramming Benefit You?*
- *Chapter 2, Metaprogramming Concepts*
- *Chapter 3, Demystifying through Existing Real-World Examples*

1

How Can Metaprogramming Benefit You?

So, what is **metaprogramming** and why should you care? If you picked up this book hoping to learn about programming in the **metaverse**, you're about to become very disappointed.

Metaprogramming is all about code treating other code as data. This could be just to understand and reason about the code, or actually create new code based on metadata implicitly through structure or explicitly added.

"But why should I care about that," you might ask? "Isn't it just enough to write the code and get it shipped?" In this chapter, we will look into the concrete benefits you can get from doing metaprogramming and how it can benefit you daily. We will also provide tips on how it can increase productivity and remove tedious tasks we developers tend to have to do.

The main objective of this chapter is to introduce you to metaprogramming and examples of use cases. In doing this, we'll see some of the building blocks .NET has for metaprogramming. In this chapter, we'll cover the following topics:

- Reasoning about your code
- Removing manual structures and processes

By the end of this chapter, you should have some good ideas and inspiration for how metaprogramming can benefit you. You should have also gained insight into what metaprogramming is all about.

Reasoning about your code

The software industry is very young. In the last 20-30 years, we've seen a dramatic increase in its usage.

Today, software is engraved into every aspect of our lives – our work, our transportation, and in our homes, down to the smart light bulbs many of us have installed.

With the breadth of applications and users using the software we make, there are expectations from the software. Users today expect far more from software than they did 20 years ago. And since software is so engraved in our lives, we are far more vulnerable, which makes it a risk factor.

In this section, we'll discuss why you, as a developer, should care about metaprogramming. We'll go through the developer concerns, how we can do some nifty automation, and cover some of the basics around metaprogramming.

Developer concerns

For us developers, we have a lot of different aspects to cover to guarantee the success of our software.

End users have high expectations of great user experiences, and they expect to be put in the pit of success. We also need to be empathetic to the different types of users our system will have and make sure it is accessible to everyone.

Our systems need to maintain the integrity of their data and help the end users do the right thing. To do this, we need to validate all the input according to what we expect or what our data model requires. In addition, we need to have business rules that enforce the integrity of the system.

The data is also something we want to protect, so security plays an important role. Users need to be authenticated and we also want to make sure the user has the correct authorization to perform the different tasks of the system.

We must also make sure that our systems don't have security flaws that would allow hackers to breach the system. The input from users also needs to be sanitized, to prevent malicious attacks through things such as **SQL injection**.

For our software to be available to our users, we need to have it running somewhere, on an on-premises server or servers with a hosting partner, or in the cloud, be it physical or virtual. This means we need to think about how we package the software and then how we get it onto the running environment.

Once it is running, we have to make sure it runs all the time and doesn't have any downtime; our users rely on it. For this, we want to consider having more than one instance of the system running so that it can fail over to a second instance if the primary one goes down.

We also need to make sure that the environment it is running in can handle the number of users it is targeting.

Instead of just having a fail-over instance, we can scale out horizontally and have a load balancing mechanism spreading the users across the different instances we have. This makes our system a distributed system.

Those are a lot of different concerns. Ideally, you want to have different people doing different aspects of the job, but this is not always the case (depending on the size of the organization, as well as its culture). Today, you'll often see in job ads that companies are looking for *full stack developers*. In many cases, this could mean the expectations are that you need to work with all of the following aspects:

- **User experience**: This is all about the interaction, flows, and how it all feels
- **Accessibility**: This involves creating empathetic software that is accessible to those with disabilities
- **Frontend code**: This is the layout, styling, and necessary logic to make the user experience come to life
- **Backend code**: This is for creating the glue that represents the domain we're working in
- **Data modeling**: This is how we store the data and model it for the usage we need
- **Authentication and authorization**: This is for making sure users are authenticated and the proper authorization policies are applied to the different features
- **Security**: This makes the application robust from any attacks and protects the data
- **DevOps**: This involves delivering features to production in a timely fashion without any ceremony

Automation

Being humans, we make mistakes and we forget things. Sometimes, this has some really bad outcomes, such as systems going down, or worse, such as being breached by hackers.

Luckily, computers are good at doing what they're told and repeating it endlessly. They never complain and don't make mistakes. This means there are great opportunities for streamlining a lot of our work. As the industry has matured over the years, we have seen improved workflows and tooling that can help us achieve what we aim to achieve, often taking away tedious and time-consuming tasks.

A great example of automation is what has happened in the last decade in cloud computing. Before this, we had to set up physical hardware and often had manual routines for getting our software onto that hardware. This has completely changed into us being able to spin up anything our hearts desire with a few clicks, connect it to some continuous deployment software that will build our software, and automatically get it onto the running environment. All this can be achieved in minutes, rather than hours or days.

Metaprogramming

Where am I going with all this? Wasn't this book supposed to be about something called metaprogramming?

Metaprogramming is all about additional information surrounding your code. This information is sometimes implicit – that is, it's already there. Sometimes, however, it needs to be added explicitly or deliberately by you, as a developer.

The computer that runs the software only understands the machine language instructions laid out in memory for the CPU to execute. For us humans, this is less than intuitive. Early on, we came up with languages that would help us write something more friendly and we could reason about more easily. This started with the **assembly language** and, later, higher-level languages that would compile down to assembly language.

With this tooling in place, we gained the ability to not just translate from one language into another, but also to reason about what was going on with our code. In 1978, Stephen C. Johnson, from Bell Labs, came up with what he called **lint** – a static code analysis tool that could be used to reason about C code and detect potential issues with it. Today, this is common with most programming languages. For web development in **JavaScript** or **TypeScript**, we could typically add tools such as **ESLint** to our build pipelines to do this. With **C#**, we have this built into the compiler, and with the Roslyn compiler, it is completely extensible with our own custom rules, something we will cover in *Chapter 17, Static Code Analysis*.

For programming languages such as **C/C++** that compile down to something that runs natively on the CPU, we're limited to what we can reason about at the compile level. However, with programming languages such as Java or C#, often referred to as managed languages, we're now running code in a managed environment. The code we write compiles down to an intermediate language that will be translated on the fly while running. These languages then carry information with them about the code we wrote – this is known as **metadata**. This lets us treat our programs or others as data at runtime and allows us to reason about the code; we can even discover code at runtime.

With C#, from *version 1*, we could add additional information and more metadata. Through the use of C# **attributes**, we could adorn things such as types, properties on types, and methods with additional information. This information would carry through to the running program and is something we can use to reason about our software.

For instance, with attributes, we can now add additional information that we can reason about both at compile time and runtime. We can do things such as marking properties on an object with validation information, such as [Required]:

```
public class RegisterPerson
{
    [Required]
    public string FirstName { get; set; }

    [Required]
    public string LastName { get; set; }

    [Required]
    public string SocialSecurityNumber { get; set; }
}
```

This code represents what is needed to register a person. All the properties that we required have the [Required] attribute as metadata.

Now that we have added metadata to the code, we can take concrete actions based on it.

Removing manual structure and process

Adding explicit metadata is great for visibility and makes it very explicit in the code for the type of metadata that has been added. However, this metadata is not actionable on its own. This means that there is nothing that will inherently deal with it – for instance, a property is required, as we've seen.

This metadata gives us the power to not only reason about the metadata surrounding our code but put it into action. We can build our systems in a way that leverages this information to make decisions for us, or we could automate tedious tasks.

One of the most common things I've seen throughout my career is what I call **recipe-driven development**. Code bases tend to settle on a certain structure and a certain set of things developers need to do when creating features in it. These *recipes* are then often written down as a part of the documentation for the code base and something everyone has to read and make sure they follow. This is not necessarily a bad thing, and I think all code bases have this to some degree.

Taking a step back, there might be some potential to improve our productivity and have to write less code. The recipes and patterns could be formalized and automated. The main reason for doing so is that following recipes can be error-prone. We can forget to do something or do it wrong or maybe even mix up the ordering of steps.

Imagine that you have an API and that for every action, you have the following recipe:

- Check if the user is authorized
- Check if all the input is valid
- Check for malicious input (for example, SQL injection)
- Check if the action is allowed by the domain logic, typically business-specific rules
- Perform the business logic
- Return the correct HTTP status code and result, depending on whether or not we're successful

Those are a lot of concerns mixed into one place. At this point, you're probably thinking that this is not how we do things in modern **ASP.NET** API development. And that is correct – they are typically split into concerns and things such as the SQL injection handled by the pipeline.

> **Important note**
> We'll revisit how ASP.NET leverages metaprogramming to make the developer experience it offers in *Chapter 3, Demystifying through Existing Real-World Examples*.

Even though these things might not be in the same method and spread out, they are still concerns we have to be aware of, and a recipe would then still state that these things would need to be done. Often, they are repetitive and could potentially be optimized for an improved developer experience and also reduce the risk of fatal errors in the system.

Maintaining software

Another aspect of this type of repetitive code is that all code we add to our system is code we need to maintain. Building out a feature might not take that long, but chances are the code needs to be maintained for years to come. It might not be maintained by you, but by others on the team or a successor to you. So, we should be optimizing our code bases for maintenance first. Getting features out the door in a timely fashion is expected of us, but if we don't consider the maintenance of the code, we, as the owners of the code, will suffer when it needs to be maintained.

Maintenance is not just about keeping the code working and delivering on its promise. It's also about its ability to change and adapt to new requirements, whether business or technical. The very beginning of a project is when you know the least about it.

So, planning for this is super hard and would require us to be able to predict the future. But we can write our code in a way that would make it more adaptable to change.

Instead of repeating all this code all over the place, we could put metadata into our code that we could leverage. This is typically what ASP.NET supports – for instance, for authorization with the [Authorize] attribute for controllers. It would require a specific policy to be fulfilled, such as the user having to be in a role. If our system has a deliberate structure for our features, you might find natural groupings of features belonging to specific roles. We could then reason about this structure by looking at the namespace metadata on the type and putting in the correct authorization rules. For developers, you replaced the need for an explicit piece of information and made it implicit through the structure. This may seem like a small thing, but throughout the lifetime of the code base, this type of mindset can have a huge impact on productivity and maintainability.

Generating code

With C#, we can go even further than just reasoning about code and making decisions based on what we find – we can generate code. Code generation can take place at compile time if we have all the information we need or are pushed to the runtime level. This opens up a lot more flexibility and gives us a vast amount of power.

As an example, if you've ever worked with XAML-based frontend technology such as **Windows Presentation Foundation** (**WPF**) or **Universal Windows Platform** (**UWP**) and have used data binding, you have probably come across the INotifyPropertyChanged interface. Its purpose is to enable the view controls so that you're notified when the value of a property has changed on an instance of an object in the view to which it is bound.

Let's say you have an object representing a person:

```
public class Person
{
    public string FirstName { get; set; }
    public string LastName { get; set; }
}
```

Now, let's say we want to make this notification appear whenever one of the properties changes. Using the INotifyPropertyChanged interface for binding purposes, the object would need to expand into the following:

```csharp
public class Person : INotifyPropertyChanged
{
    private string _firstName;
    public string FirstName
    {
        get { return _firstName; }
        set
        {
            _name = value;
            RaisePropertyChanged("FirstName");
        }
    }

    public string LastName { get; set; }
    public event PropertyChangedEventHandler
      PropertyChanged;
    protected void RaisePropertyChanged(string
      propertyName)
    {
        if (PropertyChanged != null)
        {
            PropertyChanged(this, new
                PropertyChangedEventArgs(propertyName));
        }
    }
}
```

As you can see, creating a property is now very tedious. Imagine having all the properties of an object do this. This easily becomes code that is hard to read, and there's more code to maintain, and it's not adding any business value to your code.

This can be improved upon thanks to the latest version of the C# compiler.

Microsoft rewrote the C# compiler a few years back. The compiler was given the name Roslyn. There were a couple of reasons they rewrote the compiler, with one being that they wanted to have the compiler itself be written in C# – a proof of the maturity of the language and the .NET runtime Also, as part of the move from Microsoft to open source, having a rewrite and doing it in the open and leaving the old license model behind made more sense. But the most important reason in my opinion was to make it more extensible, and not just for Microsoft themselves, but everyone.

Part of this extensibility is what is called Roslyn code generation. With it, we could go and make this code very close to the original. Let's imagine we introduce some metadata in the form of an [Bindable] attribute and we create a compiler extension that makes all private fields into properties that are needed for InotifyPropertyChanged. Here, our object would look like this:

```
[Bindable]
public class Person
{
    private string _firstName;
    private string _lastName;
}
```

We could also do this at runtime. However, at runtime, we are limited to what has been compiled and can't change the type. So, the approach would be slightly different. Instead of changing the existing type, we would need to create a new type that inherits from the original type and then extend it. This would require us to make the original properties virtual for us to override them in a generated type:

```
[Bindable]
public class Person
{
    public virtual string FirstName { get; set; }
    public virtual string LastName { get; set; }
}
```

For this to work, we would need a factory that knows how to create these objects. We would call this when we needed an instance of it.

With great power also comes great responsibility, and it needs to be a very deliberate choice to go down this path. We'll cover this in *Chapter 18, Caveats and Final Words*.

We will cover the Roslyn extensibility in more depth in *Chapter 15, Roslyn Compiler Extensions*.

Compile time safety

There are also times when we must add certain metadata for the system to work. This is a candidate for writing a code analyzer for the Roslyn compiler. The analyzer would figure out what's missing and let the developer know as soon as possible, providing a tight feedback loop rather than the developer having to discover the problem at runtime.

An example of this is in a platform I work on called **Cratis** (https://cratis.io), an event sourcing platform. For all the events being persisted, we require a unique identifier that represents the type of event. This is added as an attribute for the event:

```
[EventType("66f58b90-c027-41b3-aa2c-2cfd18e7db69")]
public record PersonRegistered(string FirstName, string LastName);
```

When calling the `Append()` method on the event log, the type has to be associated with the unique identifier. If there is no association between an event type and the .NET type, the `Append()` method will throw an exception. This is a great opportunity to perform a compile-time check of anything being sent to the `Append()` method and to check whether or not the type of the object has the `[EventType]` attribute.

We will revisit all this in *Chapter 17, Static Code Analysis*.

Summary

Hopefully, you now know of the great potential of metaprogramming. It is very powerful. This comes with great responsibility – the balance of code you don't see that magically gets added either at compile time or runtime versus the explicitness in every code file is a hard one. From my experience, new developers coming into a code base with a lot of implicit automation can run into trouble and might end up not trusting the magic.

But after a while, once they get used to it, they tend to want more magic. The benefits are clear once you have experience with them, but it might be a bit scary at first. To remedy this, you should communicate the automation you have. That will at least make it adhere more to the *principle of least surprise*.

In the next chapter, we will dive into more concrete concepts of metaprogramming and look at what's behind the concepts. We'll become familiar with how the .NET runtime sees code and the metadata it produces and how this can be leveraged in a running application. Finally, we'll learn how to extend this metadata.

2

Metaprogramming Concepts

Now that we have a few ideas about how metaprogramming can benefit you, we need to cover the basic concepts.

When working with metaprogramming, you get metadata for free from the environment it's running in, and there is the opportunity to explicitly add more. With explicitness, you can enable clarity in your code base, and a level of transparency for the developers writing and reading the code.

Some parts of your source code will benefit from more explicit metadata rather than having it implicitly and just magically do things that can be hard for developers to reason about why.

With explicitness also comes the possibility of representing the domain language of your business in code and with increasing expressiveness.

In this chapter, we will be covering the following topics:

- Implicit – using what is already there
- Explicit – additional adornment of code
- Domain-specific languages

By the end of the chapter, you should have a good feel for the different metaprogramming concepts you can leverage, when to use which concept, and the benefits of each concept.

Technical requirements

You can find all the source code used in this chapter in the GitHub repository: `https://github.com/PacktPublishing/Metaprogramming-in-C-Sharp/tree/main/Chapter2`.

Implicit – using what is already there

The compiler that compiles **C#** parses all our code and ends up creating what is referred to as **IL-code**, short for **Intermediate Language code**. This is standardized and part of the **ECMA-335** standard for the Common Language Infrastructure. You can read more about the standard here: https://www. ecma-international.org/publications-and-standards/standards/ecma-335/. This type of code is not something that the CPU in the system understands and it requires another step for the CPU to understand it. The last step of translation is done when we run our programs and the **.NET runtime** takes over, interprets the IL, and generates the necessary instructions for the CPU type of the computer the program is running on.

Looking at the binary output, you can't necessarily tell the difference. But by opening up the binary using a decompiler tool such as **ildasm**, or something more visual, such as **JetBrains dotPeek** (https:// www.jetbrains.com/decompiler/), we can get a glimpse at what our programs look like.

Take, for instance, the following program:

```
using System;

public class Program
{
    public static void Main()
    {
        Console.WriteLine("Hello world!");
    }
}
```

Compiling this will produce a **Dynamic Link Library** (**DLL**) file, and on opening the file with a decompiler, we would see something like this:

```
.class private auto ansi '<Module>'
{
}
.class public auto ansi beforefieldinit Program
    extends [System.Runtime]System.Object
{

    .method public hidebysig static
        void Main () cil managed
    {           .maxstack 8

        IL_0000: ldstr "Hello world!"
```

```
        IL_0005: call void [System.Console]System.
            Console::WriteLine(string)
        IL_000a: ret
    }
    .method public hidebysig specialname rtspecialname
        instance void .ctor () cil managed
    {
        .maxstack 8

        IL_0000: ldarg.0
        IL_0001: call instance void [System.Runtime]System.
            Object::.ctor()
        IL_0006: ret
    }
}
```

On an x86/AMD64-based CPU, this then gets translated into something like the following disassembled code:

```
L0000: mov rcx, 0x2217fb34a50
L000a: mov rcx, [rcx]
L000d: jmp 0x00007ffef72f2fc8
```

The actual `Hello world!` string is then placed in memory at the location used by the first `mov` instruction. If you're interested in trying out code and seeing how it translates yourself, I recommend heading over to `https://sharplab.io`.

In the finished compiled result, there is actually no metadata whatsoever, making it impossible to reason about our code in any meaningful way.

While the IL contains everything we wrote, all the type information is intact (type names, method names, and so forth).

With that, we are being set up for success to do some proper metaprogramming.

Leveraging the power of reflection

All this information is available to us, and it all starts with the powerful, and my personal favorite, namespace called `System.Reflection`. This holds all the C# types representing the different code elements we write. Since C# is a managed language running on top of the managed runtime, we get all the details about all the code we write.

Since every type we have created and will create is inherent of the Object type, every derived type inherently gets its methods and properties. One of these methods is called GetType(). This method returns an instance of the type of the object in the form of Type. It holds all the details about the particular type – everything from what namespace it resides in, to fields, properties, methods on it, and much more. For the type, we can even look at what it is inheriting and what interfaces it might implement. We can even see which assembly (DLL) it is defined in.

If you look at object-relational mappers such as **Microsoft's Entity Framework, Dapper, NHibernate**, or even the **MongoDB C# Driver**, they all use reflection to reason about the types you have to translate into something expected by the underlying data store. For a relational store, it would typically translate into the correct **SQL** statements, while for MongoDB, it would be the correct MongoDB **Binary JSON** (**BSON**) objects.

The same is done by things that serialize from .NET types to other formats, such as JSON. Libraries such as Newtonsoft.JSON or the built-in System.Text.Json namespace leverages reflection to know what to translate.

Let's say you have a Person type:

```
public class Person
{
    public string FirstName { get; set; }
    public string LastName { get; set; }
    public string SocialSecurityNumber { get; set; }
}
```

An extremely simplistic conversion to JSON could easily be done:

```
public string SerializeToJson(object instance)
{
    var stringBuilder = new StringBuilder();
    var type = instance.GetType();
    var properties = type.GetProperties();
    Var first = true;

    stringBuilder.Append("{\n");

    foreach( var property in properties )
    {
        if (!first)
        {
```

```
            StringBuilder.Append(",\n");
        }
        stringBuilder.Append($"    \"{property.Name}\":
          \"{property.GetValue(instance)}\"");
    }

    stringBuilder.Append("\n}");
}
```

This can then be used as follows:

```
var person = new Person
{
    FirstName = "Jane",
    LastName = "Doe",
    SocialSecurityNumber = "12345abcd"
};
Console.WriteLine(Serializer.SerializeToJson(person));
```

The output of running this would yield some nice JSON:

```
{
    "FirstName": "Jane",
    "LastName": "Doe",
    "SocialSecurityNumber": "12345abcd"
}
```

The code basically gets the type information from the instance and gets the properties on it. It outputs a string containing the property name and leverages `PropertyInfo` to get a value from the instance and just outputs its `.ToString()` representation.

Obviously, this sample is very simple and non-recursive for complex types or support arrays and doesn't recognize well-known JSON primitive types. But this proves how easily you can get to the information.

Implicit metadata and the type system of .NET can be very powerful. The further down the rabbit hole you go with reflection, the more you'll probably feel like going further and doing more. The flip side of that is for everything you do automatically, you lose the transparency of what's going on. It needs to be balanced and be as close to the element of least surprise as possible.

For some things, you're better off going with being very explicit. There is also metadata that can't be discovered with what the compiler generates, and the only way to go is to be very explicit.

Explicit – additional adornment of code

Pretty much all code elements can have additional information added to them. These are called **attributes**. Attributes are a powerful method of associating metadata with the element. Within the .NET framework itself, you'll see quite a few of these attribute types that can be used.

In the `System.ComponentModel.DataAnnotations` namespace, you can find some great examples of attributes that add metadata used by the runtime. Here, you'll find attributes used for adding validation metadata. ASP.NET picks up the usage of these attributes and checks objects being sent to controller actions for validity according to the rules applied. As we saw briefly in *Chapter 1, How Can Metaprogramming Benefit You?*, with our `RegisterPerson` type, we could instruct properties that should be required. It contains much more, for instance, `[StringLength]` and `[Range]`. These are great examples of metadata recognized by the framework and components that support them.

Some attributes in the framework are recognized by the compiler and will direct the compiler to perform certain things. For instance, the `[Flags]` attribute can be added to enums that instruct it to require every value to represent a bit field:

```
[Flags]
public enum MyEnum
{
    Flag1 = 1,
    Flag2 = 1 << 1,
    Flag3 = 1 << 2,
    Flag4 = 1 << 3
}
```

With this type of enum, we define flags, with each flag being a left bitwise shift for the number of places to move to represent the correct bit. You can also do this by giving the actual decimal or hexadecimal number of the bit (1, 2, 4, or 8, or 0x1, 0x2, 0x4, 0x8, 0x10, and so on).

The `System.Text.Json` serializer also makes use of metadata. It uses metadata to know how to serialize or deserialize what it is given. For instance, it can ignore properties in an object:

```
public class Person
{
    public string FirstName { get; set; }
    public string LastName { get; set; }

    [JsonIgnore]
    public string FullName => $"{FirstName} {LastName}";
```

```
    public string SocialSecurityNumber { get; set; }
}
```

Serializing an instance of this would leave out `FullName`.

Creating custom attributes

You can easily create your own custom attributes by adding the metadata you want for your code. All attributes can take arguments with the extra metadata you want to have associated with them. This gives you the opportunity to be very specific on what data you want to associate as metadata with the code element being adorned.

All of the metadata added to an attribute needs to be resolvable by the compiler at compile time. That limits us to only have things that are typical primitive types and constant in nature. You can't dynamically create instances of things to pass into an attribute.

An example of an attribute could, for instance, be for describing types or properties that hold **personal identifiable information** (**PII**). This can be very useful to be able to later reason about your code, to know what PII is being collected about users, which can be presented to the user themselves. With the European Union privacy law called **GDPR**, it could also be used as a reporting mechanism if your company is audited or have a GDPR-related incident and need to report it to the authorities.

A huge benefit, once you have tagged types and properties with this metadata, is that you get an opportunity for future use cases – for example, the encryption of PII data or anything else.

Creating a custom attribute is in its basic form as follows:

```
public class PersonalIdentifiableInformationAttribute :
Attribute
{
}
```

The `PersonalIdentifiableInformationAttribute` type needs to inherit the base `Attribute` type. The compiler also expects the type you create to be suffixed with `Attribute` as part of the name. However, when using your custom attribute, you can then leave out `Attribute` in the name, the compiler will map this to the full name with the suffix added to it.

The next thing you need to specify is actually a bit of metadata for the compiler. This is done using the `[AttributeUsage]` attribute. With this, we need to specify what target code elements are supported, and we can support multiple by *ORing* (the OR operation) them together.

For `PersonalIdentifiableInformationAttribute`, we'd typically want this for classes, properties, and fields:

```
[AttributeUsage(AttributeTargets.Class | AttributeTargets.
Property | AttributeTargets.Parameter, AllowMultiple = false)]
public sealed class PersonalIdentifiableInformationAttribute :
Attribute
{
}
```

In addition, we specify that we don't want to allow multiple copies of the same attribute. A good practice is to have your attributes be very specific and not create any inheritance chains of attributes. This will make your attribute a `sealed` type not allow inheritance from a C# perspective.

One of the things that GDPR mentions is to record the collection purpose. So, to add to this, we could include the purpose as optional metadata. You can do this by adding a constructor that takes the metadata as an argument, and if you want it to be optional, you can give it a default value:

```
[AttributeUsage(AttributeTargets.Class | AttributeTargets.
Property | AttributeTargets.Parameter, AllowMultiple = false)]
public sealed class PersonalIdentifiableInformationAttribute :
Attribute
{
    public PersonalIdentifiableInformationAttribute(string
      purpose = "")
    {
        Purpose = purpose;
    }

    public string Purpose { get; }
}
```

As you can see, in addition to adding the constructor with the argument for the metadata, you need to add the `Purpose` property that exposes the metadata.

With this, we can start applying the `PersonalIdentifiableInformation` attribute to properties on something, such as a `Person` object:

```
public class Person
{
    [PersonalIdentifiableInformation("First name of person")]
```

```
    public string FirstName { get; set; }

    [PersonalIdentifiableInformation("Last name of person")]
    public string LastName { get; set; }

    [PersonalIdentifiableInformation("Unique identifier for
        person")]
    public string SocialSecurityNumber { get; set; }
}
```

We will go into more depth on how we can leverage this further in *Chapter 5, Leveraging Attributes*.

We've discussed how we can reason about our code through implicit structures and also how we can add explicit additional metadata and even our own custom data. What about going the other way? By this, we mean going from something and basically generating code.

As we talked about previously, the programming language itself is basically a higher-level metadata language designed to be able to express code more efficiently.

With that mindset, there is really nothing stopping us from inventing our own language and leveraging the infrastructure to generate running code.

Domain-specific languages

The concept of creating your own **domain-specific language** (DSL) is nothing new and has been done for years by companies. This can be a very efficient way to include your domain experts in the mix and provide a way for them to contribute code in a language that is more familiar to them. The code they write is typically then on a much higher level and has a vocabulary that is supported by lower-level code constructs, which are actually doing the heavy lifting.

Think of this as a programming language and a compiler for your business, expressing your business problems.

It could also be used for technical aspects and not just for the business side – for instance, if you have complex state machines or workflows that have their own vocabulary and you want to make it into a language that is easier to reason about. You could also imagine that the language is represented in a well-known file format such as JSON, YAML, or even Excel.

The purpose of going to the length of generating the code for this higher-level representation is that you get an opportunity to make the end result more optimal, and you can make decisions to optimize the flow before it hits the runtime. You also get a snappier startup of your application, as it doesn't have to parse things at startup and hand it over to an engine that runs it. It will ultimately just be code running, just as any other code in your solution.

Gherkin – technical sample

If you're familiar with writing unit tests, the typical structure is **arrange**, **act**, and then **assert**. A test would look something like this:

```
public class CalculatorTests
{
    [Fact]
    public void Add()
    {
        // Arrange
        var left = 5;
        var right = 3;
        var expectedResult = 8;


        // Act
        var actualResult = Calculator.Add(left, right);


        Assert.Equal(expectedResult, actualResult, 0);
    }
}
```

This code tests a calculator to verify that its add functionality works as expected. It does this by setting up the inputs and expected results, then calling into the calculator, and finally, verifying the result by using assertions that claim the result should be the same as the expected result.

While this is the more traditional **test-driven development** (TDD) style, there is something called **behavior-driven design** (BDD). This approach focuses much more on the behavior of a system and interactions between parts of your system rather than its state. For expressing this interaction, a DSL was created called **Gherkin**. It is somewhat similar in its basic form with *given*, *when*, and *then*, which maps pretty much to the same as TDD's *arrange*, *act*, and *assert*. In addition, it has the concepts of features, scenarios, and steps. The goal is to write concrete functional requirements for a system.

For higher-order functionality, it is hard for domain experts to reason about C# code to verify whether we're testing the right thing or delivering what is expected.

With the correct tool, we can start articulating the functionality of a system in plain English and let it be hooked up to code snippets that perform the actual code we need to test or specify.

A great example of an implementation of this is the .NET BDD framework called **SpecFlow** (`https://specflow.org/`). When navigating to their site, you're presented with their data privacy dialog, and they've included the specification of the scenario:

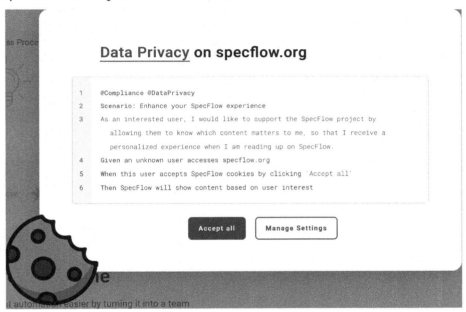

Figure 2.1 - SpecFlow data privacy dialog

SpecFlow embraces Gherkin and provides a compiler that compiles the DSL to runnable code, mixing in the necessary code to call for the feature under test.

We will be looking at how we can do this at runtime using dynamic code generation emitting IL code into the running application in *Chapter 6, Dynamic Proxy Generation*, and also how we can leverage .NET Expression to create code and how these can be compiled on the fly in *Chapter 8, Building and Executing Expressions*. In *Chapter 16, Generating Code*, we will be looking at how we can really make this fly by doing it at the compiler level.

Summary

You should now have a clearer idea of the different concepts of metaprogramming and a better understanding of when to use what. You'll see health warnings throughout the book about being careful about doing too many implicit or magical things that the developers might not understand. This balance can be very hard to get right, and there is also a certain level of maturity involved for individual developers and teams as a whole involved as well.

The .NET compiler and what it produces give a lot of power to you as a developer. Use it wisely.

In order to demystify and demonstrate more day-to-day use of metaprogramming, we will look into how Microsoft's ASP.NET leverages metaprogramming techniques in the next chapter. This should give you some security in feeling it is not too exotic, and also get a feel for how it can make you more productive and be of help.

3

Demystifying through Existing Real-World Examples

In this chapter, we will look into how Microsoft's **ASP.NET** leverages metaprogramming in order to automate tedious configuration.

Since the first release of **ASP.NET MVC** back in 2009, there has been quite a lot of automation going on to make developers more productive. The main objective of this chapter is to demystify what metaprogramming is by showing that you might already be leveraging something that takes advantage of metaprogramming.

In this chapter, we will cover the following topics:

- ASP.NET controllers
- ASP.NET validation

By the end of this chapter, you will understand how ASP.NET leverages metaprogramming with a non-intrusive approach and see the benefits of automation.

Technical requirements

To follow the instructions in this chapter, you will need the following:

- A computer with either Windows, macOS, or Linux installed
- The **.NET 6 SDK**
- Preferably, a code editor or IDE (such as Visual Studio Code, Visual Studio, or JetBrains Rider)

The finished code for this chapter can be found here: `https://github.com/PacktPublishing/Metaprogramming-in-C-Sharp/tree/main/Chapter3`

Prerequisites for your system

In this chapter, we'll dive concretely into code, so you need to have your system prepared.

The first thing we'll need is the Microsoft .NET SDK. Go to `https://dot.net` and download the SDK by clicking the **Download** button.

> **Important note**
> This book is based on *version 7* of the .NET SDK.

To create and edit files, it all depends on your own preferences and also what system you're running on. Visual Studio Code and JetBrains Rider are both available on Windows, macOS, and Linux. Visual Studio is only available for Windows and macOS. You can download any of these editors from the following links; if you don't have a preference, VSCode is lightweight and will get you up and running very fast:

- **VSCode** (`https://code.visualstudio.com/`)
- **JetBrains Rider** (`https://www.jetbrains.com/rider/`)
- **Visual Studio** (`https://visualstudio.com/`)

Once you've picked your editor, go ahead and follow the installation process relevant to the product you chose.

To call on APIs, you can use the web browser, **Wget**, or **cURL**, but I recommend using **Postman** (`https://www.postman.com/`) for this. Samples in this book will use Postman.

ASP.NET controllers

Being explicit with registering artifacts of your application is very common among different frameworks. Discovering the artifacts and just doing an automated self-registration of them is becoming more popular. But it's very common that you will have to go and explicitly add everything manually.

Although it is very clear what is going on with these registrations, the downside of manual registration is that you are basically adding code that is not directly contributing to the business value you're trying to achieve. It is also code that is highly repeatable and tends to end up in large files with all the initialization going on.

For instance, with **ASP.NET Core 6** we got a brand-new minimal API, which is designed to have a smaller footprint and less ceremony to get started. You can start creating a Web API with three lines of setup code and then add your API as HTTP methods with routes at will.

This is all fine and dandy, but can quite easily become unmaintainable as the project grows.

Let's dive more concretely into how this works.

Create a new folder for this on your system called Chapter 3. In this folder, we want to create a simple ASP.NET web application. This can be done in various ways, depending on the editor/IDE choice you made and also your personal preferences. However, throughout the book, we'll just stick with doing it from the command line, as that will work in all environments.

Open up a command-line interface (Windows CMD, macOS Terminal, Linux bash, or similar). Navigate to the folder you created for this (Chapter 3). Then run the following command:

```
dotnet new web
```

This will produce a minimal setup to get started. Open the folder/project in your editor/IDE. Your Program.cs file should look like this:

```
var builder = WebApplication.CreateBuilder(args);
var app = builder.Build();


app.MapGet("/", () => "Hello World!");


app.Run();
```

It basically sets up a web application and adds a route at the root level that will return "Hello World!" when navigating to it using your web browser.

The app.MapGet() call is a very simple way to expose an endpoint and could in fact be used to build simple REST APIs. Let's create a simple one for returning employees of a system.

Custom HTTP Get handler

Start by creating a new file called Employee.cs and adding the following to the file:

```
namespace Chapter3;
public record Employee(string FirstName, string LastName);
```

This holds just a simple representation of an employee with their first and last name. Obviously, in a proper system, you would add more properties to this. But for the sake of this sample, this will suffice.

With the Employee type in place, we can now change our Get action to a different route and also just return a collection of the Employee type. Swap out the .MapGet() method call with the following:

```
app.MapGet("/api/employees", () => new Employee[]
        {
                new("Jane", "Doe"),
```

```
        new("John", "Doe")
    });
```

At the top of the file, you also need to add a using statement for the Chapter3 namespace. The new Program.cs file should look like the following:

```
using Chapter3;
var builder = WebApplication.CreateBuilder(args);
var app = builder.Build();
app.MapGet("/api/employees", () => new Employee[]
        {
            new("Jane", "Doe"),
            new("John", "Doe")
        });
app.Run();
```

You can run this using dotnet run from your terminal/console or if you prefer to run it with your IDE, you should get a running program listing something like this:

```
info: Microsoft.Hosting.Lifetime[14]
      Now listening on: https://localhost:7027
info: Microsoft.Hosting.Lifetime[14]
      Now listening on: http://localhost:5016
info: Microsoft.Hosting.Lifetime[0]
      Application started. Press Ctrl+C to shut down.
info: Microsoft.Hosting.Lifetime[0]
      Hosting environment: Development
info: Microsoft.Hosting.Lifetime[0]
      Content root path: /Users/einari/Projects/
Metaprogramming-in-C/Chapter3/
```

The two lines saying Now listening on: will have different ports on your computer, as it is randomly assigned when creating the project. Combine the URL with /api/employees from the .MapGet() method. It should be something like https://localhost:7027/api/employees or the non-HTTPS http://localhost:5016/api/employees, just remember to put your ports into it. Take this combined URL and navigate to it in your browser. You should see the following:

```
[{"firstName":"Jane","lastName":"Doe"},
{"firstName":"John","lastName":"Doe"}]
```

Obviously, if you're adding a bunch of these API endpoints right there in the program file with additional logic within the handler method, this file will become big and hard to read and maintain.

This is where we can improve a lot and let ASP.NET be clever. Let's start by creating a controller for this instead.

Controller

Add a new file called `EmployeesController.cs` to the project. Make the file look like this:

```
using Microsoft.AspNetCore.Mvc;

namespace Chapter3;

[Route("/api/employees")]
public class EmployeesController : Controller
{
    [HttpGet]
    public IEnumerable<Employee> AllEmployees()
    {
        return new Employee[]
        {
            new("Jane", "Doe"),
            new("John", "Doe")
        };
    }
}
```

This will now create a Web API controller that leverages explicit metadata using the available C# attributes found in ASP.NET. In front of the `EmployeesController` class, you have the `[Route]` attribute, which tells at which base route the controller will be located. Then we have a method we want to represent a particular HTTP verb; this is the `[HttpGet]` attribute.

We have now rigged our code to be automatically discovered and configured by the ASP.NET engine itself. All we need to do is change the startup of this application and instruct ASP.NET to add controllers to our system. Open the `Program.cs` file and replace the content with the following:

```
var builder = WebApplication.CreateBuilder(args);
builder.Services.AddControllers();
var app = builder.Build();
```

```
app.MapControllers();
app.Run();
```

The `builder.Services.AddControllers()` call will instruct ASP.NET to discover all the controllers in the current assembly. The second call you'll notice is `app.MapControllers()`. This call maps all the controllers to the routes specified in the metadata.

By running this application and navigating the browser to the same URL as before, we should see the exact same result.

The beauty now with this model is that we can quite easily add a second controller without having to go into the configuration of our application to get it configured. It will just be discovered and automatically be there.

That means we can now concentrate on building out the business value and it is by default more manageable and maintainable, especially when you bring other developers into it to work together or if someone is inheriting your code base.

ASP.NET validation

When doing HTTP requests against ASP.NET, it goes through a pipeline consisting of different middlewares with specific responsibilities. This pipeline is completely configurable and extensible by you as a developer. Out of the box, it comes pre-configured with a specific middleware that handles the validation of objects sent to a request. The validation engine behind this recognizes rules in the form of metadata that can be applied to the objects. This metadata again is based on C# attributes.

Let's start by changing our `Employee` object a bit. Open the `Employee.cs` file and make it look like the following:

```
public record Employee(
    [Required]
    string FirstName,

    [Required]
    string LastName);
```

This makes the `FirstName` and `LastName` properties required by adding the `[Required]` attribute to them. The ASP.NET pipeline will pick this up and check any input being sent to see if these properties have values.

However, ASP.NET does not decide for you how to treat invalid objects; it just populates an object called `ModelState` for you to decide how you want to deal with this.

For us to deal with something like registering a new employee, we need to have an action in our controller that deals with that. Open `EmployeesController` and add the `Register` method as follows:

```
using Microsoft.AspNetCore.Mvc;

namespace Chapter3;

[Route("/api/employees")]
public class EmployeesController : Controller
{
    [HttpPost]
    public IActionResult Register(Employee employee)
    {
        if (!ModelState.IsValid)
        {
            return ValidationProblem(ModelState);
        }

        // ...
        // Do some business logic
        // ...

        return Ok();
    }
}
```

Notice the `ModelState.IsValid` statement. If there are validation rules that are not valid, it will return `ValidationProblem` as the result containing the errors found in `ModelState`.

Run the application and open Postman as discussed earlier. In Postman, you can create a new request by clicking on the button with the + sign on it:

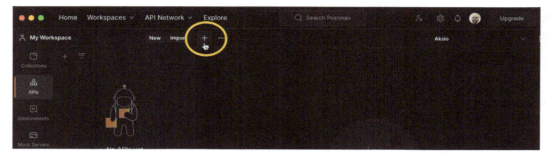

Figure 3.1 -Creating a new request in Postman

This will create a new tab, much like a regular web browser that contains everything for the request. Select **POST** as an HTTP verb in the left dropdown of the request, then enter the URL for our API. Now you can simply click the **Send** button and see the result in the lower part:

Figure 3.2 – Creating a new tab that contains the request details

Since we're not really passing it an object, none of the properties are set. The errors listed will therefore say that the properties are required.

Automatically hooking up model state handling

In ASP.NET, everything revolves around what is known as middlewares – small, special-purpose code blocks that perform a single task and then hand over to the next middleware. Every HTTP request that is handled by ASP.NET has these, and even the code that handles the controller is one of these. Every middleware can decide whether it should continue to the next middleware or whether it should exit with or without an error.

Controller handlers are just one of many formalized middlewares we can tap into.

You can find more details on middlewares here:

https://learn.microsoft.com/en-us/aspnet/core/fundamentals/middleware/?view=aspnetcore-7.0

If you never want to allow an invalid state to enter your controllers and want to get rid of the possibility of developers doing this manually, then there is a particular middleware we can put into the pipeline that allows us to stop it before we even hit the controller.

ASP.NET has the concept of an **action filter**. This gets called before the controller performs any action and lets us decide whether we want to continue with the pipeline or not. You can read more about action filters here: https://learn.microsoft.com/en-us/aspnet/core/mvc/controllers/filters?view=aspnetcore-7.0.

Let's create a new file called ValidationFilter.cs and make it look like the following:

```
using Microsoft.AspNetCore.Mvc;
using Microsoft.AspNetCore.Mvc.Filters;

namespace Chapter3;

public class ValidationFilter : IAsyncActionFilter
{
    public async Task
OnActionExecutionAsync(ActionExecutingContext context,
ActionExecutionDelegate next)
    {
        if (context.ModelState.IsValid)
        {
            await next();
```

```
        }
        else
        {
            context.Result = new BadRequestObjectResult(new
ValidationProblemDetails(context.ModelState));
        }
    }
}
```

This takes over the checking of whether ModelState is valid. The line with await next() is the continuation of the pipeline. So by only calling this when things are valid, we avoid getting to the controller if we're in an invalid state. Instead, we then create the same object the ASP.NET pipeline creates when calling the ValidationProblem method from the controller and return this.

We can then simplify the controller to look like the following:

```
using Microsoft.AspNetCore.Mvc;

namespace Chapter3;

[Route("/api/employees")]
public class EmployeesController : Controller
{
    [HttpPost]
    public IActionResult Register(Employee employee)
    {
        // ...
        // Do some business logic
        // ...

        return Ok();
    }
}
```

This code does not need to consider ModelState at all and just assumes it is taken care of, simplifying the implementation of every controller and making it focus on its single purpose of registering an employee. For most controllers, this would be fine and, in fact, you're now removing the possibility of developers forgetting to check for validity before doing their business logic.

The last piece of the puzzle is to hook it up in the ASP.NET pipeline. Open the `Program.cs` file and change the content to the following:

```
using Chapter3;

var builder = WebApplication.CreateBuilder(args);
builder.Services.AddControllers(mvcOptions => mvcOptions.
Filters.Add<ValidationFilter>());
var app = builder.Build();
app.MapControllers();
app.Run();
```

The `.AddControllers()` call takes a delegate that lets us configure `MvcOptions`. Within this, we can add our new action filter.

Run the application and verify that you get the exact same result by clicking the **Send** button inside postman.

Summary

In this chapter, we learned how an existing piece of technology leverages the power of the .NET runtime to make it easier for developers using the technology to do so. From the use of metadata in the right context, we get to focus on delivering business value and don't have to worry about how it is all configured. It also automatically gives us a certain structure to abide by, which in the long run will yield a more maintainable, extensible, and predictable code base. By adding the action filter as we did, we added what we call a cross-cutting concern, something we will revisit in more detail in *Chapter 13*, *Applying Cross-Cutting Concerns*.

In the next chapter, we will dive into how frameworks such as ASP.NET are capable of doing discovery and automation, and how we can leverage the .NET runtime type system to discover types and metadata to achieve something similar.

Part 2:
Leveraging the Runtime

In this part, you will see how powerful the .NET runtime is and dive into the details of its capabilities for metaprogramming. You'll see the different metaprogramming models the runtime provides and get an idea of how they can be leveraged with real-world examples.

This part has the following chapters:

- *Chapter 4, Reasoning about Types Using Reflection*
- *Chapter 5, Leveraging Attributes*
- *Chapter 6, Dynamic Proxy Generation*
- *Chapter 7, Reasoning about Expressions*
- *Chapter 8, Building and Executing Expressions*
- *Chapter 9, Taking Advantage of the Dynamic Language Runtime*

4

Reasoning about Types Using Reflection

Now that we have covered some of the basics of how metaprogramming can benefit you, its core concepts, and a real-world example, it's time to look inside the .NET runtime and see how we can leverage its power.

In this chapter, we will have a look at the implicit metadata provided by the compiler and the runtime. We'll see how we can collect all types in a running system and use it for discovery.

We will cover the following topics:

- Assembly discovery in the running process
- Leveraging library metadata to get project-referenced assemblies
- Discovering types
- Open/closed principle applied

By the end of this chapter, you will understand how you can use the powerful APIs of the .NET runtime to reason about the types already in the system. You'll learn how this can then be applied to make a more elastic and dynamic code base that can grow and ensure its maintainability is preserved.

Technical requirements

The source code specific to this chapter can be found on GitHub (`https://github.com/PacktPublishing/Metaprogramming-in-C-Sharp/tree/main/Chapter4`) and builds on top of the Fundamentals code found at `https://github.com/PacktPublishing/Metaprogramming-in-C-Sharp/tree/main/Fundamentals`.

Assembly discovery in the running process

In .NET, everything we compile ends up inside what is called an **assembly**. This is the binary that holds the compiled code in the form of **Intermediate Language** (IL). Alongside this, there is metadata that goes with it to identify types, methods, properties, fields, and any other symbols and metadata.

All of these artifacts are discoverable through APIs, and it all starts with the `System.Reflection` namespace. Within this namespace, there are APIs that allow you to reflect on what's running. In other languages, this is often referred to as **introspection**.

Looking at any instance of any type you'll see that there is always a `GetType()` method you can call. This is part of the reflection capabilities and is implemented in the base type of `Object`, which all types implicitly inherit from.

The `GetType()` method returns a `Type` type that describes the capabilities of the particular type – its fields, properties, methods, and more. It also holds information about what possible interfaces it implements or a base type it is inheriting from. These are very powerful constructs that we will leverage later in this chapter.

Instead of starting with individual types, let's take a step back and see how, from no type, we can discover what we have in our running process.

Assembly

One of the types in the `System.Reflection` namespace is `Assembly`. This is the type representing an assembly, typically a `.dll` file containing the IL code. On the `Assembly` type, there are a few static methods. We want to focus on one particular method: `.GetEntryAssembly()`. This method lets us, at any time, get the assembly that was the starting point, the entry point that the .NET runtime called to start our application:

1. Let's create a folder called `Chapter4`. For this chapter, we will create a few projects, so let's start by creating another folder called `AssemblyDiscovery`.

2. Change into this folder in your command-line interface and create a new console project:

    ```
    dotnet new console
    ```

3. This will set up the necessary artifacts for the project. Open the `Program.cs` file and replace its content with the following:

    ```
    using System.Reflection;

    var assembly = Assembly.GetEntryAssembly();
      Console.WriteLine(assembly.FullName)
    ```

The code is accessing the `GetEntryAssembly()` static method on `Assembly` to get the assembly that serves as the entry point of the application.

By running this program now, you should get an output that is similar to the following:

```
AssemblyDiscovery, Version=1.0.0.0, Culture=neutral,
   PublicKeyToken=null
```

This just prints out the name of the assembly, its version, information about the culture the assembly is for, and, if the assembly was signed, its public key.

From the entry assembly, we can now start looking at what assemblies have been referenced. Replace the code in `Program.cs` with the following:

```
using System.Reflection;

var assembly = Assembly.GetEntryAssembly();
Console.WriteLine(assembly!.FullName);
var assemblies = assembly!.GetReferencedAssemblies();
var assemblyNames = string.Join(", ", assemblies.Select(_
   => _.Name));
Console.WriteLine(assemblyNames);
```

The code gets the referenced assemblies from the entry assembly and prints them out. You should be see something like the following:

```
AssemblyDiscovery, Version=1.0.0.0, Culture=neutral,
   PublicKeyToken=null
System.Runtime, System.Console, System.Linq
```

Since we haven't explicitly referenced any assemblies, we only see `System.Runtime`, `System.Consol`, and `System.Linq` as the available assemblies.

This is all very basic but demonstrates the starting point of reasoning about your applications and what they're built from. But we can do so much more.

Leveraging library metadata to get project referenced assemblies

If you are going to gather metadata across a running process, chances are that you're only interested in the assemblies that are part of your solution and not all the .NET framework libraries or third-party libraries. There is a performance impact of looking through all assemblies for metadata, so filtering down might be a good idea.

In .NET projects, we can add package references, typically from sources such as **NuGet** or your own package sources, but we can also add local project references. These are references to other `.csproj` files representing something that we want to package in its own assembly. Inside a `.csproj` file, you can identify the different references by their XML tags – `<PackageReference/>` or `<ProjectReference/>`. Inside Visual Studio or Rider, you will typically see these tags in the explorer view as well.

The **C#** compiler produces additional metadata to distinguish the different types of references all projects have. This can be leveraged in code.

Reusable fundamentals

Let's build a reusable library that we can leverage and expand on throughout the following chapters. Let's call this project `Fundamentals`:

1. Create a new folder at the root of where you started building out the chapters and call it `Fundamentals`. Change into this folder and create the new project:

    ```
    dotnet new classlib
    ```

    This creates a new project and adds a file called `Class1.cs`. Remove this file as we don't need it at all.

2. In order for us to be able to get to the proper metadata enabling us to distinguish between package or project references, we need to add a NuGet package reference.

    The package we're looking for is `Microsoft.Extensions.DependencyModel`. In the terminal, you add the reference by doing the following:

    ```
    dotnet add package
       Microsoft.Extensions.DependencyModel
    ```

3. Now that we have the package, we want to create a system that is capable of discovering project references and any additional package references we explicitly tell it to load. From these, we want to get all the types so that we can start making some serious discoveries about our system.

    Start by creating a file called `Types.cs`. Then add the following code to it:

    ```
    namespace Fundamentals;

    public class Types
    {
    }
    ```

    Within this new class, we want to be able to expose all the discovered types. Before we can do that, we need to discover them.

4. At the top of the `Types.cs` file before the namespace declaration, add the following using statements:

    ```
    using System.Reflection;
    using Microsoft.Extensions.DependencyModel;
    ```

5. Add a private method called `DiscoverAllTypes()` and start by making it look as follows:

```
IEnumerable<Type> DiscoverAllTypes()
{
    var entryAssembly = Assembly.GetEntryAssembly();
    var dependencyModel =
      DependencyContext.Load(entryAssembly);
    var projectReferencedAssemblies =
      dependencyModel.RuntimeLibraries
                     .Where(_ => _.Type.Equals
                       ("project"))
                     .Select(_ => Assembly.Load
                       (_.Name))
                     .ToArray();
}
```

This code will get the entry assembly and then leverage `DependencyContext` from the package you referenced. This model contains more metadata around the assemblies (or libraries, as they are called in the `DependencyModel` extension). The last thing we do is to load the assemblies we find. For the most part, the assemblies are already loaded. But this will guarantee they are loaded and return an instance of the assembly. It won't load it again if it is already loaded.

The result of this is that we have all the project-referenced assemblies in an array. That might not be all you want. If for instance you're maintaining a set of common packages that are shared within your organization and you want to discover from these, a common pattern is to have your organization name as part of the assembly name, typically at the beginning. That means it's easy to add something that includes all assemblies that are prefixed with a certain string.

6. Change the signature for the `DiscoverAllTypes()` method to be able to include a collection of assembly prefixes for collecting types for discovery:

```
IEnumerable<Type> DiscoverAllTypes(IEnumerable<string>
  assemblyPrefixesToInclude)
{
    // ... leave the content of this method as before
}
```

7. In the `DiscoverAllTypes()` method, add the following at the end:

```
var assemblies = dependencyModel.RuntimeLibraries
              .Where(_ =>
            _.RuntimeAssemblyGroups.Count > 0 &&
            assemblyPrefixesToInclude.Any(asm
            => _.Name.StartsWith(asm)))
              .Select(_ =>
              {
                  try
```

```
        {
            return Assembly.Load
                (_.Name);
        }
        catch
        {
            return null!;
        }
    })
    .Where(_ => _ is not null)
    .Distinct()
    .ToList();
```

The code looks at the same RuntimeLibraries, but this time specifically for assemblies that start with the prefixes. There is also error-handling functionality here: some assemblies can't be loaded with the regular Assembly.Load() method and we just ignore them, as they are not of interest.

Since we call .ToList() at the end of the LINQ query, we can easily combine the two collections of assemblies and all the types from all the loaded assemblies and return them from the DiscoverAllTypes() method. Add the following at the end of the DiscoverAllTypes() method:

```
assemblies.AddRange(projectReferencedAssemblies);
return assemblies.SelectMany(_ => _.GetTypes())
    .ToArray();
```

8. Now that we have collected all assemblies and their types and returned them, it's time to expose them to the outside world. We do this by adding a public property returning IEnumerable of Type. We don't want this to be potentially mutated from the outside:

```
public IEnumerable<Type> All { get; }
```

9. The last piece of the puzzle for the Types class is to add a constructor. We want the constructor to take any assembly prefixes for the DiscoverAllTypes() method:

```
public Types(params string[]
    assemblyPrefixesToInclude)
{
    All = DiscoverAllTypes(assemblyPrefixesToInclude);
}
```

We have now encapsulated a type registry that we can leverage for other use cases. Now that we have some basic building blocks. Let's go ahead and create a multi-project application.

Business app

Now that we have some basic building blocks. Lets go ahead and create a multi project application.

Inside the Chapter4 folder, create a folder called BusinessApp. In this folder, we're going to create multiple projects that will make up the application. Within the BusinessApp folder, create one folder called Domain and another called Main. The Domain folder will represent the domain logic of our application and should be a class library project. Go ahead and create a new .NET project in the Domain folder:

```
dotnet new classlib
```

Delete the Class1.cs file that is generated. Then, in the Main folder, we want to create a console app:

```
dotnet new console
```

Within the Main project you should now add references to the Fundamentals project and also the Domain project:

```
dotnet add reference ../../../Fundamentals/Fundamentals.csproj
dotnet add reference ../Domain/Domain.csproj
```

In the Program.cs file, inside the Main project, replace the content with the following:

```
using Fundamentals;

var types = new Types();
var typeNames = string.Join("\n", types.All.Select(_ =>
  _.Name));
Console.WriteLine(typeNames);
```

This code now leverages the Types class we put into Fundamentals, which will look at all our project reference assemblies and give us all the types. Running this should give you an output similar to this:

```
Program
<>c
EmbeddedAttribute
NullableAttribute
NullableContextAttribute
EmbeddedAttribute
NullableAttribute
NullableContextAttribute
Types
```

You'll notice that some of these types aren't types you have created at all. These are types the C# compiler has put into the projects.

Go and add a folder called `Employees` in the `Domain` project and within it, create a file called `RegisterEmployee.cs` and add the following content:

```
namespace Domain.Employees;

public class RegisterEmployee
{
    public string FirstName { get; set; } = string.Empty;
    public string LastName { get; set; } = string.Empty;
    public string SocialSecurityNumber { get; set; } =
        string.Empty;
}
```

By running the `Main` project again, you should now see the added type:

```
Program
<>c
EmbeddedAttribute
NullableAttribute
NullableContextAttribute
RegisterEmployee     <-- New
EmbeddedAttribute
NullableAttribute
NullableContextAttribute
Types
```

With this, we have the beginning of a strong foundation for working with types. We just need to improve its capabilities to make it even more useful.

Discovering types

With the `Types` class, we now have a raw approach to get all the types in a running system. This can be very helpful on its own as you can now use this to perform **Language Integrated Query** (**LINQ**) queries on top of finding types that match specific criteria you'd be interested in.

A very common scenario in code in general is that we have base classes or interfaces that represent characteristics of known artifact types in our system and we create specialized versions that override virtual or abstract methods, or just implement a specific interface to represent what it is. This is the power of object-oriented programming languages.

With this, we are adding additional implicit metadata into our systems that we can leverage. For instance, in *Chapter 3*, *Demystifying through Existing Real-World Examples*, we looked at how ASP. NET does this by discovering all classes that have `Controller` as their base type.

From my own experience, this is the typical pattern that has been used the most on the projects I've been doing these things on. In fact, it is so common that it is a good idea to optimize the lookup of types on this to avoid the complexity when looking up types based on inheritance. An optimized lookup will improve performance significantly.

It would be a bit too verbose to do a full walkthrough of the full lookup cache mechanism as there are quite a few moving parts to it. You can find the full code here: `https://github.com/PacktPublishing/Metaprogramming-in-C-Sharp/blob/main/Fundamentals/ContractToImplementorsMap.cs`.

The interface represented by `ContractToImplementorsMap` is as follows:

```
public interface IContractToImplementorsMap
{
    IDictionary<Type, IEnumerable<Type>>
      ContractsAndImplementors { get; }
    IEnumerable<Type> All { get; }
    void Feed(IEnumerable<Type> types);
    IEnumerable<Type> GetImplementorsFor<T>();
    IEnumerable<Type> GetImplementorsFor(Type contract);
}
```

The purpose of the API of `IContractToImplementorsMap` is to give a fast way of getting implementations of a specific type, be it a base class or an interface. The implementation of `IContractToImplementorsMap` takes all types it is fed and maps these correctly in this cache.

You'll notice that there is a method called `Feed()`. We will have to call this in our `Types` class. In addition, we want to have some methods that make discovering different types a lot more helpful; for instance, the following methods would be helpful:

```
public Type FindSingle<T>();
public IEnumerable<Type> FindMultiple<T>();
public Type FindSingle(Type type);
public IEnumerable<Type> FindMultiple(Type type);
public Type FindTypeByFullName(string fullName);
```

These methods allow us to find methods that implement a specific interface or inherit from a base type. They allow us to find a single instance or multiple implementors, based on type either by generic parameter or by passing in the `Type` object. Also for convenience, there is a method for finding a type by its name.

You can find the full implementation in the `Fundamentals` folder at the link specified at the beginning of the chapter.

Back to business

Moving back to our business sample, let's add a second class in the `Employee` folder within the `Domain` project called `SetSalaryLevelForEmployee.cs`. Make it look like the following:

```
namespace Domain.Employees;

public class SetSalaryLevelForEmployee
{
    public string SocialSecurityNumber { get; set; } =
        string.Empty;
    public decimal SalaryLevel { get; set; }
}
```

The RegisterEmployee and SetSalaryLevelForEmployee classes both represent the data we need to perform the specific actions in our domain business logic. These types of actions are often called commands. If we wanted to discover all of our commands, we could create an empty interface that we can use for all our commands to implement to make it easy for us to discover them. These types of empty interfaces used in this way are often referred to as marker interfaces.

In the Fundamentals project, add a file called ICommand.cs and make it look like the following:

```
namespace Fundamentals;

public interface ICommand
{
}
```

We now need to have a project reference to the Fundamentals project from the Domain project. Run the following from the Domain project:

```
dotnet add reference ../../../Fundamentals/
    Fundamentals.csproj
```

With the new ICommand interface, we can mark the RegisterEmployee and SetSalaryLevelForEmployee commands with it. Open the files for both RegisterEmployee and SetSalaryLevelForEmployee and add the following using statements at the top of each of the files:

```
using Fundamentals;
```

For both of the class definitions, add : ICommand at the end to make them implement the ICommand interface.

Open the Program.cs file in the Main project and change it with the following content:

```
using Fundamentals;

var types = new Types();
var commands = types.FindMultiple<ICommand>();
var typeNames = string.Join("\n", commands.Select(_ => _.Name));
Console.WriteLine(typeNames);
```

Running the `Main` project should now yield the following result:

```
SetSalaryLevelForEmployee
RegisterEmployee
```

Effectively we have now reproduced the necessary infrastructure to mimic what ASP.NET is doing for its discovery of items. With this, we have opened our software to be more open to expansion.

Domain concepts

The most boring types in most programming languages are the primitives that come with the language; typically, your integers, booleans, strings, and such. They offer absolutely no interesting or meaningful metadata. They are nothing but very primitive.

It's easy to fall into the trap of using these and end up with primitive obsession. Not only are you losing valuable metadata, but it also creates code that can at times be unclear and also potentially be error prone as two properties of the same primitive type are interchangeable.

For applications, there is a great opportunity to move away from primitives and bring back meaning to your domain by encapsulating the primitives into meaningful types in your domain.

The beauty of this is that you'll not only make your code more readable but also understandable and less ambiguous. Doing so moves you away from being primitive-obsessed to a place where you will get compiler errors if you do something wrong, putting developers on the right foot from the start. On top of all this, you'll also be bringing in tons of metadata that can be leveraged.

Key characteristics of primitives are that they are value types. This means you can have two instances of the same value and equality checks would indicate that they are the same. In **C# 9.0**, we got a new construct called `record`. This enables us to create types that are complex types but bare the same characteristics as value types. Comparing two complex `record` types with the same values on them will be considered equal.

Let's introduce a base type that can be used for concepts. In the `Fundamentals` project, add a file called `ConceptAs.cs` and make it look like the following:

```
namespace Fundamentals;

public record ConceptAs<T>
{
    public ConceptAs(T value)
    {
        ArgumentNullException.ThrowIfNull(value,
          nameof(value));
        Value = value;
    }
```

```
public T Value { get; init; }

public static implicit operator T(ConceptAs<T> value)
    => value.Value;
}
```

This implementation gives you a way to encapsulate domain concepts. It's built using generics letting you specify the inner type of the value the concept is representing. It is strict on not allowing null values within the encapsulation. If you want to allow null values in your code, it should not be within the concept but rather on the instance of the concept. Further, the implementation provides a convenience operator for automatic conversion to the primitive.

Typically, when you're working with databases or you are transferring data across the wire in different formats, you want to strip away the concept wrapper and just get the primitive. Having the common base type is then a fantastic piece of type information that these serializers can work with.

In the Fundamentals link that was at the beginning of the chapter, you'll find an example of how to create a JsonConverter for System.Text.Json that will automatically convert any implementations of a concept to the underlying value during serialization and back to the concept type when deserializing. With the ConceptAsJsonConverterFactory implementation in the same location in the Fundamentals link, you'll see that it recognizes whether a type can be converted if it is a concept based on the ConceptAs base type and creates the correct converter to serialize and deserialize the concepts.

With the ConceptAs construct, we can now go and create domain-specific implementations. As you'll find in the code for this chapter (https://github.com/PacktPublishing/ Metaprogramming-in-C-Sharp/tree/main/Chapter4/BusinessApp), you can create specific concepts. For instance, for the RegisterEmployee command we created earlier, instead of just using primitives, you can create specific types like the following:

```
public record FirstName(string Value) :
    ConceptAs<string>(Value);
public record LastName(string Value) :
    ConceptAs<string>(Value);
public record SocialSecurityName(string Value) :
    ConceptAs<string>(Value);
```

Then, you can alter RegisterEmployee from before to the following:

```
namespace Domain.Employees;

public class RegisterEmployee
{
    public FirstName FirstName { get; set; } =
        new(string.Empty)
    public LastName LastName { get; set; } = new(string.Empty);
```

```
    public SocialSecurityNumber SocialSecurityNumber { get;
      set; } = new(string.Empty);
}
```

This will remove any potential mistakes in the code. There is no way you could accidentally put `FirstName` into `LastName` or vice versa, as the compiler will tell you they're not of the same type.

Cross-cutting concerns

With something like a concept in place, we are really starting to enrich our application code with meaningful metadata. This creates new opportunities. As mentioned earlier for serialization, by having the base type that everything uses, we can easily handle serialization in one place for concept types. This is what we mean when we talk about cross-cutting concerns: creating constructs or behavior once that can be applied across multiple things, automatically.

The possibilities are endless with these things. We could automatically create validation rules that are applied for the type whenever it is being used. Or we could go ahead and apply authorization policies based on types when they are used. For the command pattern and a powerful pipeline-based framework such as ASP.NET, this means we can go ahead and create action filters or middleware that can be injected into the pipeline that deals with these things automatically – just because we now have the metadata we need.

Take security, the one thing you really want to get right. Don't get us wrong, we aim to get everything we do right – but security is the one thing you don't want to mess around with. With the richness of the type system and all the metadata that goes with it, you gain access to some great opportunities to make it simpler for developers to do the right thing.

One thing that could be done, for instance, is creating authorization policies based on namespaces. If you have a command coming in and it belongs to a namespace that requires a certain role or claim for the user, you could do that check in one place, and by convention, just let developers drop commands or other artifacts into the correct place and they'd be secure.

Compliance is another area you really want to get right. It can be extremely costly if your software is not compliant. Probably the most talked-about compliance law over the last few years has been the EU regulation called **GDPR**. If you're not compliant with this, you could end up being fined.

The whole idea of the GDPR is to protect the privacy of the end users of computer systems. A lot of systems collect what is known as **Personally Identifiable Information**, or **PII** for short. Things such as your name, address, birth date, social security number, and a lot more are classified as PII. There is also a requirement for transparency for the end users to know what data you have on them and also to know the reason for collecting the data. If your company gets audited, you have to also show what type of data you're collecting in a report.

Building on what you just learned about concepts, we can take it even further and create a specialized version of the base `ConceptAs<>` type. Let's call it `PIIConceptAs<>`:

```
namespace Fundamentals;

public record PIIConceptAs<T>(T Value) : ConceptAs<T>
  (Value)
{
}
```

As you can see, it inherits from `ConceptAs<>`, giving us the opportunity to create serializers and other tooling around this base type once, but it adds metadata saying this is a specialized concept for PII.

At runtime in your application, you can quite easily present to the user all this information, as well as to any auditor or law enforcement agency.

Take the `SocialSecurityNumber` type we made into a concept earlier. Change that to be `PIIConceptAs<>` instead:

```
public record SocialSecurityName(string Value) :
PIIConceptAs<string>(Value);
```

As you can see from the code, it doesn't take much to enrich it with metadata that can be leveraged. And with the powerful type discovery you built at the beginning of the chapter, you now have the power to quite easily create a simple console report of all this:

```
Console.WriteLine("GDPR Report");
var typesWithConcepts = types.All
                        .SelectMany(_ =>
                          _.GetProperties()
                           .Where(p =>
                             p.PropertyType
                              .IsPIIConcept()))
                        .GroupBy(_ => _.DeclaringType);

foreach (var typeWithConcepts in typesWithConcepts)
{
    Console.WriteLine($"Type: {typeWithConcepts
      .Key!.FullName}");
    foreach (var property in typeWithConcepts)
    {
        Console.WriteLine($"  Property : {property.Name}");
    }
}
```

The first thing the code does is do a LINQ query collecting all properties in the system from all types that are of the `PIIConceptAs<>` type. As you can see, it uses an extension method, which is part of the fundamentals (https://github.com/PacktPublishing/Metaprogramming-in-C-Sharp/tree/main/Fundamentals). Since it selects all the properties with `.SelectMany()`, we group it together based on the declaring type. Then it just loops through all the types and then all the properties and printing out the information.

It should yield the following result:

```
GDPR Report
Type: Domain.Employees.RegisterEmployee
   Property : FirstName
   Property : LastName
   Property : SocialSecurityNumber
```

With a fairly low amount of code, we've gone from having no additional metadata to a much richer model that opens up the opportunity of applying logic in our code across the board. In fact, with it, we're future-proofing our code to a certain extent. We could come back to it at a later stage and decide we want to change security. Without changing the actual code at all, we could just apply a new rule based on the metadata we already have. This is powerful and makes for flexible, extensible, and highly maintainable systems.

Open/closed principle applied

The **open/closed principle** is a principle credited to Bertrand Meyer after its appearance in his 1988 book called *Object-Oriented Software Construction*. This is a principle regarding types we can apply in our software:

- A type is open if it can be extended
- A type is closed when it is available to other types

Classes in C# are open for extension by default. We can inherit from them and add new meanings to them. But the base class we're inheriting from should be closed, meaning that there shouldn't be any need for changes in the base type for the new type to work.

This helps us design our code for extensibility and keep responsibilities in the right place.

Taking a step back, we can apply some of this same thinking on the system level. What if our systems can just be extended with new capabilities without having to add configuration at the heart of a type for it to know about the additions?

This type of thinking is what we did earlier with ICommand and the implementations. The two commands we added were not known by any parts of the system, but by virtue of implementing the ICommand interface, we could see both types through an introspective of our system.

Summary

In this chapter, we have learned about the power of looking inward into our running process and collecting all the referenced assemblies and all the types of these assemblies. We've looked at how we can leverage even more metadata to gain access to the types of reference the assemblies are, be they package references or project references.

From this, we are empowered to start reasoning about types in a more meaningful way and really take advantage of the type system. Interfaces can serve as a very powerful method to mark types. The interfaces can, of course, enforce implementations of members that need to be there, but they can also just act as empty marker interfaces, serving as a way to bring explicit metadata into the assemblies.

In the next chapter, we will dive into how we can make full use of custom attributes to provide explicit metadata for your applications.

5

Leveraging Attributes

We briefly touched on the concept of C# attributes in *Chapter 2, Metaprogramming Concepts*. They are an obvious choice for adding explicit metadata to your source code. This is what they are intended for. Attributes should not carry heavy logic with them and should be viewed as just metadata.

In this chapter, we will look into how you can leverage them in your code base, providing mechanisms for adorning types and members with valuable, rich information that can be used for different scenarios.

We will cover the following topics:

- What is an attribute and how can it be applied?
- Finding types with specific attributes
- Generic attributes

From this chapter, you should understand the power of attributes as a building block for metaprogramming, how to create your own custom attributes, and how you can discover them being used.

Technical requirements

The source code specific to the chapter can be found on GitHub (`https://github.com/PacktPublishing/Metaprogramming-in-C-Sharp/tree/main/Chapter5`) and it builds on top of the **Fundamentals** code, which is found at `https://github.com/PacktPublishing/Metaprogramming-in-C-Sharp/tree/main/Fundamentals`.

What is an attribute and how can it be applied?

An **attribute** is a special type that the C# compiler understands. It can be used to associate metadata to assemblies, types, and any member of a type. During compilation, the compiler will pick up the attributes and add them to the compiled assembly as metadata. You can place more than one attribute on every item.

Creating your own custom attribute is as simple as this:

```
public class CustomAttribute : Attribute
{
}
```

And then using it is done as follows:

```
[Custom]
public class MyClass
{
}
```

Notice that you create the attribute with the `Attribute` postfix in the name. While using it, you don't need it and you only have `[Custom]`. The C# compiler has a convention built into it saying you have to have the postfix, but it will ignore it when it's used. This is a little bit weird and definitely violates the principle of least surprise.

The nice thing about attributes is that they live outside the scope of the element itself, meaning that you don't have to create an instance of the type with the metadata to access the metadata.

Attributes can take parameters to give them specific information you want to capture. However, all parameters must be available at compile time. This means you can't create new objects dynamically for any of the parameters.

For instance, we can add a parameter to the attribute by taking the instance of another type:

```
public class CustomAttribute : Attribute
{
    public CustomAttribute(SomeType instance)
    {
    }
}
```

The compiler will allow the attribute to take the type – after all, it is a valid C# type. However, when you try to use it, you're not allowed to create a new instance:

```
[Custom(new SomeType())] // Will give you a compiler error
public class MyClass
{
}
```

This is because the compiler needs the values to be available at compile time. Even though attributes are ultimately instantiated at runtime, the information captured and added to the compiled assembly is never executed. This means that you're limited to things the compiler can resolve, such as primitive types (for example, `int`, `float`, and `double`) and things such as strings – anything that can be represented as constants and not have to be created by the runtime to work.

A valid parameter could be a string:

```
public class CustomAttribute : Attribute
{
    public CustomAttribute(string information)
    {
    }
}
```

With the constructor now taking a string, it will work not just at compile time but also at runtime.

Since strings can be literal constants, you are allowed to use them:

```
[Custom("I'm a valid parameter")]
public class MyClass
{
}
```

Already, you can see the power of attributes – the ability to have additional information sitting there that your code can reason about and you can use to make decisions or even use for reporting.

Limiting attribute usage

For attributes, you can also add metadata to them, which feels a little bit like inception; metadata for the metadata. The metadata that you add is to limit the scope of how the attribute can be used.

You can be very specific about what elements in your code the attribute is for (class, property, field, and so on).

The [AttributeUsage] attribute allows you to be specific about the attribute. Let's say you want to limit the usage to only classes – you can do the following:

```
[AttributeUsage(AttributeTargets.Class)]
public class CustomAttribute : Attribute
{
}
```

If you then try to add the attribute to something else other than a class, you will get a compiler error:

```
public class MyClass
{
    [Custom] // Compiler error
    public void SomeMethod()
    {
    }
}
```

The [AttributeUsage] type is an enum holding different values for the different code elements attributes support. Every value in the enum represents a flag, making it possible to combine them and target multiple code element types.

Let's limit the code elements to Class, Method, and Property by applying the [AttributeUsage] attribute with these specified for the custom attribute:

```
[AttributeUsage(
    AttributeTargets.Class |
    AttributeTargets.Method |
    AttributeTargets.Property)]
public class CustomAttribute : Attribute
{
}
```

As you can see, using the bitwise **OR** construct (|) you can add all the elements you want to support.

A little fun fact about [AttributeUsage] is that it uses itself to tell the compiler that it can only be used for classes. Again, a little bit of inception there; the [AttributeUsage] attribute is using [AttributeUsage] to provide metadata about itself.

In addition to limiting the code elements an attribute can be associated with, you can also tell whether or not you allow multiple instances of the attribute to be applied. You can also specify whether or not you allow the attribute to be available as metadata for types inheriting from the type that has the attribute applied to it.

The [AttributeUsage] attribute does, however, only take one parameter in its constructor. That means we have to use its properties explicitly.

By default, attributes are limited to only being associated once per code element type. Trying to associate the attribute more than once will give you a compiler error:

```
[Custom]
[Custom] // Compiler error
public class MyClass
{
}
```

This behavior can be changed by simply using the AllowMultiple property:

```
[AttributeUsage(AttributeTargets.Class, AllowMultiple =
  true)]
public class CustomAttribute : Attribute
{
}
```

Compiling the same code will now be allowed.

The other property you can use for limiting the usage of the attributes is the `Inherited` property. Setting this to `false` will tell the compiler that the associated attribute is only the specific type it is being used explicitly and not for the derived type:

```
[AttributeUsage(AttributeTargets.Class, Inherited = false)]
public class CustomAttribute : Attribute
{
}
```

As you saw earlier, you can add the attribute in a normal way to the class:

```
[Custom]
public class MyClass
{
}
```

You can add a class that inherits from the type with the `[Custom]` attribute applied to it:

```
public class MyOtherClass : MyClass
{
}
```

The metadata associated with the `MyClass` base type will not be associated with `MyOtherClass` when the `Inherited` property is set to `false`. This is, by default, turned on, meaning that the derived type will have the same metadata associated with it.

To create an attribute, inheriting from `Attribute` and applying `[AttributeUsage]` is all you need to do. However, you might want to bring more clarity and explicitness to your metadata by not allowing inheritance from your attribute. Sealing your class will disable anyone inheriting from your custom attribute.

Sealing your attribute class

Since attributes represent specific metadata, they're not a regular code construct that you use for holding logic. Therefore, you will find that you don't need to create base attributes that other, more specific attributes inherit from. In fact, it could make your metadata unclear if you use inheritance as your metadata will lose explicitness and you would bring implicitness into it.

Because of this, it is considered good practice to not allow for the inheritance of attributes and stop it at a compiler level by making the attribute class `sealed`:

```
public sealed class CustomAttribute : Attribute
{
}
```

If you then try to create a more specific attribute that inherits from it, you will get a compiler error.

Now that we've covered all the mechanics involved in creating custom attributes and how you can make them very specific to your use case, you are probably eager to start actually discovering them and putting them to good use.

Finding types with specific attributes

Since attributes are created at compile time and do not require you to have an instance of a type that has been associated with attributes, you can discover attributes using the type system.

If you look at the `System.Type` type, you'll see that it implements a type called `MemberInfo` that sits in the `System.Reflection` namespace. This base class serves as the base class for `PropertyInfo`, `MethodInfo`, `FieldInfo`, and most of the specific info types representing code elements we can discover through the type system.

On the `MemberInfo` type, you find a method called `GetCustomAttributes()`. This lets you get a collection of attributes associated with the particular code element.

Take the class we had before:

```
[Custom]
public class MyClass
{
}
```

You can then quite easily get to the custom attributes on a type and loop through them and perform the actions you want to:

```
foreach( var attr in typeof(MyClass).GetCustomAttributes() )
{
    // Do something based on the attribute
}
```

Using `typeof()` is very explicit and can be used just for this type. For a more dynamic solution, you can discover what types have a specific attribute, which you can leverage for the work we did in *Chapter 4, Reasoning about Types Using Reflection*.

Personal Identifiable Information (PII)

Let's go back to the GDPR theme we touched on in previous chapters. In *Chapter 4, Reasoning about Types Using Reflection*, we used types to discover what was personally identifiable information. Another approach could be to use custom attributes as an explicit metadata approach. With attributes, we can associate more than what we did with a base type in *Chapter 4, Reasoning about Types Using Reflection*. You can add metadata about the reason for collecting the data.

You can capture this with an attribute like the following:

```
[AttributeUsage(AttributeTargets.Class |
  AttributeTargets.Property | AttributeTargets.Parameter,
    AllowMultiple = false, Inherited = true)]
public class PersonalIdentifiableInformationAttribute :
  Attribute
{
    public PersonalIdentifiableInformationAttribute(string
      reasonForCollecting = "")
    {
        ReasonForCollecting = reasonForCollecting;
    }

    public string ReasonForCollecting { get; }
}
```

The code creates an attribute that can be applied to classes, properties, and parameters. It does not allow multiple instances of itself to be applied to the code element it will be applied to. It allows the metadata to be available for any type that inherits from the type that has this metadata applied to it or its members. One of the things it is interesting to know about GDPR is the reason the system collects specific data – the attribute, therefore, has this as optional metadata.

> **Important note**
> You'll find this implementation in the Fundamentals project in the GitHub repository.

Start by creating a folder called Chapter 5. Change into this folder in your command-line interface and create a new console project:

```
dotnet new console
```

The next thing you'll need to do is to reference the Fundamentals project. If you have the project next to the Chapter5 folder, do the following:

```
dotnet add reference ../Fundamentals/Fundamentals.csproj
```

With that in place, let's say you want to create an object that encapsulates an employee:

```
public class Employee
{
    public string FirstName { get; set; } = string.Empty;
    public string LastName { get; set; } = string.Empty;
    public string SocialSecurityNumber { get; set; } =
      string.Empty;
}
```

This type clearly holds properties that would be identifiable for the person; let's add the appropriate metadata for its members:

```
using Fundamentals.Compliance.GDPR;

public class Employee
{
    [PersonalIdentifiableInformation("Employment records")]
    public string FirstName { get; set; } = string.Empty;

    [PersonalIdentifiableInformation("Employment records")]
    public string LastName { get; set; } = string.Empty;

    [PersonalIdentifiableInformation("Uniquely identifies
      the employee")]
    public string SocialSecurityNumber { get; set; } =
      string.Empty;
}
```

With this, we now have enough information to discover any type in the system that holds this type of information.

Building on the assembly and type discovery system introduced in *Chapter 4, Reasoning about Types Using Reflection*, we can query specifically for this.

Since every member on a type inherits from the `MemberInfo` type found in the `System.Reflection` namespace, we can easily create a convenience extension method allowing us to check whether a member has a specific attribute associated with it.

You can then create a simple extension method that allows you to check whether an attribute is associated with a member:

```
public static class MemberInfoExtensions
{
    public static bool HasAttribute<TAttribute>(this
      MemberInfo memberInfo) where TAttribute : Attribute
        => memberInfo.GetCustomAttributes<TAttribute>()
          .Any();
}
```

> **Important note**
>
> You'll find this implementation in the `Fundamentals` project in the GitHub repository.

With this in place, you can discover all the types with this information:

```
using Fundamentals;
```

```
var types = new Types();

var piiTypes = types.All.Where(_ => _
                        .GetMembers()
                        .Any(m => m.HasAttribute<Personal
                            IdentifiableInformation
                                Attribute>()));
var typeNames = string.Join("\n", piiTypes.Select(_ =>
    _.FullName));
Console.WriteLine(typeNames);
```

The `HasAttribute<>` extension method is a powerful little helper that you'll find handy in all scenarios where you want to do simple querying of type metadata based on attributes.

To create a GDPR report with the reason for collecting information, change the `Program.cs` file look like the following:

```
using System.Reflection;
using Fundamentals;

var types = new Types();

Console.WriteLine("\n\nGDPR Report");
var typesWithPII = types.All
                        .SelectMany(_ =>
                            _.GetProperties()
                                .Where(p => p.HasAttribute
                                <PersonalIdentifiable
                                    InformationAttribute>()))
                        .GroupBy(_ => _.DeclaringType);

foreach (var typeWithPII in typesWithPII)
{
    Console.WriteLine($"Type: {typeWithPII.Key!
      .FullName}");
    foreach (var property in typeWithPII)
    {
        var pii = property.GetCustomAttribute<
          PersonalIdentifiableInformationAttribute>();
        Console.WriteLine($"  Property : {property.Name}");
        Console.WriteLine($"    Reason :
          {pii.ReasonForCollecting}");
    }
}
```

The code leverages the type discovery introduced in *Chapter 4, Reasoning about Types Using Reflection*, and uses LINQ extension methods to select all the types that have properties with `[PersonalIdentifiableInformationAttribute]` applied. It then groups them by type so that you can easily loop through and present the members with the attribute per type.

Running this will yield the following result:

```
GDPR Report
Type: Main.Employee
   Property : FirstName
      Reason : Employment records
   Property : LastName
      Reason : Employment records
   Property : SocialSecurityNumber
      Reason : Uniquely identifies the employee
```

This type of metadata is very valuable for a business. If your business gets a query from the government about a GDPR audit, with your code fully loaded with metadata you can easily create a report on what type of data you're collecting and the reason for collecting it.

You could also present this type of information to the end users of your system. It is very valuable for a user to know what the system collects about them. This builds a trusting relationship between the system and your users.

GDPR is a very good use case for getting very useful metadata into your code base, but it is just one of many use cases. You can, of course, make use of metadata in a more actionable way other than just for reporting.

Generic attributes

One of the limitations of C# attributes that we used to have is that attributes could not be generic types taking generic arguments. Prior to C# 11, you would get a compiler error if you added a generic argument to your attribute class. This limitation is lifted with the release of **C# 11**.

Up till C# 11, the only way you could collect type information was for the attribute to have parameters or properties that were of type `System.Type`. This became very verbose:

```
public class CustomAttribute : Attribute
{
    public CustomAttribute(Type theType)
}
```

And then adorning a type with the attribute would be as follows:

```
[Custom(typeof(string))]
public class MyClass
{
}
```

With C# 11, now you can improve how you get type information:

```
public class CustomAttribute<T> : Attribute
{
}
```

When you adorn a type with the attribute, you use the generic argument:

```
[Custom<string>]
public class MyClass
{
}
```

If you're looking to have a parameter that is dynamic in type, you can do the following:

```
[AttributeUsage(AttributeTargets.Class, AllowMultiple =
    true)]
public class CustomAttribute<T> : Attribute
{
    public CustomAttribute(T someParameter)
    {
        SomeParameter = someParameter;
    }

    public T SomeParameter { get; }
}
```

The code defines an attribute that takes a generic argument and it then requires a parameter for the attribute, which will then be of the generic type. It then uses the same generic type when exposing the metadata as a property on the attribute.

When adorning types with the attribute, you specify the type and the parameter because the attribute has to be of the type specified:

```
[Custom<int>(42)]
[Custom<string>("Forty two)]
public class MyClass
{
}
```

> **Important note**
>
> Normally the C# compiler is very good at inferring the type for generic arguments based on the type passed in. But with generic attributes, you have to explicitly give it the generic type every time.

Generic attributes can be another powerful metadata collection approach. It adds flexibility to how you can construct your metadata.

Summary

In this chapter, we've looked at what C# attributes are and how powerful they are for describing explicit metadata in your code. We've looked at all the mechanics of how you can create your own custom attributes and apply them very to different code elements. From this type of metadata, you can now enrich your code.

With the enrichment looked at in this chapter, you've seen how you can quite easily discover this metadata and put it to good use for your business.

In our next chapter, we will dive further into the capabilities of the .NET runtime and look at how you can dynamically generate code based on metadata, making you more productive as a developer in doing so.

Dynamic Proxy Generation

In the previous chapters, we looked at how powerful it is to have the type of metadata that the .NET runtime provides us with, combining that with the power of creating your own metadata, the capability to analyze it, and turn it into useful information or take actions based on it. We're now going to explore even further and let code make new code based on metadata.

In this chapter, we will look into how we can take advantage of the fact that your code runs in a managed runtime environment and how that can be used to create new code at runtime after your code has been compiled.

We will cover the following topics:

- An introduction to IL and Reflection.Emit
- Creating a dynamic assembly and module
- Virtual members and overrides
- Implementing an interface

Upon completion of this chapter, you should understand the power of the .NET runtime and how you can turn metadata into new code to make you more productive.

Technical requirements

The source code specific to the chapter can be found on GitHub (https://github.com/PacktPublishing/Metaprogramming-in-C-Sharp/tree/main/Chapter6).

An introduction to IL and Reflection.Emit

In *Chapter 2, Metaprogramming Concepts*, we touched on what the C# compiler turns your code into. **IL**, short for **Intermediate Language**, is a representation of instructions the .NET runtime understands and translates to CPU instructions for the target CPU your code is running on.

Since the .NET runtime operates dynamically on your code in this manner, it means that it is not a too far a jump to conclude that you should be able to generate code as your program executes. And luckily, that is the case. The .NET APIs include a whole namespace dedicated to generating code – `System.Reflection.Emit`.

With the `Emit` APIs, you can go and create any constructs you want from scratch, introduce new types that do not exist in any source code, or create new types that inherit from other types and add new capabilities.

For all the different types of artifacts, you can create class, method, properties, and more. There are specific builder types – `TypeBuilder` for classes and `MethodBuilder` for methods. Properties are also considered methods and are based on a convention of a prefix having the name of `get_` or `set_`, which then represents a `get` or `set` method respectively.

With a builder, you can call a method called `.GetILGenerator()`. This method will then return a type called `ILGenerator`. The `ILGenerator` method is where all the magic happens. This is the type you can use to generate the actual code. The primary method you use is the `.Emit()` method. The `.Emit()` method has several overloads to it and is the method used to add instructions that constitute your program. Instructions are referred to as an **op-code**, and there is a class with all the allowed instructions, or op-codes, called `OpCodes`.

All the different op-codes are well defined and well documented, and you can find the documentation for all of them on Microsoft's documentation pages (`https://learn.microsoft.com/en-us/dotnet/api/system.reflection.emit.opcodes?view=net-7.0#fields`).

Even though they're well defined and well documented, the preparation involved to get the right instructions in the right order can be hard and daunting. Therefore, it's a good idea to derive the instructions from real code instead. A great resource for doing so is to use something such as **Sharplab** (`https://sharplab.io`). With Sharplab, you can take regular C# code and see the instructions needed to be able to reproduce it.

In order to get to the point of actually generating IL code, you need to jump through a couple more hoops.

Creating a dynamic assembly and module

When your code has gone through the compiler and been outputted to a binary that runs. That code is considered static and cannot be modified. The binary represented as an assembly is completely static; not only can you not modify code in it but you also cannot add to it either. It would be a security risk if arbitrary code could go and modify running code.

To overcome this, you have to explicitly create a new assembly on the fly that only exists in memory. This is known as a **dynamic assembly**.

All assemblies have also the concept of modules. An assembly must have at least one module. A module is a container that holds the concrete IL code and only metadata related to it, while an assembly is a higher-order abstract container that contains more metadata and could, in fact, refer to multiple .dll files. Generally, you'll only see a one-to-one relationship between an **assembly** and a **module**.

It is very easy to get started with this:

```
using System.Reflection;
using System.Reflection.Emit;

var assemblyName = new AssemblyName("MyDynamicAssembly");
var dynamicAssembly = AssemblyBuilder.Define
  DynamicAssembly(assemblyName, AssemblyBuilderAccess.Run);
var dynamicModule = dynamicAssembly.DefineDynamicModule
  ("MyDynamicModule");
```

The code defines the two containers you need – first, the .DefineDynamicAssembly() method creates the dynamic assembly, and you tell it to give you an assembly that you will use to run code from. Once you have the dynamic assembly, you call .DefineDynamicModule() to get the container where you'll generate the actual code that will run.

One thing you should take into consideration is the name of both the dynamic assembly and dynamic module. Assembly names need to be unique within a running process, and within an assembly, every module needs a unique name as well. So, if you're going to create multiple dynamic assemblies and multiple modules within them, you need to guarantee unique names.

The simplest way to do that is to leverage Guid and mix it into your name. The following code will give a unique name:

```
static string CreateUniqueName(string prefix)
{
    var uid = Guid.NewGuid().ToString();
    uid = uid.Replace('-', '_');
    return $"{prefix}{uid}";
}
```

The code generates a new Guid and combines it with a prefix. The purpose of the prefix is to be able to recognize the different assemblies with a friendly name. There are some limitations to what characters can be used in an assembly name; that's why you see that - is replaced with _.

If your code only needs one dynamic assembly and a dynamic module within it, the need to create a unique name might not be needed, as you can quite easily just give it a unique name.

You might not even need to have multiple dynamic assemblies and, most likely, not even multiple modules within the dynamic assembly. It is perfectly fine to have one global dynamic assembly. It all depends on your code and whether or not you'll be generating types with the same name for different purposes that should then be grouped into specific assembly/module pair containers.

With a dynamic assembly and a dynamic module in place, we can start generating some code.

Let's dynamically create a simple type without its source code that can print out a message. The target type we're aiming for would look something like the following if we wrote it in C#:

```csharp
public class MyType
{
    public void SaySomething(string message)
    {
        System.Console.WriteLine(message);
    }
}
```

If we put this into Sharplab (https://sharplab.io), we can see the IL code that is behind it and use it as the template for what we're trying to achieve:

Figure 6.1 – IL code

1. Start by creating a folder called Chapter6. Open this folder in your command-line interface and create a new console project:

    dotnet new console

    Add a file called MyTypeGenerator.cs. Start by making the file look like the following:

    ```csharp
    using System.Reflection;
    using System.Reflection.Emit;

    namespace Chapter6;

    public class MyTypeGenerator
    ```

```
    {
        public static Type Generate()
        {
            // Do the generation
        }
    }
```

2. As you can see, we have pulled in two namespaces – `System.Reflection` and `System.Reflection.Emit`. These hold the APIs we will be needing.

   The first thing we want to do is create the assembly and module, and add the following to the `Generate` method:

   ```
   var name = new AssemblyName("MyDynamicAssembly");
   var assembly = AssemblyBuilder.DefineDynamicAssembly(name,
     AssemblyBuilderAccess.Run);
   var module = assembly.DefineDynamicModule
     ("MyDynamicModule");
   ```

   From the module, we can create a new type, and within the type, a method. Then, we append the following to the `Generate` method after the module has been defined:

   ```
   var typeBuilder = module.DefineType("MyType",
     TypeAttributes.Public | TypeAttributes.Class);
   var methodBuilder = typeBuilder.DefineMethod
     ("SaySomething", MethodAttributes.Public);
   methodBuilder.SetParameters(typeof(string));
   methodBuilder.DefineParameter(0, ParameterAttributes.None,
     "message");
   ```

   The code creates a public class called `MyType` and then defines a public method called `SaySomething`. In the method, we then set that it has parameters. The method accepts `param` that allows us to define one or more parameter types. The last thing we do is define the parameter. This is done by giving it the parameter index it has and a name.

Important note

The `ParameterAttributes` value you give the parameter indicates that there is nothing special with it; it is a regular parameter. If you wanted it to be an `out` or `ref` parameter, you would tell it that.

---

3. You now have the definition in place of the method with the expected signature. It is now time for you to fill in the actual code.

   The code for this method is very simple, as we're just taking the parameter coming in and passing it to another method.

With the method definition in place, you can start building out the code. Append the following code to the `Generate` method:

```
var consoleType = typeof(Console);
var writeLineMethod = consoleType.GetMethod(nameof
  (Console.WriteLine), new[] { typeof(string) })!;

var methodILGenerator = methodBuilder.GetILGenerator();
methodILGenerator.Emit(OpCodes.Ldarg_1);
methodILGenerator.EmitCall(OpCodes.Call, writeLineMethod,
  new[] { typeof(string) });
methodILGenerator.Emit(OpCodes.Ret);
```

The code starts off by getting the `System.Console` type and the method called `WriteLine`, which accepts a simple `string`. The method is what you are going to use to call and forward the incoming parameter that will eventually produce the message in the console. Once you have the `WriteLine` method, you need `ILGenerator` for the `SaySomething` method you're building. Then, the first thing you do is to emit an instruction to load the actual argument given to the parameter into what is known as the **evaluation stack**. `OpCodes.Ldarg_1` refers to 1, which might seem counterintuitive. In the context of an instance type, `OpCodes.Ldarg_0` would represent the value of `this`. With the argument loaded onto the stack, you emit code that calls the `WriteLine` method on `Console`, giving it the type of parameter to use. Finishing off your method, you emit a return instruction from the method.

4. The last piece of the `Generate` method is building out the actual `Type` and returning it. Append the following to the `Generate` method:

```
return typeBuilder.CreateType()!;
```

The full listing of the `MyTypeGenerator` class should now look like the following:

```
using System.Reflection;
using System.Reflection.Emit;

namespace Chapter6;

public class MyTypeGenerator
{
    public static Type Generate()
    {
        var name = new AssemblyName("MyDynamicAssembly");
        var assembly = AssemblyBuilder.DefineDynamic
            Assembly(name, AssemblyBuilderAccess.Run);
        var module = assembly.DefineDynamicModule
            ("MyDynamicModule");
        var typeBuilder = module.DefineType("MyType",
            TypeAttributes.Public | TypeAttributes.Class);
```

```
        var methodBuilder = typeBuilder.DefineMethod
          ("SaySomething", MethodAttributes.Public);
        methodBuilder.SetParameters(typedoc(string));
        var parameterBuilder = methodBuilder
          .DefineParameter(0, ParameterAttributes.None,
            "message");

        var consoleType = typeof(Console);
        var writeLineMethod = consoleType.GetMethod
          (nameof(Console.WriteLine), new[] { typeof
            (string) })!;

        var methodILGenerator = methodBuilder
          .GetILGenerator();
        methodILGenerator.Emit(OpCodes.Ldarg_1);
        methodILGenerator.EmitCall(OpCodes.Call,
          writeLineMethod, new[] { typeof(string) });
        methodILGenerator.Emit(OpCodes.Ret);

        return typeBuilder.CreateType()!;
    }
}
```

With your first code generator in place, you want to take it out for a spin. Since this is a type that is completely unknown to the compiler, there is really no way to write standard C# code that can call it. You will have to revert to reflection to do so.

In the Program.cs file of the Chapter6 project, replace the existing code with the following:

```
using Chapter6;

var myType = MyTypeGenerator.Generate();
var method = myType.GetMethod("SaySomething")!;
var myTypeInstance = Activator.CreateInstance(myType);
method.Invoke(myTypeInstance, new[] { "Hello world" });
```

The code calls into your new generator to get the generated Type. Next, it asks the generated type to get the method called SaySomething. You then go and create an instance of the type by using the Activator type in .NET. From the method, you can then invoke it and give the instance as the first parameter, and then add in the parameter it is expecting in the array that follows.

Running this using dotnet run or, if you prefer, your IDE, you should get a simple message:

Hello world

The intermediate language and how the runtime actually works with instructions is logical, but it might not be intuitive compared to writing C#. However, it gives you great powers and enables new scenarios.

Virtual members and overrides

From my own experience, generating new types from scratch that didn't exist at compile time is not the most common use case. I've found myself, more often than not, just wanting to automate something that I find tedious and forced upon me from libraries that I have to use.

When that is the case, it is common to take a type and create a new one that inherits from this and then starts overriding behavior.

Since C# doesn't have all its members as virtual, as the case is with Java, members have to be explicitly virtual. An example of a method that is virtual is one that all objects inherit – the ToString method.

Let's continue the work on the MyTypeGenerator code by adding an override of the ToString method, just to see the mechanics of how it is done:

1. In the Generate method of the MyTypeGenerator class, before you return the type, you need to define a new method that will be the MyType implementation of the ToString method:

    ```
    var toStringMethod = typeof(object).GetMethod(nameof
      (object.ToString))!;
    var newToStringMethod = typeBuilder.DefineMethod(nameof
      (object.ToString), toStringMethod.Attributes,
        typeof(string), Array.Empty<Type>());
    var toStringGenerator = newToStringMethod.GetILGenerator();
    toStringGenerator.Emit(OpCodes.Ldstr, "A message from
      ToString()");
    toStringGenerator.Emit(OpCodes.Ret);
    typeBuilder.DefineMethodOverride(newToStringMethod,
      toStringMethod);
    ```

    First, the code gets a reference to the method it wants to override from the base class. Since this type doesn't have a specific base type, it will implicitly just be object. Then, you start defining the new ToString method and specify that it will return a string type. Since the ToString method doesn't take any parameters, you just pass it an empty array of Type. From the method definition, you go and do as before – get ILGenerator. You then simply load the string into the evaluation stack, which will be the only thing there, and return from the method. To make it an override method, you then call .DefineMethodOverride() on the type builder to tell it which method you're overriding and give it the original ToString method.

2. Open the Program.cs file and add a line of code that will invoke the ToString method to see that it works:

    ```
    using Chapter6;

    var myType = MyTypeGenerator.Generate();
    var method = myType.GetMethod("SaySomething")!;
    var myTypeInstance = Activator.CreateInstance(myType);
    ```

```
method.Invoke(myTypeInstance, new[] { "Hello world" });
Console.WriteLine(myTypeInstance); // Added line
```

Running the program should then print out the message:

A message from ToString()

With what you've learned thus far in this chapter, you should now have the basic building blocks to create types with members on them and also override virtual members from inherited base types. All of these things will get you pretty far. Now that we've looked at the mechanics of how to generate code, let's make a more concrete example.

Implementing an interface

In addition to overriding virtual members from a base type, there is often the need to implement interfaces that satisfy a need for a third-party library you are using. The implementation of the interface might not be important to your own code, but it is something that is forced on you to enable certain behaviors.

Anyone who has been doing any XAML-flavored development will have come across an interface called INotifyPropertyChanged. The INotifyPropertyChanged interface is something that the data binding engine recognizes and will automatically use if a type implements it. Its purpose is to notify anyone using your object when a property changes. This is very useful when you have a UI element automatically reflecting changes being done in the data behind the scenes.

The INotifyPropertyChanged interface itself is very simple and looks like this:

```
public interface INotifyPropertyChanged
{
    event PropertyChangedEventHandler? PropertyChanged;
}
```

For an object implementing INotifyPropertyChanged, it means it needs to implement the logic for every property when its value is set. This can be very tedious and will bloat your code base with code that is not part of your domain.

Let's say you have an object representing a person:

```
public class Employee
{
    public string FirstName { get; set; }
    public string LastName { get; set; }
}
```

With the INotifyPropertyChanged requirement for binding purposes, the object would, for just one of the properties, need to explode into the following:

```csharp
using System.ComponentModel;

public class Employee : INotifyPropertyChanged
{
    private string _firstName;
    public string FirstName
    {
        get { return _firstName; }
        set
        {
            _firstName = value;
            RaisePropertyChanged("FirstName");
        }
    }

    public event PropertyChangedEventHandler
      PropertyChanged;
    protected void RaisePropertyChanged(string
      propertyName)
    {
        if (PropertyChanged != null)
        {
            PropertyChanged(this, new Property
                ChangedEventArgs(propertyName));
        }
    }
}
```

As you can see, the code goes from simple one-liners per property to something that explicitly has a getter, setter, and private field to hold the actual value. In the setter, you have to then raise the PropertyChanged event, and a typical pattern is to have a convenience method that is reused for all properties to do that.

Thanks to code generation, you can make it all go away and get your code back to being readable and more maintainable, making you more productive in the process.

In the Chapter6 folder, go and create a new file called Person.cs and make it look like the following:

```csharp
namespace Chapter6;

public class Employee
{
    public virtual string FirstName { get; set; }
    public virtual string LastName { get; set; }
}
```

The `Person` class now represents the target version without any of the `INotifyPropertyChanged` things. At compile-time, it does not implement the `INotifyPropertyChanged` interface, but we will make it do so at runtime.

Since we've made the properties `virtual`, we can create a new type that inherits from the `Person` type and overrides the properties to do what we want.

NotifyObjectWeaver class

To be able to do what we want, we need to do the following:

1. Create a new type.
2. Inherit from the existing type.
3. Implement the `INotifyPropertyChanged` interface.
4. Add a method that handles the logic for when a property is changed.
5. Override any virtual methods and implement the code needed for notification when properties change.

In addition to this, it is also common to have properties that are dependent on other properties – for instance, to compose multiple properties together. These should also notify you of their change, so you want something to handle that as well.

Start by adding a file called `NotifyObjectWeaver.cs` in the `Chapter6` project. Then, add the following to the file:

```
using System.ComponentModel;
using System.Linq.Expressions;
using System.Reflection;
using System.Reflection.Emit;

namespace Chapter6;

public static class NotifyingObjectWeaver
{
    const string DynamicAssemblyName = "Dynamic Assembly";
    const string DynamicModuleName = "Dynamic Module";
    const string PropertyChangedEventName = nameof
      (INotifyPropertyChanged.PropertyChanged);
    const string OnPropertyChangedMethodName =
      "OnPropertyChanged";
    static readonly Type VoidType = typeof(void);
    static readonly Type DelegateType = typeof(Delegate);

    const MethodAttributes EventMethodAttributes =
```

```
            MethodAttributes.Public | MethodAttributes
              .HideBySig | MethodAttributes.Virtual;

        const MethodAttributes OnPropertyChanged
          MethodAttributes =
              MethodAttributes.Public | MethodAttributes
                .HideBySig;
    }
```

The code adds the common constants and statics you'll be using in the code generation, ensuring that you do not have to repeat them throughout and that they gather at the top for better structure.

With this, you now have the start of the NotifyObjectWeaver class.

Creating the type

The first thing you're going to start with is the code to define the type. It is pretty much what you've done before, only that we are now going to make your dynamically created type inherit from a base type and also implement an interface:

```
static TypeBuilder DefineType(Type type)
{
    var name = $"{type.Name}_Proxy";
    var typeBuilder = DynamicModule.DefineType(name,
      TypeAttributes.Public | TypeAttributes.Class);

    typeBuilder.SetParent(type);
    var interfaceType = typeof(INotifyPropertyChanged);
    typeBuilder.AddInterfaceImplementation(interfaceType);
    return typeBuilder;
}
```

The call to .SetParent() is the key to the inheritance. It instructs the builder to take the Type input given to the method as the parent. The next thing you do is to instruct the builder that you will be implementing the INotifyPropertyChanged interface.

Implementing the INotifyPropertyChanged interface

The INotifyPropertyChanged interface only has one field on it, the PropertyChanged event field that we need to implement. We need to add code that defines the event and also implements the logic to add and remove event handlers from the event.

In the NotifyObjectWeaver class, add the following method:

```
static void DefineEvent(TypeBuilder typeBuilder, Type
  eventHandlerType, FieldBuilder fieldBuilder)
```

```
{
    var eventBuilder = typeBuilder.DefineEvent(nameof
      (INotifyPropertyChanged.PropertyChanged),
        EventAttributes.None, eventHandlerType);
    DefineAddMethodForEvent(typeBuilder, eventHandlerType,
      fieldBuilder, eventBuilder);
    DefineRemoveMethodForEvent(typeBuilder,
      eventHandlerType, fieldBuilder, eventBuilder);
}
```

The DefineEvent method defines the actual event on the type and then calls two methods to define the add and remove methods for the event.

Add the following method to the NotifyObjectWeaver class:

```
static void DefineAddMethodForEvent(TypeBuilder
  typeBuilder, Type eventHandlerType, FieldBuilder
  fieldBuilder, EventBuilder eventBuilder)
{
    var combineMethodInfo = DelegateType.GetMethod
      ("Combine", BindingFlags.Public |
        BindingFlags.Static, null,
          new[] { DelegateType, DelegateType }, null)!;

    var addEventMethod = string.Format("add_{0}",
      PropertyChangedEventName);
    var addMethodBuilder = typeBuilder.DefineMethod
      (addEventMethod, EventMethodAttributes, VoidType,
        new[] { eventHandlerType });
    var addMethodGenerator = addMethodBuilder
      .GetILGenerator();
    addMethodGenerator.Emit(OpCodes.Ldarg_0);
    addMethodGenerator.Emit(OpCodes.Ldarg_0);
    addMethodGenerator.Emit(OpCodes.Ldfld, fieldBuilder);
    addMethodGenerator.Emit(OpCodes.Ldarg_1);
    addMethodGenerator.EmitCall(OpCodes.Call,
      combineMethodInfo, null);
    addMethodGenerator.Emit(OpCodes.Castclass,
      eventHandlerType);
    addMethodGenerator.Emit(OpCodes.Stfld, fieldBuilder);
    addMethodGenerator.Emit(OpCodes.Ret);
    eventBuilder.SetAddOnMethod(addMethodBuilder);
}
```

The code adds a method that by convention will be used when event handlers are added, add_
PropertyChanged. It uses the Delegate type that you added at the beginning of the class to
get the Combine method that will be called.

It then generates the needed IL code that adds the incoming callback to be called when a change
happens, by calling the retrieved Combine method.

You should also, for good measure, add the opposite – the method that will remove a callback that
has been added. Add the following method to the NotifyObjectWeaver class:

```
static void DefineRemoveMethodForEvent(TypeBuilder
  typeBuilder, Type eventHandlerType, FieldBuilder
    fieldBuilder, EventBuilder eventBuilder)
{
    var removeEventMethod = string.Format("remove_{0}",
      PropertyChangedEventName)!;
    var removeMethodInfo = DelegateType.GetMethod("Remove",
      BindingFlags.Public | BindingFlags.Static, null,
        new[] { DelegateType, DelegateType }, null)!;
    var removeMethodBuilder = typeBuilder.DefineMethod
      (removeEventMethod, EventMethodAttributes, VoidType,
        new[] { eventHandlerType });
    var removeMethodGenerator = removeMethodBuilder
      .GetILGenerator();
    removeMethodGenerator.Emit(OpCodes.Ldarg_0);
    removeMethodGenerator.Emit(OpCodes.Ldarg_0);
    removeMethodGenerator.Emit(OpCodes.Ldfld,
      fieldBuilder);
    removeMethodGenerator.Emit(OpCodes.Ldarg_1);
    removeMethodGenerator.EmitCall(OpCodes.Call,
      removeMethodInfo, null);
    removeMethodGenerator.Emit(OpCodes.Castclass,
      eventHandlerType);
    removeMethodGenerator.Emit(OpCodes.Stfld,
      fieldBuilder);
    removeMethodGenerator.Emit(OpCodes.Ret);
    eventBuilder.SetRemoveOnMethod(removeMethodBuilder);
}
```

The implementation of remove is pretty much the same as for add, with the difference of getting the
Remove method from the Delegate type and calling .SetRemoveOnMethod().

The OnPropertyChanged method

With the event logic in place, you now need a private method that all properties will call – an
OnPropertyChanged method that will be doing all the heavy lifting.

Start by adding the following method in the `NotifyObjectWeaver` class:

```
static MethodBuilder DefineOnPropertyChangedMethod
  (TypeBuilder typeBuilder, FieldBuilder
    propertyChangedFieldBuilder)
{
    var onPropertyChangedMethodBuilder =
      typeBuilder.DefineMethod(OnPropertyChangedMethodName,
        OnPropertyChangedMethodAttributes, VoidType,
    new[] { typeof(string) });
    var onPropertyChangedMethodGenerator =
      onPropertyChangedMethodBuilder.GetILGenerator();

    var invokeMethod = typeof(PropertyChangedEventHandler)
      .GetMethod(nameof(PropertyChangedEventHandler
        .Invoke))!;
}
```

The code defines the `OnPropertyChanged` method with a signature that takes `string`, with the name of the property that changed.

Then, add the following at the end of `DefineOnPropertyChangedMethod` to declare a local variable that holds the type of event args the code will create:

```
var propertyChangedEventArgsType = typeof(
  PropertyChangedEventArgs);
onPropertyChangedMethodGenerator.DeclareLocal(
  propertyChangedEventArgsType);
```

Now, you need code that checks whether the `PropertyChanged` event field is null or not and has the `propertyChangedNullLabel` label that the code can jump to if the value is null.

Add the following code at the end of the `DefineOnPropertyChangedMethod` method:

```
var propertyChangedNullLabel = onPropertyChangedMethod
  Generator.DefineLabel();
onPropertyChangedMethodGenerator.Emit(OpCodes.Ldnull);
onPropertyChangedMethodGenerator.Emit(OpCodes.Ldarg_0);
onPropertyChangedMethodGenerator.Emit(OpCodes.Ldfld,
  propertyChangedFieldBuilder);
onPropertyChangedMethodGenerator.Emit(OpCodes.Ceq);
onPropertyChangedMethodGenerator.Emit(OpCodes.Brtrue_S,
  propertyChangedNullLabel);
```

Now, you need to add code that creates the `PropertyChangedEventArgs` instance with the argument that was passed into the `OnPropertyChanged` method. Then, call the `invoke` method:

```
onPropertyChangedMethodGenerator.Emit(OpCodes.Ldarg_1);
onPropertyChangedMethodGenerator.Emit(OpCodes.Newobj,
  propertyChangedEventArgsType.GetConstructor(new[] {
    typeof(string) })!);
onPropertyChangedMethodGenerator.Emit(OpCodes.Stloc_0);

onPropertyChangedMethodGenerator.Emit(OpCodes.Ldarg_0);
onPropertyChangedMethodGenerator.Emit(OpCodes.Ldfld,
  propertyChangedFieldBuilder);
onPropertyChangedMethodGenerator.Emit(OpCodes.Ldarg_0);
onPropertyChangedMethodGenerator.Emit(OpCodes.Ldloc_0);
onPropertyChangedMethodGenerator.EmitCall(OpCodes.Callvirt,
  invokeMethod, null);
```

The last piece of the puzzle is to mark the label that the null check will jump to if it is null, and then return from the method. Add the following to the end of the `DefineOnPropertyChangedMethod` method:

```
onPropertyChangedMethodGenerator.MarkLabel(propertyChanged
  NullLabel);
onPropertyChangedMethodGenerator.Emit(OpCodes.Ret);
return onPropertyChangedMethodBuilder;
```

The code to define the `OnPropertyChanged` method is now done. Now, you need to define the properties.

The overriding properties

One of the requirements we had at the beginning was that we wanted to be able to notify other properties to make composites or, if it's relevant, for another property to re-evaluate:

1. Add a file called `NotifyChangedForAttribute.cs` and make it look like the following:

    ```
    namespace Chapter6;

    [AttributeUsage(AttributeTargets.Property)]
    public class NotifyChangesForAttribute : Attribute
    {
        public NotifyChangesForAttribute(params string[]
          propertyNames)
        {
            PropertyNames = propertyNames;
        }
    ```

```
    public string[] PropertyNames { get; }
}
```

This custom attribute takes a `param` array of property names that will be called for a change, in addition to the property that changed.

2. For convenience, you should add a method to get the properties to notify, based on `PropertyInfo` for the property. In the `NotifyingObjectWeaver` class, add the following method:

```
static string[] GetPropertiesToNotifyFor(PropertyInfo
   property)
{
    var properties = new List<string>
    {
        property.Name
    };

    foreach (var attribute in (NotifyChangesForAttribute[])
      property.GetCustomAttributes(typeof(NotifyChangesFor
        Attribute), true))
    {
        properties.AddRange(attribute.PropertyNames);
    }
    return properties.ToArray();
}
```

The code combines the name of the property, looks for the `NotifyChangesForAttribute` attribute, and adds the declared names.

3. You're now ready to add the method that defines all the properties on the new type. Add the following method to the `NotifyingObjectWeaver` class:

```
static void DefineProperties(TypeBuilder typeBuilder, Type
   baseType, MethodBuilder onPropertyChangedMethodBuilder)
{
    var properties = baseType.GetProperties();
    var query = from p in properties
                where p.GetGetMethod()!.IsVirtual && !p
                   .GetGetMethod()!.IsFinal
                select p;

    foreach (var property in query)
    {
        DefineGetMethodForProperty(property, typeBuilder);
        DefineSetMethodForProperty(property, typeBuilder,
           onPropertyChangedMethodBuilder);
    }
```

```
}
```

The code looks at the base type and gets all the properties and filters down to only virtual methods. Then, for all the properties it found, it goes and defines the `get` and `set` methods for the property.

4. Add the following method to the `NotifyingObjectWeaver` class:

```
static void DefineSetMethodForProperty(PropertyInfo
  property, TypeBuilder typeBuilder, MethodBuilder
  onPropertyChangedMethodBuilder)
{
    var setMethodToOverride = property.GetSetMethod();
    if (setMethodToOverride is null)
    {
        return;
    }
    var setMethodBuilder = typeBuilder.DefineMethod
      (setMethodToOverride.Name, setMethodToOverride
        .Attributes, VoidType, new[] { property
          .PropertyType });
    var setMethodGenerator = setMethodBuilder
      .GetILGenerator();
    var propertiesToNotifyFor = GetPropertiesToNotifyFor
      (property);

    setMethodGenerator.Emit(OpCodes.Ldarg_0);
    setMethodGenerator.Emit(OpCodes.Ldarg_1);
    setMethodGenerator.Emit(OpCodes.Call,
      setMethodToOverride);

    foreach (var propertyName in propertiesToNotifyFor)
    {
        setMethodGenerator.Emit(OpCodes.Ldarg_0);
        setMethodGenerator.Emit(OpCodes.Ldstr,
          propertyName);
        setMethodGenerator.Emit(OpCodes.Call,
          onPropertyChangedMethodBuilder);
    }

    setMethodGenerator.Emit(OpCodes.Ret);
    typeBuilder.DefineMethodOverride(setMethodBuilder,
      setMethodToOverride);
}
```

The `set_*` method is the method that will perform the notification. The code defines the method and first adds a call to the base type's set method so that the base type can handle the value being set for itself. Then, it loops through all the properties to notify for and adds code to call the OnPropertyChanged method with the name of the property.

5. Getting the value is slightly different, as you only want it to read through to the base type and get the value from it.

    Add the following method to the NotifyingObjectWeaver class:

```
static void DefineGetMethodForProperty(PropertyInfo
  property, TypeBuilder typeBuilder)
{
    var getMethodToOverride = property.GetGetMethod()!;
    var getMethodBuilder = typeBuilder.DefineMethod
      (getMethodToOverride.Name, getMethodToOverride
        .Attributes, property.PropertyType,
          Array.Empty<Type>());
    var getMethodGenerator = getMethodBuilder
      .GetILGenerator();
    var label = getMethodGenerator.DefineLabel();

    getMethodGenerator.DeclareLocal(property.PropertyType);
    getMethodGenerator.Emit(OpCodes.Ldarg_0);
    getMethodGenerator.Emit(OpCodes.Call,
      getMethodToOverride);
    getMethodGenerator.Emit(OpCodes.Stloc_0);
    getMethodGenerator.Emit(OpCodes.Br_S, label);
    getMethodGenerator.MarkLabel(label);
    getMethodGenerator.Emit(OpCodes.Ldloc_0);
    getMethodGenerator.Emit(OpCodes.Ret);
    typeBuilder.DefineMethodOverride(getMethodBuilder,
      getMethodToOverride);
}
```

You now have all the code for doing the code generation needed for the properties and also the method to raise the PropertyChanged event.

Initialization and public API

The last piece of the puzzle will be to do the main initialization that defines the dynamic assembly and module.

Add the following in the NotifyingObjectWeaver class:

```
static readonly AssemblyBuilder DynamicAssembly;
static readonly ModuleBuilder DynamicModule;
```

```
static readonly Dictionary<Type, Type> Proxies = new();

static NotifyingObjectWeaver()
{
    var assemblyName = new AssemblyName
      (DynamicAssemblyName);
    DynamicAssembly = AssemblyBuilder
      .DefineDynamicAssembly(assemblyName,
        AssemblyBuilderAccess.Run);
    DynamicModule = DynamicAssembly.DefineDynamicModule
      (DynamicModuleName);
}
```

The code introduces a private `Proxies` field. This will serve as a cache to avoid generating the same type multiple times every time one needs a proxy of a type.

You now need a public API that can be called from the outside to get a proxy type of another type.

Add the following code to the `NotifyingObjectWeaver` class:

```
public static Type GetProxyType(Type type)
{
    Type proxyType;
    if (Proxies.ContainsKey(type))
    {
        proxyType = Proxies[type];
    }
    else
    {
        proxyType = CreateProxyType(type);
        Proxies[type] = proxyType;
    }

    return proxyType;
}
```

The `GetProxyType` method checks first whether there is a proxy type for the given type and returns the existing one if that's the case, creating the proxy type if it doesn't have it in the cache.

Using NotifyingObjectWeaver

You now have a fully functional object weaver. Let's take it out for a spin. In the `Program.cs` file, add the following code:

```
var type = NotifyingObjectWeaver.GetProxyType
  (typeof(Person));
Console.WriteLine($"Type name : {type}");
```

```
var instance = (Activator.CreateInstance(type) as
  INotifyPropertyChanged)!;
instance.PropertyChanged += (sender, e) =>
  Console.WriteLine($"{e.PropertyName} changed");

var instanceAsViewModel = (instance as Person)!;
instanceAsViewModel.FirstName = "John";
```

The code asks for a wrapped-up type and then creates an instance of it. Since it now implements INotifyPropertyChanged, we can simply cast it to that type and interact with the PropertyChanged event.

And since the new type inherits from the Person class, we can also cast it to that type and set the property on it.

When you run this program, you should see the following:

```
Type name : Person6e46bfa7_e47a_4299_8ae6_f928b8a027ee
FirstName changed
```

Now would be a good time to try out the NotifyChangesFor functionality you added. Open the Person.cs file and change it to look like the following:

```
public class Person
{
    [NotifyChangesFor(nameof(FullName))]
    public virtual string FirstName { get; set; } =
      string.Empty;

    [NotifyChangesFor(nameof(FullName))]
    public virtual string LastName { get; set; } =
      string.Empty;

    public virtual string FullName => $"{FirstName}
      {LastName}";
}
```

Since FullName is a composite of both FirstName and LastName, it makes sense to be notified if either of those properties changes.

Running the program should now give you the following:

```
Type name : Person6e46bfa7_e47a_4299_8ae6_f928b8a027ee
FirstName changed
FullName changed
```

The code in the GitHub repository has more capabilities that sit there as a reference. For instance, if the base type has a constructor that takes parameters, you should implement the same constructor in the type and pass along the constructor parameters to the base constructor.

Another common occurrence you may run into is the need to be able to ignore properties. Since the implementation in this chapter is an **opt-out** model, all virtual properties are considered properties that notify about changes. This might not be true, but it is most likely what you need from most properties. Therefore, you want to have a way to ignore these.

Look at the complete listing in the GitHub repository, where you can see how these things are implemented.

Summary

In this chapter, we have learned about the power of having a managed runtime environment, seeing how we can take full advantage of it by dynamically creating code that will be executed in the same premises as pre-compiled code.

The possibilities are pretty much endless with such a power. It is super helpful as a way to automate tedious tasks and optimize the developer experience, but it can be used for so much more. For instance, if you have a system that dynamically connects to other systems and the types are dynamically created through configuration or similar, instead of going through untyped mechanisms such as the `Dictionary<,>` type to hold property values, an optimization would be to create types on the fly. The benefit is that you'd have something that was type-safe within the runtime. It could also prove to be a performance boost to your system, as you wouldn't be looking up values from the dictionary.

In the next chapter, we will dive into a constructor called `Expression`, how it can be used to represent code and logic, and how you can extract information from an `Expression`.

7

Reasoning about Expressions

So far, we've looked at the powerful metadata that is captured and how we can access it using reflection. We've also looked at how we can leverage this same metadata and generate code on the fly at runtime.

Using reflection and generating code as techniques in metaprogramming are extremely powerful, but they're not applicable to all scenarios. It can also be very involved and produce hard-to-read and maybe even hard-to-maintain code going deep with reflection and proxy generation.

C# expressions can, for a lot of scenarios, represent a better approach or an additional approach for specific scenarios for doing runtime discovery and extraction of metadata.

We will cover the following topics in this chapter:

- What are expressions?
- Traversing an expression tree
- Using expressions as descriptors of members on types

From this chapter, you should understand what expressions are and how you can leverage them as a technique to reason about the running code at runtime.

Technical requirements

The source code specific to the chapter can be found on GitHub (https://github.com/PacktPublishing/Metaprogramming-in-C-Sharp/tree/main/Chapter7), and it builds on top of the Fundamentals code that is found at https://github.com/PacktPublishing/Metaprogramming-in-C-Sharp/tree/main/Fundamentals.

> **Important note**
> Both the GetMemberExpression() and GetPropertyInfo() methods can be found in the ExpressionExtensions.cs file in Fundamentals in the GitHub repository.

What are expressions?

C# 3.0 was introduced in late 2007, and its killer feature was something called **Language-Integrated Query (LINQ)**. With the underlying API model and combination of new capabilities in C#, it introduced a programming paradigm that bridges into the more functional programming space. The fluent interfaces and its use of lambdas can feel foreign if you're used to more object-oriented approaches.

What it brought to the table was a way of expressing queries for data in a more natural native C# way. Not only does it do this for your in-memory collections, but also for any other data source, such as a database. It basically gave developers a uniform way of expressing queries, filters, and projections.

It did this by recognizing that a query operation consists of the following three distinct parts:

- The data source
- The query expression
- Executing the query

Let's look at an example without LINQ and compare it to how you could do the same with LINQ in a more expressive way:

```
int[] items = { 1, 2, 3, 42, 84, 37, 23 };

var filtered = new List<int>();
foreach (var item in items)
{
    if( item >= 37 )
    {
        filtered.Add(item);
    }
}
Console.WriteLine(string.Join(',', filtered));
```

Running this would print out 42, 84, 37, as expected. The challenge with something like this is that it is very verbose and coupled to the data source and gives no room for optimization.

With LINQ and the recognition of the three distinct parts mentioned earlier that make up a query, there is a concept of **deferred execution**. The actual execution of the query does not happen until you start enumerating it. That means you can build on the query while its final execution won't occur until we really need the data. The execution is performed by the query provider, which could be the default in-memory one or something that represents a data source such as a database.

Representing the previous sample with LINQ is much more expressive:

```
int[] items = { 1, 2, 3, 42, 84, 37, 23 };

var selectedItems =
    from i in items
    where i >= 37
    select i;

Console.WriteLine(string.Join(',', selectedItems));
```

The code becomes much more readable, but what happens behind the scenes is that it also becomes much more flexible in how it runs and makes it possible to optimize the execution as it sees fit for the data source the query is running against.

LINQ is a language feature of C#, and it can't work without support from the .NET class libraries and the .NET runtime. This is where expressions come in.

As part of the base class libraries that were released at the same time, there was a new namespace called System.Linq and another within it called System.Linq.Expressions. This is where the *magic sauce* lies.

The C# compiler translates the native LINQ code using another feature that was introduced in C# 3.0 called extension methods. Extension methods are just static methods that look like they're members of the actual type they extend, they can be used to form a fluent interface that can chain method calls.

Taking the previous LINQ code, we can express it using expressions and the extension methods that are found in the System.Linq namespace:

```
int[] items = { 1, 2, 3, 42, 84, 37, 23 };

var selectedItemsExpressions = items
    .Where(i => i >= 37)
    .Select(i => i);

Console.WriteLine(string.Join(',',
  selectedItemsExpressions));
```

All three approaches discussed so far do the same thing and print out the same result. The biggest difference is readability.

Since our data source is just an in-memory array, the extension methods will reflect that and you'll notice the signature of the .Where() method it uses:

```
public static IEnumerable<TSource> Where<TSource>(this
   IEnumerable<TSource> source, Func<TSource, bool>
      predicate);
```

The first parameter is the source it extends, IEnumerable<TSource>, and the second parameter is Func<int, bool>. This means that you're giving it a callback that will be called to decide whether or not the specific value, while it iterates through them, should be included or not.

This doesn't really bring out the topic of this chapter. Let's change it up a little to bring out the real magic.

Expression

For LINQ to work as intended with regard to different data sources and deferred execution, there is an interface called IQueryable. The IQueryable interface is something a data source can implement, and instead of having an imperative approach to just iterating the data source, it can now get the query represented as an expression.

An IQueryable interface gives us different extension methods that expose Expression as a type. Let's change the array filtering up a little bit and introduce the concept of a queryable:

```
int[] items = { 1, 2, 3, 42, 84, 37, 23 };

var selectedItemsExpressions = items
    .AsQueryable()  // Making the array a queryable
    .Where(i => i >= 37)
    .Select(i => i);

Console.WriteLine(string.Join(',', selectedItems
   Expressions));
```

The .AsQueryable() array changes from an array, or more exactly, IEnumerable<int> becomes IQueryable<int>. That means we get access to a whole set of LINQ extension methods that are extending IQueryable<>.

If you look closer at the .Where() method, you'll notice that one of the extension methods now has the following signature:

```
public static IQueryable<TSource> Where<TSource>(this
   IQueryable<TSource> source, Expression<Func<TSource,
      bool>> predicate);
```

The first parameter is the source it extends, and the second parameter is Expression<Func<TSource, bool>>. This is the most significant part. The C# compiler recognizes anything that is an expression type, and instead of just creating a callback that gets called, it expands it into an expression.

In order for us to investigate what the compiler does, we can take the `where` clause and separate it into its own line of code, enabling us to set a breakpoint in the debugger and look at what is going on:

```
int[] items = { 1, 2, 3, 42, 84, 37, 23 };

// Extracted expression
Expression<Func<int, bool>> filter = (i) => i >= 37;

var selectedItemsExpressions = items
    .AsQueryable()
    .Where(filter)
    .Select(i => i);

Console.WriteLine(string.Join(',', selectedItems
  Expressions));
```

With the expression extracted into its own line of code, we can easily see what the compiler generates for us. By setting a breakpoint after the `filter` variable construction and looking at the `filter` variable in the watch view of your debugger, you can see the following:

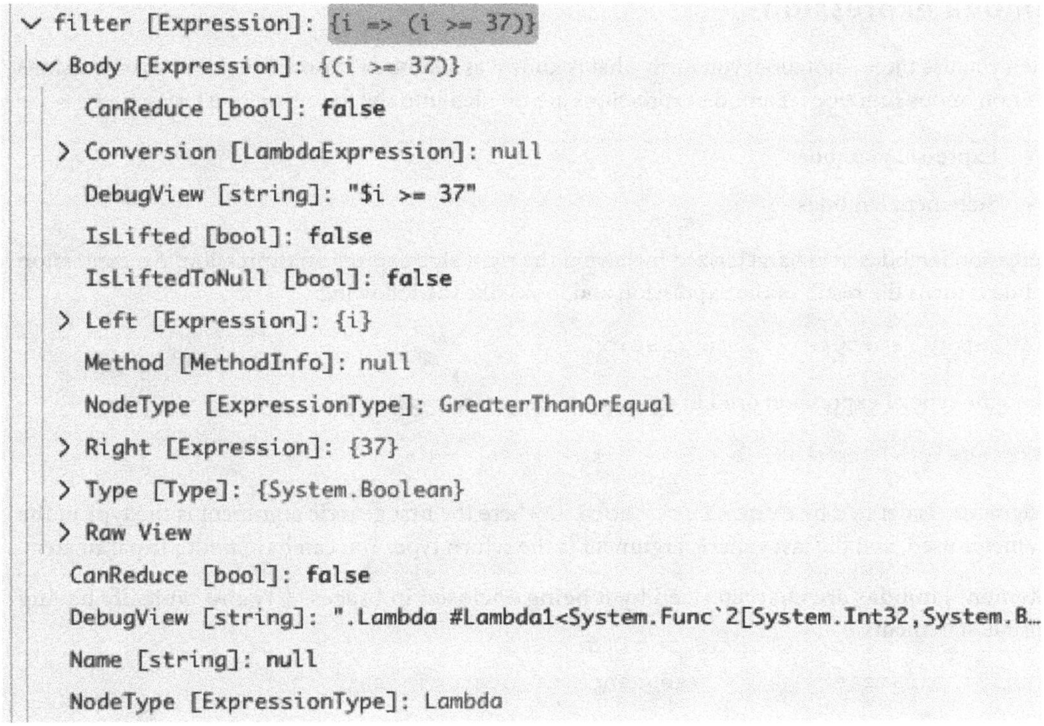

```
v filter [Expression]: {i => (i >= 37)}
  v Body [Expression]: {(i >= 37)}
      CanReduce [bool]: false
    > Conversion [LambdaExpression]: null
      DebugView [string]: "$i >= 37"
      IsLifted [bool]: false
      IsLiftedToNull [bool]: false
    > Left [Expression]: {i}
      Method [MethodInfo]: null
      NodeType [ExpressionType]: GreaterThanOrEqual
    > Right [Expression]: {37}
    > Type [Type]: {System.Boolean}
    > Raw View
      CanReduce [bool]: false
      DebugView [string]: ".Lambda #Lambda1<System.Func`2[System.Int32,System.B...
      Name [string]: null
      NodeType [ExpressionType]: Lambda
```

Figure 7.1 – The filter expression

As you can see, it is no longer just a callback. It has captured all the details of what you are expressing. Notice the `Body` property. This is the inner expression. The type, in our case, is translated into `LogicalBinaryExpression`, which holds three things of importance:

- `Left`
- `NodeType`
- `Right`

The `Left` property represents what is on the left-hand side of the expression, and the `Right` property represents what is on the right-hand side. And in the middle of this, the operator, `NodeType`, tells us the action it will be performing.

For both the `Left` and `Right` properties, you also see that their type is `Expression`. The `Left` expression, in this case, is `PrimitiveParameterExpression`, representing the parameter, the value that will be passed if we are iterating or calling the expression. While the `Right` expression becomes `ConstantExpression`, holding the concrete value, the `NodeType` property is set to `GreaterThanOrEqual`, which is what was expressed by `>=`.

Lambda expression

When you use the `=>` notation, you form what is known as a **lambda expression**. Lambda expressions are anonymous functions. Lambda expressions are divided into the following two types:

- Expression lambdas
- Statement lambdas

Expression lambdas are characterized by having the right side express an expression. An expression lambda returns the result of the expression and looks like the following:

```
(input parameters) => expression
```

This is the type of expression used in the expression you saw earlier:

```
Expression<Func<int, bool>> filter = (i) => i >= 37;
```

Its signature is defined by `Func<int, bool>`, where the first generic argument is the type of the parameter used, and the last generic argument is the return type. You can have multiple parameters.

Statement lambdas are characterized by it being enclosed in braces, `{ }`, and typically having multiple statements:

```
(input parameters) => { <sequence of statements> }
```

This could be something like the following code snippet:

```
(string name) =>
{
    var message = $"Hello {name}";
    Console.WriteLIne(message);
}
```

With a statement, a lambda is typically something that is not possible to reason about, as it will not form an expression tree but rather have multiple statements within it.

Lambdas represent a very powerful construct that can be used to gain insight into what is going on. It's also a great way to help understand how expressions work and can be constructed.

Traversing an expression tree

An Expression is a simple construct that represents a node in a tree. The expression has a node type, and the implementation decides what the node type expresses and means. This forms a tree that can be recursively traversed and reasoned about.

For lambda expressions, it means it has a body that consists of an expression that is of a specific type; this type could be a **Binary Expression** that holds a left and a right and the node itself representing the operand (equals, not equals, and so forth):

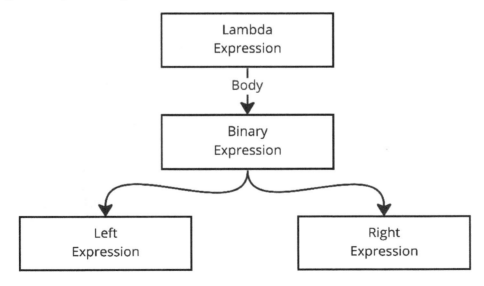

Figure 7.2 – Binary expression

Taking the example of the filter:

```
Expression<Func<int, bool>> filter = (i) => i >= 37;
```

Visually it looks like the following:

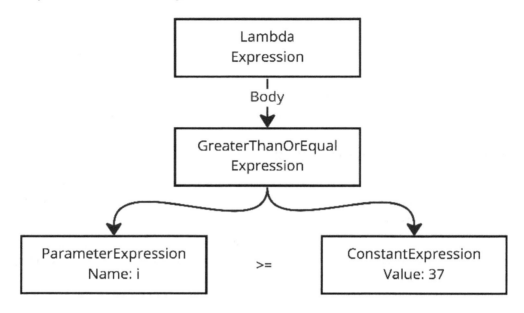

Figure 7.3 - A parameter larger than the constant expression

The operand is greater than or equal, the left-hand side accesses the parameter passed into it, and the right-hand side holds the constant value of 37.

Expressions can also represent accessing a member on the type being passed in as a parameter.

Let's say we have an object called Employee that looks like the following:

```
public record Employee(string FirstName, string LastName);
```

A filter accessing the first name and looking for a person called Jane would look like the following:

```
Expression<Func<Employee, bool>> employeeFilter =
    (employee) => employee.FirstName == "Jane";
```

Dissecting the expression tree, we will see that it now changes into the following:

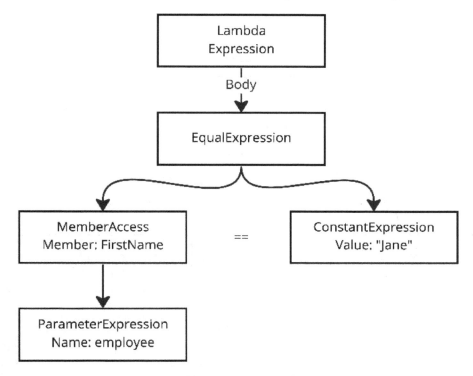

Figure 7.4 – Member access equal constant expression

Since we're now accessing a member, the left-hand expression is now MemberAccessExpression. MemberAccessExpression has an expression on it that represents the source that holds the member, in our case, a parameter being passed in. To get the actual member, MemberAccessExpression holds a property called Member. Since the member we're accessing is a property, it will be the actual PropertyInfo.

Expressions are not just used for filters; they can represent other operations as well. We could have an expression that represents adding values, such as the following:

```
Expression<Func<int, int>> addExpression = (i) => i + 42;
```

The expression itself now returns int instead of bool, takes the parameter passed to it, and adds 42.

The expression tree is shown in the following diagram:

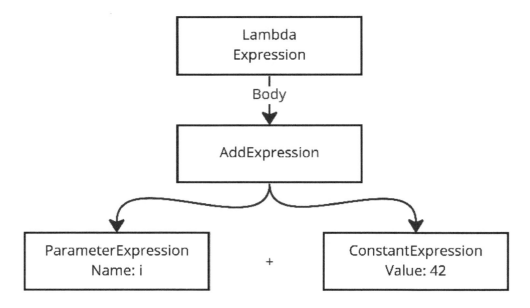

Figure 7.5 – Parameter adding constant expression

As you can see, the node type is Add. This is just one of many types of expressions you can use. You can create really complex structures and represent in an abstract way the core functionality of what the .NET runtime itself is capable of running. We will see more of the different types in *Chapter 8, Building and Executing Expressions*.

Using expressions as descriptors of members on types

Expressions represent a way of describing intent in a declarative fashion. Rather than with an imperative approach where we tell the computer exactly what to do, we can declaratively describe it and let the code decide the best way to approach it.

As we saw earlier with the filtering of numbers, the imperative approach using foreach does not open for any other execution than what we have put in. While with the LINQ and expression approach, we describe what we want, and the execution is deferred, how it is handled and executed, we don't know – but the results are the same.

This type of declarative thinking can be a very powerful way to describe what you want for your system and can also make your code more readable and easier for others to reason about. Imperative code requires you to thoroughly read and understand what the code does, while a declarative approach describes the desired outcome and is much easier to reason about.

Obviously, a declarative model is limited in its capabilities, while an imperative approach is fully flexible, and you can leverage the full power of the C# language. Combining the two methods is best if you can declaratively describe things using something such as a fluent interface and take full advantage of the C# extension methods to hold methods that represent the imperative actions.

Let's take a look at a library called `FluentValidation` (`https://docs.fluentvalidation.net/en/latest/`). It is a library that lets you fluently write validation of input. It takes full advantage of expressions and gives you a declarative model that is extensible using extension methods for describing your intent.

The following is the sample from their documentation:

```
public class CustomerValidator : AbstractValidator<Customer>
{
  public CustomerValidator()
  {
    RuleFor(x => x.Surname).NotEmpty();
    RuleFor(x => x.Forename).NotEmpty().WithMessage("Please
      specify a first name");
    RuleFor(x => x.Discount).NotEqual(0).When(x =>
      x.HasDiscount);
    RuleFor(x => x.Address).Length(20, 250);
    RuleFor(x => x.Postcode).Must(
      BeAValidPostcode).WithMessage("Please specify a
      valid postcode");
  }

  private bool BeAValidPostcode(string postcode)
  {
    // custom postcode validating logic goes here
  }
}
```

The validator inherits from a base type called `AbstractValidator<>`, and on this type, there is a method called `RuleFor()`. This method is the starting point for describing rules for properties on the type passed in as a generic argument to `AbstractValidator<>`. The `RuleFor()` signature looks like the following:

```
public IRuleBuilderInitial<T, TProperty>
  RuleFor<TProperty>(Expression<Func<T, TProperty>>
    expression);
```

As you can see, the parameter for `RuleFor()` is an expression. The expected expression is one that takes the type that was passed to `AbstractValidator<>` as a parameter and returns any type. `TProperty` will automatically be inferred by the C# compiler from the expression.

FluentValidation uses this expression to know what property you're validating by inspecting the expression.

In Fundamentals part of the code for the book, you'll find a class called ExpressionExtensions that has helper extension methods for doing the same type of inspection that FluentValidation does.

Since expressions can describe all kinds of members and the code for finding the member it represents is the same, there is a method for getting the expression that represents the member:

```
public static MemberExpression GetMemberExpression(this
  Expression expression)
{
    var lambda = expression as LambdaExpression;
    if (lambda?.Body is UnaryExpression)
    {
        var unaryExpression = lambda.Body as
          UnaryExpression;
        return (MemberExpression)unaryExpression!.Operand!;
    }

    return (MemberExpression)lambda?.Body!;
}
```

The code assumes that the incoming expression is LambdaExpression and then checks whether this is a UnaryExpression that holds the member. If it is not UnaryExpression, we assume it is MemberExpression.

If it is not MemberExpression, this will cause an invalid cast exception. You might want to consider checking types and throw a more specific exception.

The reason for the check for UnaryExpression is that for expressions that have the type of the value as object and the actual value is a type that needs converting, casting, or unboxing for it to become the object type, the compiler can decide to put in a unary expression that performs this action.

Once you have the member expression, we can get the actual member as the System.Reflection type that represents a property, PropertyInfo:

```
public static PropertyInfo GetPropertyInfo(this Expression
  expression)
{
    var memberExpression = GetMemberExpression(expression);
    return (PropertyInfo)memberExpression.Member!;
}
```

The code calls GetMemberExpression() and casts Member to PropertyInfo. If the member is not PropertyInfo, this will throw an exception. You might want to check for correctness and throw a more specific exception.

With `PropertyInfo` returned, you now have all the information you need about the described property, its name and type, and more.

Summary

In this chapter, we learned about a valuable member of the .NET class libraries called expressions. Thanks to the symbiosis of the C# compiler and the runtime, you get another approach to reason about the running code.

Expressions represent a structured approach for representing, well, expressions. There is somewhat of a resemblance to an abstract syntax tree, which all code compilers produce when parsing code. Something we'll get more familiar with in *Chapter 15, Roslyn Compiler Extensions*.

As we've seen in this chapter, the type of expressions can be for just capturing information, but they can also be more powerful and capture operations that can be executed.

In the next chapter, we will dive deeper into expressions and see how you can build out expressions at runtime that you can then execute dynamically.

8

Building and
Executing Expressions

Expressions in C# are not just great to use as a means of capturing metadata and reason about code; you can also generate expression trees, either based on code represented as lambdas, as we saw in *Chapter 7, Reasoning about Expressions*, or by programmatically adding the different expression node types yourself.

The expressions that you build can then be executed. And with the breadth of capabilities offered with expressions, they're almost as powerful as generating intermediate language code, as we saw in *Chapter 6, Dynamic Proxy Generation*. Since every expression is code that sits inside the specific expression that is executed and performs the task of the expression, you can't expect the same level of performance as with generating intermediate language that runs natively on the .NET runtime. So, it depends on your use case whether or not you should pick expression generation over proxy generation.

In this chapter, we will look into how we can leverage expressions to express our intent and execute them, and hopefully get some inspiration as to what they can be useful for.

We will cover the following topics:

- Creating your own expressions
- Creating expressions as delegates and executing them
- Creating a query engine

From this chapter, you should understand how expression trees are constructed and how you can leverage them to generate logic dynamically that can then be executed.

Technical requirements

The source code specific to the chapter can be found on GitHub (`https://github.com/PacktPublishing/Metaprogramming-in-C-Sharp/tree/main/Chapter8`) and it builds on top of the `Fundamentals` code that is found here: `https://github.com/PacktPublishing/Metaprogramming-in-C-Sharp/tree/main/Fundamentals`.

Creating your own expressions

Expressions are pretty much as powerful and capable as the .NET runtime. That means that we can express all operations that the intermediate language holds and eventually the runtime executes. Constructs are very different from the intermediate language, as we saw in *Chapter 7, Reasoning about Expressions*. They're all focused around a tree structure with left and right expressions representing the nodes in the tree.

With expressions, we don't necessarily need to limit ourselves to using them as a means to filter data, but we could in fact use them to hold logic that performs operations. Since they are just as powerful as the intermediate language, we could go and generate very complex expression trees.

But with great power comes great responsibility. Even though this is possible, it doesn't mean it's necessarily a good idea. The structures can be hard to understand and debug, so I would recommend not going all in and treating it as a new programming language.

Let's say we have a type we want to manipulate the property of. For simplicity, let's make our type a simple type with a string property that we want to set:

```
public class MyType
{
    public string StringProperty { get; set; } =
        String.Empty;
}
```

For this sample, we want to manipulate the `StringProperty` property, so we're making it a `class` rather than a `record`, enabling us to manipulate its state.

To create an expression representing the property we need to build, start off with something that represents the type the property belongs to. The owning type will also be represented by an expression. For this sample, we don't want the expression to create an instance of the `MyType` type but rather manipulate an existing one. The instance it will be working on is represented by a parameter for the expression:

```
var parameter = Expression.Parameter(typeof(MyType));
```

The parameter takes the type of the parameter. But you can also give it a name with one of the overloads of the `.Parameter()` method, which can be very useful for debugging information if one has multiple parameters.

For us to work with the property, we need to use C# reflection to get the `PropertyInfo` for the property we want to manipulate:

```
var property = typeof(MyType).GetProperty
  (nameof(MyType.StringProperty))!;
```

With the parameter representing the instance, we will manipulate the actual property. We can now create an expression representing the property on the type:

```
var propertyExpression = Expression.Property
    (parameter,property);
```

The last thing we want to do is then to do the actual assignment. For this, we use the `Expression.Assign()` method:

```
var assignExpression = Expression.Assign(
    propertyExpression,
    Expression.Constant("Hello world"));
```

The `Expression.Assign()` method takes the left-hand expression representing the target while the right-hand expression is the source. In the code, we assign it a constant of `Hello world`.

Obviously, this is a very simple sample and doesn't really do much. You can really go to town with expressions and leverage things such as `Expression.IfThen()` and `Expression.IfElse()` for `if`/`else` statements and you can even go and do `Expression.Call()` to invoke methods, passing along arguments and dealing with the result. Results can be manipulated with things such as `Expression.Add()` and `Expression.Subtract()`. Anything you can imagine can be done. For this book, we'll just keep it simple with regard to building expressions representing logic.

Expressions aren't really useful unless we can invoke them and get the result. What we want to do is build out the expression tree we want and then be able to quite easily call them with standard C# code.

Creating expressions as delegates and executing them

We can think of expressions as methods or functions we can call. They might have parameters or not and they might return results or not. We can represent the expressions as either `Action` or `Func`. Both are delegate types found in the `System` namespace. `Action` represents a parameter-less action that can, if you need to, return results. While `Func` represents a function that has one or more parameters and can return a result. Both of these delegate types can take generic parameters representing the input parameter types and the result type.

Delegates are basically just representations of methods. They define a callable signature. We can invoke delegates as methods directly.

With expressions, we can turn them into a callable expression. This is done through `Expression.Lambda()`. Let's build on the property assign expression we had earlier:

```
var parameter = Expression.Parameter(typeof(MyType));
var property = typeof(MyType).GetProperty
    (nameof(MyType.StringProperty))!;
var propertyExpression = Expression.Property
    (parameter,property);
```

```
var assignExpression = Expression.Assign(
    propertyExpression,
    Expression.Constant("Hello world"));
```

We can create the following lambda:

```
var lambdaExpression = Expression.Lambda<Action<MyType>>
  (assignExpression, parameter);
```

The `Expression.Lambda()` method takes a generic parameter – the type of delegate. This delegate can be whatever delegate type you want – your own custom delegate or just use either `Action` or `Func`. For this example, we'll use `Action<MyType>` since we are going to just call the expression and it will manipulate the instance we give it. We pass along the expression representing the assignment of the value and then the definition of the parameter.

With the lambda expression in place, we can compile the expression down to a callable delegate and call it:

```
var expressionAction = lambdaExpression.Compile();
var instance = new MyType();
expressionAction(instance);
Console.WriteLine(instance.StringProperty);
```

The code calls the `.Compile()` method, which will then compile the expression down into a delegate we can invoke directly. It creates an instance of the `MyType` type and passes it along to the delegate. Running the program, you should now see the following:

```
Hello world
```

This is pretty straightforward and this example probably doesn't show the full potential.

Creating a query engine

Let's switch gears a little bit and increase the complexity a couple of levels and make it a little bit more relevant. One thing we could use expressions for is as a way to do dynamic querying of data. Some applications might want to even give the end user the ability to create arbitrary queries for your data. I've worked on solutions that offered this type of power to the end user, which can be a tough problem to solve if you're providing a flexible query system for the end user without something such as expressions. I've seen solutions that basically just expose SQL directly to the end user instead of trying to tackle this problem. Giving this level of power to the end user can cause problems in the future. What you end up doing is completely obliterating all abstractions between your data storage and your end users. Good luck changing technologies or supporting multiple data storage mechanisms. But luckily, we have the power of expressions in our hands, giving us the opportunity to create an abstraction that puts us in the pit of success.

Expressions, as discussed in *Chapter 7, Reasoning about Expressions*, are disconnected from how they are translated for execution for the target data source. As long as we keep our expression trees simple enough, it should be possible to execute them optimally for the data source.

Building out an interactive query user interface is involved, so for this book, let's make it a bit more developer-centric and make our query interface a JSON document. We want to create a data store that can hold data with the capability of being queried with a defined query language.

A MongoDB-like database

Let's build something that resembles a document database. MongoDB can be a good blueprint for this. Obviously, we're not going to be building a fully capable document database but will use the characteristics of one and also be inspired by them.

MongoDB has a query language that is very much like JSON, meaning that you construct the different clauses as key/value expressions. Let's say we have a document in JSON that looks like the following:

```
{ "FirstName": "Jane", "LastName": "Doe", "Age": 57 }
```

With a MongoDB-like syntax, we can do a query that does an equals match for the `LastName` property as follows:

```
{
    "LastName": "Doe"
}
```

To add more properties that needs to match – a typical **And** operation – you just simply add another property as a key/value with the value you want it to be:

```
{
    "LastName": "Doe",
    "Age": 57
}
```

Sometimes you have **Or** statements, saying *this* or *this*, with MongoDB that would be expressed as follows:

```
{
    "LastName": "Doe",
    "$or": [
        {
            "Age": 57
        }
    ]
}
```

If you want to do queries that need a value to be greater than, less than, or similar to, you would need an object structure for the right-hand side:

```
{
    "Age": {
        "$gt": 50
    }
}
```

As you can see, in MongoDB, keywords are prefixed with $. We're not going to implement them all, but just a few – enough to make it interesting.

Building a simple query engine

With the requirements in place, we're now ready to start building out the engine that will be able to parse queries and create expressions that we can call from code.

Start by creating a folder called Chapter8. Change into this folder in your command-line interface and create a new console project:

```
dotnet new console
```

Add a file called QueryParser.cs. Add the following to the file:

```
using System.Linq.Expressions;
using System.Text.Json;

namespace Chapter8;

public static class QueryParser
{
    static readonly ParameterExpression
    _dictionaryParameter = Expression.Parameter(typeof
    (IDictionary<string, object>), "input");
}
```

The code adds the namespaces we're going to need for this to work and then adds a class that holds, for now, a representation of the parameter we're going to pass into the query evaluation expression that we will have at the end.

One of the characteristics of document databases is that, by default, they don't have a definition of the shape of objects being put into them, unlike a SQL database, which has a table definition with columns. To mimic that behavior, you're going to be using a key/value dictionary represented as IDictionary<string, object>. This is the parameter of the expression.

The query expressions will have the following structure:

```
left-hand (operand) right-hand
```

Here's an example:

```
LastName equals Doe
```

That means we need to build the correct left value expression and right value expression. Add the following method to the `QueryParser` class:

```
static Expression GetLeftValueExpression(JsonProperty
  parentProperty, JsonProperty property)
{
    var keyParam =
      Expression.Constant(parentProperty.Name);
    var indexer = typeof(IDictionary<string,
      object>).GetProperty("Item")!;
    var indexerExpr = Expression.Property(
      _dictionaryParameter, indexer, keyParam);

    return property.Value.ValueKind switch
    {
        JsonValueKind.Number =>
          Expression.Unbox(indexerExpr, typeof(int)),
        JsonValueKind.String =>
          Expression.TypeAs(indexerExpr, typeof(string)),
        JsonValueKind.True or JsonValueKind.False =>
          Expression.TypeAs(indexerExpr, typeof(bool)),
        _ => indexerExpr
    };
}
```

The code is based on the fact that your query is coming in as a JSON construct. It's built for recursion, which is why it takes a `parentProperty` and a `property`. This is to support more than the **equals** operand and support the nested **greater than** type of operands. At the top level, the `parentProperty` and `property` will be the same, while when we do the nested ones, we need the `parentProperty` and not the `property` in the nested expression as that represents the operand and value.

The first thing the code does is create an expression that accesses the dictionary. This is done by using the `Item` property that exists on `IDictionary<string, object>`. The `Item` property is not a property you'll see on the interface. It represents the indexer when you typically index using `["SomeString"]`. Indexers are properties that take an argument. The code, therefore, sets up an `IndexerExpression` by using one of the overloads of the `Expression.Property()` method. It passes the indexer property and a constant that represents the property on the document.

The last thing the code needs to do is make sure the value being returned is of the correct type. Since we have IDictionary<string, object>, the values are represented as object. You do this to be able to use the different operands (=, >, <). If you don't do this, you'll get an exception because it will not know how to deal with comparing **object** to the actual type of the right-hand expression.

Numbers are value types and need to be unboxed, while strings and Booleans need to cast to their actual type.

> **Important note**
>
> JSON numbers are hardcoded to be an int. This is just a simplification for this sample. Numbers could be more than that, such as float, double, Int64, and more.

Now that you have your left-hand expression, you'll need the right-hand expression:

```
static Expression GetRightValueExpression(JsonProperty
  property)
{
    return property.Value.ValueKind switch
    {
        JsonValueKind.Number =>
          Expression.Constant(property.Value.GetInt32()),
        JsonValueKind.String => Expression.Constant(
          (object)property.Value.GetString()!),
        JsonValueKind.True or JsonValueKind.False =>
          Expression.Constant((object)property.Value
          .GetBoolean()),
        _ => Expression.Empty()
    };
}
```

The code creates constant expressions that get the value in the correct type. On the JsonProperty type, the Value property is the JsonElement type. It has methods for getting the actual value in the type you're expecting. Since the query engine is somewhat limited in types, it just supports int, string, and bool.

With the right-hand side also in place, you're going to need something that builds on both the left- and right-hand expressions and puts them together as an expression you can use. The defined query capabilities include being able to do **greater than**, **less than**, and more and we have defined that as a complex object as the value in the key/value part of the query JSON. With that, you need a method that builds the correct expressions.

Add the following method to the `QueryParser` class:

```
static Expression GetNestedFilterExpression(JsonProperty
    property)
{
    Expression? currentExpression = null;

    foreach (var expressionProperty in
      property.Value.EnumerateObject())
    {
        var getValueExpression = GetLeftValueExpression(
          property, expressionProperty);
        var valueConstantExpression =
          GetRightValueExpression(expressionProperty);
        Expression comparisonExpression =
          expressionProperty.Name switch
        {
            "$lt" => Expression.LessThan(
              getValueExpression, valueConstantExpression),
            "$lte" => Expression.LessThanOrEqual(
              getValueExpression, valueConstantExpression),
            "$gt" => Expression.GreaterThan(
              getValueExpression, valueConstantExpression),
            "$gte" => Expression.GreaterThanOrEqual(
              getValueExpression, valueConstantExpression),
            _ => Expression.Empty()
        };

        if (currentExpression is not null)
        {
            currentExpression = Expression.And(
              currentExpression, comparisonExpression);
        }
        else
        {
            currentExpression = comparisonExpression;
        }
    }

    return currentExpression ?? Expression.Empty();
}
```

The code enumerates the object given and makes it possible to have more than one clause. It groups these as **And** operations. It leverages the methods you created earlier to get the left- and right-hand expressions and then for each supported operand, uses these to create the correct operand expression.

Since the `GetNestedFilterExpression` method is only dealing with the nested filter clauses based on an object, you need a method that will deal with the top-level clause and call into the nested one if it's a nested object:

```
static Expression GetFilterExpression(JsonProperty
  property)
{
    return property.Value.ValueKind switch
    {
        JsonValueKind.Object =>
        GetNestedFilterExpression(property),
        _ => Expression.Equal(GetLeftValueExpression(
        property, property), GetRightValueExpression(
        property))
    };
}
```

Based on the kind of value, the code chooses to use the nested expression only if it's an object representation. For everything else, it creates a simple **equal** expression.

Earlier, we discussed having the ability to do Or operations and not just And operations. Add the following method to the `QueryParser` class:

```
static Expression GetOrExpression(Expression expression,
  JsonProperty property)
{
    Foreach (var element in property.Value.EnumerateArray())
    {
        var elementExpression = GetQueryExpression(element);
        expression = Expression.OrElse(expression,
          elementExpression);
    }

    return expression;
}
```

We defined the Or expressions as an array of expressions. The code enumerates the value as an array and for each element, it calls `GetQueryExpression` – the next method we'll be needing. From the result, it creates an OrElse expression. The reason for the `OrElse` expression is that we only want to evaluate the Or if the prior expression evaluates to `false`.

Go ahead and add the following method to the `QueryParser` class:

```
static Expression GetQueryExpression(JsonElement element)
{
    Expression? currentExpression = null;
```

```
foreach (var property in element.EnumerateObject())
{
    Expression expression = property.Name switch
    {
        "$or" => GetOrExpression(currentExpression!,
          property),
        _ => GetFilterExpression(property)
    };

    if (currentExpression is not null && expression is
      not BinaryExpression)
    {
        currentExpression = Expression.And(
          currentExpression, expression);
    }
    else
    {
        currentExpression = expression;
    }
}

return currentExpression ?? Expression.Empty();
}
```

Since the query JSON can consist of multiple statements, the code enumerates the object and evaluates each property. If it is an Or expression, it calls the `GetOrExpression` method. Anything else goes to the `GetFilterExpression`. This is the place you could be adding more operations. For each of the properties in the query, it will And them together.

With the `GetQueryExpression` method in place, we have all the logic for the query engine in place. Now we need an entry point from the outside.

Add the following method to the `QueryParser` class:

```
public static Expression<Func<IDictionary<string, object>,
  bool>> Parse(JsonDocument json)
{
    var element = json.RootElement;
    var query = GetQueryExpression(element);
    return Expression.Lambda<Func<IDictionary<string,
      object>, bool>>(query, _dictionaryParameter);
}
```

The `Parse` method takes a JSON document representing the query and returns an expression that is meant to be used with single documents where each document is `IDictionary<string, object>`. It calls into `GetQueryExpression` to create the actual expression based on the root element of the JSON and then wraps the expression in a callable **lambda** expression that takes a dictionary as a parameter.

Now that you have your query engine in place, it's time to create some data and a query, and some code to test it out.

Add a file called `data.json` and add the following or your own content to it:

```
[
    { "FirstName": "Jane", "LastName": "Doe", "Age": 57 },
    { "FirstName": "John", "LastName": "Doe", "Age": 55 },
    { "FirstName": "Michael", "LastName": "Corleone",
      "Age": 47 },
    { "FirstName": "Anthony", "LastName": "Soprano",
      "Age": 51 },
    { "FirstName": "Paulie", "LastName": "Gualtieri",
      "Age": 58 }
]
```

For the query itself, add a file called `query.json` and add the following or your own query to it:

```
{
    "Age": {
        "$gte": 52
    },
    "$or": [
        {
            "LastName": "Doe"
        }
    ]
}
```

You then want to have code that parses these files and creates an expression from the `query.json`.

To be able to parse the `data.json` file and get a nice collection of `Dictionary<string, object>` types, we need a JSON converter. By default, if you try to deserialize JSON into this, the serializer will give you a `JsonElement` for the value. We want the actual value. The JSON converter listing and walk-through have no value in this context. They can be found in the GitHub repository referenced at the beginning of the chapter.

In the `Program.cs` file, replace everything with the following:

```
var query = File.ReadAllText("query.json");
var queryDocument = JsonDocument.Parse(query);
var expression = QueryParser.Parse(queryDocument);
```

```
var documentsRaw = File.ReadAllText("data.json");
var serializerOptions = new JsonSerializerOptions();
serializerOptions.Converters.Add(new Dictionary
  StringObjectJsonConverter());
var documents = JsonSerializer.Deserialize<Ienumerable
  <Dictionary<string, object>>>(documentsRaw,
    serializerOptions)!;

var filtered = documents.AsQueryable().Where(expression);
foreach (var document in filtered)
{
    Console.WriteLine(JsonSerializer.Serialize(document));
}
```

The code loads the `query.json` and the `data.json` files and parses them. For the query, you need it as a `JsonDocument` before it's passed into the `QueryParser.Parse()` method, while the data is deserialized into a collection of `Dictionary<string, object>`.

Since the documents are `IEnumerable`, you don't get the `.Where()` extension methods you're looking for. The code therefore does a `.AsQueryable()` first and then passes the parsed query expression into it.

The filtered objects can then be enumerated.

Running the code should give you the following result:

```
{"FirstName":"Jane","LastName":"Doe","Age":57}
{"FirstName":"John","LastName":"Doe","Age":55}
{"FirstName":"Paulie","LastName":"Gualtieri","Age":58}
```

The benefit of this approach rather than presenting something such as SQL to the end user is that you now have an abstraction that works with different data stores. You can even apply the same expression in memory as you would for a database.

Summary

In this chapter, we have learned about the power of building out expressions and expression trees. Not only can they represent queries but, in fact, they can be just as powerful as generating intermediate language code.

With expressions, you get an alternative to intermediate language. They do have some limitations over generating intermediate language code, such as you can't simply create types and implement interfaces or override the behavior of virtual methods inherited. But as a tool for expressing simpler actions, they are really great.

In the next chapter, we will look at yet another approach to dynamically creating types and implementations by leveraging the capabilities of the **Dynamic Language Runtime**.

9

Taking Advantage of the Dynamic Language Runtime

C# is a statically typed language, which means we take our code in text form and run it through a compiler, and it produces a binary that is then executed later. The code does not change after the compiler is done. Not all languages are like this; languages such as Ruby, Python, and JavaScript are dynamic languages and do not compile to binary before execution. They are interpreted at runtime, meaning that they can also change gradually during runtime. This is a very powerful trait.

In this chapter, we will look into how we can make use of the dynamic language runtime part of the .NET runtime and create code dynamically and differently from how we've done it thus far.

We will cover the following topics:

- Understanding the DLR
- Reasoning about a dynamic type
- Creating a DynamicObject and providing metadata

By the end of the chapter, you will understand what the dynamic language runtime is and how you can make use of it to dynamically create types and reason about them.

Technical requirements

The source code specific to the chapter can be found on GitHub (https://github.com/PacktPublishing/Metaprogramming-in-C-Sharp/tree/main/Chapter9), and it builds on top of the Fundamentals code that is found here: https://github.com/PacktPublishing/Metaprogramming-in-C-Sharp/tree/main/Fundamentals.

Understanding the DLR

The **Dynamic Language Runtime** (**DLR**) was introduced in .NET 4 back in 2010. It runs on top of the .NET runtime, **Common Language Runtime** (**CLR**), providing language services for dynamic languages such as Python and Ruby through the IronPython and IronRuby implementations. With the DLR, it is also possible to interop between the different languages, effectively making it possible to have C# and Python, Ruby, or any other dynamic language that is supported run side by side in the same process.

The CLR at a glance

Before diving into the DLR, it's helpful to understand the constraints it has to work with. The CLR is at the heart of everything .NET, which means that everything running has to abide by the rules of the CLR. That becomes very interesting when looking at the traits of the CLR.

Just-in-Time (JIT) compilation

The CLR compiles the **Intermediate Language** (**IL**) code into native code for the specific machine and operating system at runtime, using the JIT compiler. This process enables better optimization, faster execution, and cross-platform compatibility.

Automatic memory management

The CLR manages memory allocation and deallocation using garbage collection, which automatically frees up memory occupied by objects that are no longer in use. This helps prevent memory leaks and optimizes memory usage.

Type safety

The CLR ensures type safety by enforcing strict rules during code execution. This helps prevent invalid memory operations, such as accessing a memory location that has not been initialized or using an object of one type as another type.

Exception handling

The CLR provides a consistent and robust exception-handling mechanism across all .NET languages, allowing developers to handle runtime errors gracefully and maintain application stability.

Cross-language Interoperability

The CLR supports interoperability between .NET languages, allowing developers to use components written in different languages within the same application. This promotes code reusability and simplifies the development process.

Versioning and assembly management

The CLR manages the versioning of assemblies (compiled code units), helping to prevent issues such as "DLL hell," where conflicting versions of shared libraries cause application instability. It also provides features such as side-by-side execution, allowing multiple versions of an assembly to coexist on the same system.

Reflection

The CLR enables developers to inspect and interact with metadata about types, objects, and assemblies at runtime. This allows dynamic type creation, method invocation, and other advanced programming techniques.

Debugging and profiling

The CLR provides integrated support for debugging and profiling .NET applications, enabling developers to diagnose and optimize code efficiently.

The DLR building blocks

For any of the dynamic languages to work, the DLR needs to support a few things that are very different from the more static world of the CLR. The following traits are needed.

Dynamic type system

A dynamic runtime needs to be able to create types on the fly. A type is never static and should be able to be expanded on.

Dynamic dispatching of methods

A dynamic runtime should allow calling methods that aren't known beforehand.

Dynamic code generation

A dynamic runtime should allow for code generation at runtime, allowing you to add code based on input or the result of other code dynamically. It should also allow you to modify code.

From a CLR perspective, these types of traits seem very unaligned. The engineers at Microsoft extended the core functionality and put in place a dynamic runtime that works well with the CLR.

From a metaprogramming perspective, the traits of a dynamic runtime are perfect. As part of the DLR, there is a collection of constructs and APIs that enables you to dynamically create types and also reason about any dynamic type that fulfills the traits we're looking for.

Since the .NET runtime itself is a static runtime and relies on well-known types with fixed members, the DLR needs to work with this constraint. The DLR, therefore, provides a set of classes and interfaces to represent dynamic objects, their properties, and operations, such as `IDynamicMetaObjectProvider`, `DynamicMetaObject`, `DynamicObject`, and `ExpandoObject`.

For the DLR to work with dynamic languages, it needs a way to represent the language semantics. The DLR uses expression trees, which we looked at in more detail in *Chapter 7, Reasoning about Expressions*, and *Chapter 8, Building and Executing Expressions*. With the DLR comes a set of extensions to LINQ expressions that give us control flow, assignment, and other language-modeling nodes.

From a compiler perspective, the C# compiler has a keyword called `dynamic` that lets you say that a particular variable or argument is of a dynamic type. That tells the compiler to not evaluate any member accesses during compile time for the instance. Instead, it translates all this into the appropriate `Expression` that will execute.

To get started with leveraging the DLR and its dynamic capabilities, the easiest way is to use the `ExpandoObject` type. `ExpandoObject` provides a type that can be dynamically expanded on; it will hold anything you tell it to and can expand as you proceed:

```
dynamic person = new ExpandoObject();
person.FirstName = "Jane";
person.LastName = "Doe";
```

The code creates an instance of `ExpandoObject` and then starts setting values on it. `ExpandoObject` does not have `FirstName` or `LastName` as part of its type, but by setting them, the values will be there.

Accessing these members will be the same; the compiler understands that `ExpandoObject` is `dynamic` and will try to bind to the members at runtime rather than at compile time. The following code will be completely valid:

```
Console.WriteLine($"{person.FirstName} {person.LastName}");
```

The result will be as expected:

```
Jane Doe
```

`ExpandoObject` does this by implementing the `IDynamicMetaObjectProvider` interface. With `IDynamicMetaObjectProvider`, it provides its own implementation of `DynamicMetaObject` that really holds all the magic of doing the actual binding of the operations we tell it to do.

The `ExpandoObject` type also implements the `IDictionary<string, object?>` interface, which is how it represents all the members given to it and also how it can dynamically grow. Through its implementation of `DynamicMetaObject`, it basically just works on the internal dictionary. In fact, it is fully possible to work with `ExpandoObject` as a dictionary if you want:

```
var person = new ExpandoObject() as IDictionary<string, object?>;
person["FirstName"] = "Jane";
person["LastName"] = "Doe";
```

If you're using `dynamic` for data objects, this can be really handy, as it gives you a simple way to reason about an object and its content and, at the same time, a convenient programming experience by treating it as a dynamic object with properties.

Call sites and binders

Whenever you want to perform an operation on a dynamic object – for instance, a get or set property or a method call – it goes through something called a **call site**. A call site is effectively the location at runtime of the code that will execute. For compiled C#, this will be the memory location where the IL code typically resides. For other languages, such as Ruby or Python, this would be the location in the textual code. Every language has its own call site representation.

The big difference between static languages and dynamic languages is that the static languages are compiled, and at runtime, they're either executing some sort of intermediate language or actual machine language. Alternatively, a dynamic language will interpret code at runtime and execute the result. The benefit of a dynamic language then is that it can change its own code dynamically, obviously with the downside of a loss in performance.

Once you have the location, or the call site, you can bind to the member and then perform the operation you want.

There are binders for the typical operations you want to perform on an object – the get and set properties, invoke methods, indexing, and so on. Throughout the book, we've looked at the power of metadata and how we can reason about the running code; the DLR poses some challenges with this.

Reasoning about a dynamic type

The DLR is very limited in what it is possible to reason about for a dynamic type. Primarily, the DLR is built to be able to host dynamic languages. Naturally with dynamic languages, you don't really know what's going on with a dynamic type, and it can change over time, so even though a member is already there, the DLR can't provide you a reflective experience by giving you any details, such as type information, about the member.

One thing we can do, however, is ask it what members it has. Every dynamic object implements an interface called `IDynamicMetaObjectProvider`. On this, you can call the `GetMetaObject()` method to get an object that allows us to interact with the dynamic object.

Let's look at `ExpandoObject` with the following properties:

```
dynamic person = new ExpandoObject();
person["FirstName"] = "Jane";
person["LastName"] = "Doe";
```

Since ExpandoObject does, in fact, implement IDynamicMetaObjectProvider, we can ask it for its meta-object and then its members:

```
var provider = (person as IDynamicMetaObjectProvider)!;
var meta = provider.GetMetaObject(Expression.Constant(person));
var members = string.Join(',', meta.GetDynamicMemberNames());
Console.WriteLine(members);
```

Running this code will give you the following result:

FirstName,LastName

The code itself assumes it is IDynamicMetaObjectProvider by casting it to a type, in order for us to call GetMetaObject(). The Expression we create represents the instance of the person that we're getting the meta-object for. Then, we call GetDynamicMemberNames(), which returns a collection of strings with all its member names.

This is the extent of what it is possible to reason about.

However, we can dynamically invoke the members, which comes in handy when you don't know the shape of the object. It can be a bit challenging to invoke when you don't really know what the object holds, and if you want to support everything, you'll need fallback mechanisms, as the runtime will throw RuntimeBinderException if it can't bind the way you want to.

DynamicMetaObject has a set of methods with all the binding you can do. These *bind* methods require an actual binder, which you can get from the call site. After bind, you will get a new DynamicMetaObject. It is possible to use all of these things to get to the actual value, but let's jump directly to the C# binder, get the binder we want, and use that instead.

In the Microsoft.CSharp.RuntimeBinder namespace, there is a class called Binder. This class holds a set of static methods to get specific binders. The types of binders you can use are as follows:

BinaryOperation	Used for binary operations
Convert	Used to convert to a specific type
GetIndex	Used to get an index
GetMember	Used to get a member's value
Invoke	Used to invoke a method
InvokeConstructor	Used to invoke/construct a constructor
SetIndex	Used to set an index
SetMember	Used to set a member to a value
UnaryOperation	Used for unary operations

Since the object we have only has properties, we will use the GetMember binder to get the property value and, ultimately, the actual value through the call site:

```
foreach (var member in meta.GetDynamicMemberNames())
{
    var binder = Binder.GetMember(
        CSharpBinderFlags.None,
        member,
        person.GetType(),
        new[] {
            CSharpArgumentInfo.Create(CsharpArgumentInfoFlags
            .None, null) });
    var site = CallSite<Func<CallSite, object,
      object>>.Create(binder);
    var propertyValue = site.Target(site, person);
    Console.WriteLine($"{member} = {propertyValue}");
}
```

The code builds on the `meta` instance we got from `GetMetaObject()` and iterates through the member names returned by `GetDynamicMemberNames()`. For each member, you can then get the binder for it – in our case, the `GetMember` binder – passing default values to it with `member` and the `person` type.

In the `System.Runtime.CompilerService` namespace, you'll find a class called `CallSite<>`. This is a dynamic site type that can be used to create a call site for the binder dynamically. In our case, the dynamic site will be a delegate, `Func<>`, that allows us to call it with `person` and get a value back. The types going in and out are both `object`, since the actual type is unknown.

Running this code should give you this:

```
FirstName = Jane
LastName = Doe
```

> **Important note**
>
> The code assumes that all members are properties, which can fail with `RuntimeBinder Exception`. If you need to support more member types, you would need to handle that exception and fall back to the ones you want to support.

Another approach you could use is to use expressions. The `Expression` class has a `Dynamic` method that lets you pass in the binder and then create a `Lambda` expression, which gives you a similar `Func<>` delegate that can be invoked.

The following gives you a method that can be called to create `Func<>`, which we can call to get the values of members:

```
Func<object, object> BuildDynamicGetter(Type type, string
propertyName)
```

```
{
    var binder = Binder.GetMember(
        CSharpBinderFlags.None,
        propertyName,
        type,
        new[] {
            CSharpArgumentInfo.Create(CsharpArgumentInfoFlags
            .None, null) });
    var rootParameter =
      Expression.Parameter(typeof(object));
    var binderExpression = Expression.Dynamic(binder,
      typeof(object), Expression.Convert(rootParameter,
      type));
    var getterExpression = Expression.Lambda<Func<object,
      object>>(binderExpression, rootParameter);
    return getterExpression.Compile();
}
```

The code gets the `GetMember` binder and then creates `DynamicExpression`, which involves a conversion of the instance we will pass to `object`. Then, the code creates a `Lambda` expression, which we then compile for more performant execution.

This new method can then be used in the following way:

```
var firstNameExpression = BuildDynamicGetter(person.GetType(),
"FirstName");
var lastNameExpression = BuildDynamicGetter(person.GetType(),
"LastName");
Console.WriteLine($"{firstNameExpression(person)}
{lastNameExpression(person)}");
```

The output of this would be as follows:

```
Jane Doe
```

Since the DLR itself is limited in discoverability and reasoning about what is there, it might be a good idea in some use cases to provide the metadata yourself, using other formats and approaches.

Creating DynamicObject and providing metadata

Sometimes, you don't have the luxury of having your types represented in code. This could be if you're calling an external API of some sort, be it a REST API, SOAP service, or similar. However, the third party you're calling might have a representation of the type in a standard format, such as a WSDL or JSON schema.

Even though dynamic objects can be very flexible, in the real world the shape of data tends to be stricter. So, instead of using ExpandoObject for everything, you could represent these types with a custom dynamic object that gets its metadata from a well-known format. It's very common today to use JSON as a data carrier, and it's also common to represent the shape of data by leveraging JSON schemas. Let's look at how that could be a provider of metadata.

Building a JSON schema type

Start by creating a folder called Chapter9. Change into this folder in your command-line interface and create a new console project:

```
dotnet new console
```

We will rely on a third-party library, giving us an easy way of working with JSON schemas. Add the package to the project by running the following:

```
dotnet add package NJsonSchema
```

A JSON schema is a simple structure that describes a type, its properties, and the type of every property. It is, however, limited to the types available to JSON:

- String
- Number
- Boolean
- Array
- Object

However, a JSON schema does support a concept of *format* that can be used as a sub-type for types. For instance, dates are not part of the JSON type system, but having a property of type string and a format of type date would allow you to support any type you want, since strings can hold anything.

JSON schemas can also hold sub-schemas, which makes it possible to have strongly typed object definitions within an object.

For this sample, we're going to keep it very simple and stick with simple types.

Add a file called person.json to your project and add the following to it:

```
{
    „$schema": „http://json-schema.org/draft-04/schema#",
    "title": "Person",
    "type": "object",
    "additionalProperties": false,
    "properties": {
```

```
    "FirstName": {
      "type": "string"
    },
    "LastName": {
      "type": "string"
    },
    "Birthdate": {
      "type": "string",
      "format": "date"
    }
  }
}
```

In the JSON, you'll find the `title` property, which is the name of the type, and the `type` property is set to `object`, since it describes an object. The schema then contains three properties with the following types:

Property	Type
FirstName	String
LastName	String
Birthdate	Date

Table 9.1 – A schema for a person

Add a file called `JsonSchemaType.cs`, and add the following code to it:

```
using System.Dynamic;
using NJsonSchema;

namespace Chapter9;

public class JsonSchemaType : DynamicObject
{
    readonly IDictionary<string, object?> _values = new
      Dictionary<string, object?>();
    readonly JsonSchema _schema;

    public JsonSchemaType(JsonSchema schema)
    {
        _schema = schema;
    }
```

The code creates a new type called `JsonSchemaType` that inherits from the `DynamicObject` type found in the `System.Dynamic` namespace. This particular type is a helper type, created to make it easier to implement dynamic objects. To represent the actual content of the type, the code adds `Dictionary<string, object?>`. This gives you the flexibility of putting anything into it, much like `ExpandoObject` does. The reason for `object?` as the value type is to allow anything and also make it explicit that we allow null values in it. The constructor takes a `JsonSchema` type from the `NJsonSchema` dependency you added earlier.

Validating properties

Since JSON schemas give you a full description of a type, its properties, and the types for the properties, it gives you an opportunity to validate the values being set on the object.

Let's introduce some basic validation into the object. Start by adding a new file that will give us an explicit exception describing the problem that can occur. Add a file called `InvalidTypeForProperty.cs`, and add the following code to it:

```
public class InvalidTypeForProperty : Exception
{
    public InvalidTypeForProperty(string type, string
      property) : base($"Property '{property}' on '{type}'
      is invalid.")
    {
    }
}
```

The custom exception takes two properties – the name of the type that owns the errored property and then the actual property that was wrong. You could also include for good measure the type it was trying to set and what was expected, but to keep the sample simple, let's just go with this.

To do the actual validation, you'll need something that translates from the .NET type to `JsonObjectType`. Go back to the `JsonSchemaType.cs` file and add a method that does the necessary translations from the .NET type to a `JsonObjectType`. Add the following method to the `JsonSchemaType` class:

```
JsonObjectType GetSchemaTypeFrom(Type type)
{
    return type switch
    {
        Type _ when type == typeof(string) =>
          JsonObjectType.String,
        Type _ when type == typeof(DateOnly) =>
          JsonObjectType.String,
        Type _ when type == typeof(int) =>
          JsonObjectType.Integer,
```

```
        Type _ when type == typeof(float) =>
            JsonObjectType.Number,
        Type _ when type == typeof(double) =>
            JsonObjectType.Number,
        _ => JsonObjectType.Object
    };
}
```

The code uses a simple pattern matching and converts from the .NET type to JsonObjectType. It defaults to JsonObjectType.Object for anything it doesn't have an explicit conversion for.

> **Important note**
>
> This implementation is very simplistic and does not cover all the .NET types, and you should probably make it a bit more sophisticated for production. Hopefully, though, it gives you a general idea.

Now that you have a way of converting from a CLR type to JsonObjectType, you need a way to actually do the validation. Add the following method to the JsonSchemaType class:

```
void ValidateType(string property, object? value)
{
    if (value is not null)
    {
        var schemaType = GetSchemaTypeFrom(
            value.GetType());
        if (!_schema.ActualProperties[property]
            .Type.HasFlag(schemaType))
        {
            throw new InvalidTypeForProperty(_schema.Title,
                property);
        }
    }
}
```

The code only validates a value if it is not null, since you wouldn't be able to know its type unless it has a value. With the type, it gets the actual schema type and then checks whether or not the property has this type. JsonObjectType is an enum of flags, and combinations are allowed, which is why you have to use the HasFlag method. If it's not the correct type, the code throws the InvalidTypeForProperty exception.

> **Important note**
>
> A tip here would be to also validate whether null is allowed or not. This information is also supported by JSON schemas. Some types also inherently don't allow nulls, such as integers or Booleans, and you should probably not allow that.

Implementing getting and setting properties

With the constructor and validation in place, you're now ready to override some of the default behavior of the `DynamicObject` type. The `DynamicObject` type offers a set of virtual methods that can be overridden for the different operations that can be performed, such as getting or setting properties and invoking methods.

In this sample, we will focus primarily on properties. Add the following method to the `JsonSchemaType` class:

```
public override bool TrySetMember(SetMemberBinder binder, object?
value)
{
    if (!_schema.ActualProperties.ContainsKey(binder.Name))
    {
        return false;
    }
    ValidateType(binder.Name, value);
    _values[binder.Name] = value;
    return true;
}
```

The `TrySetMember` signature takes `SetMemberBinder`, which holds the information about the property being set. It also gets the value, which can be null. The code then first validates whether or not the property actually exists in the schema by looking into the `ActualProperties` dictionary. If it does not exist, it immediately returns `false`, and if you were to try to set an unknown property, you would then get `RuntimeBinderException`. When the property exists, the code validates the type of the value. If the type is correct, the code then sets the value in its private dictionary.

Once you have set a property, you also want to read it. Add the following method to the `JsonSchemaType` class:

```
public override bool TryGetMember(GetMemberBinder binder, out object?
result)
{
    if (!_schema.ActualProperties.ContainsKey(binder.Name))
    {
        result = null!;
        return false;
    }
```

```
        result = _values.ContainsKey(binder.Name)
            ? result = _values[binder.Name] : result = null!;
        return true;
    }
```

Similar to the `TrySetMember`, the code adds a check on whether or not the schema has the property. However, since this is a **get** operation and the signature of the method dictates that the result should be given as an `out` parameter, we need to explicitly set it to `null`!. The code then checks whether the private dictionary contains a value for the property and returns it if it does or returns a `null`! value if not.

Important note

In a production system, you would typically not want to return just `null` if the value is not set. It should be set to either the default value of the type or, if the JSON schema holds additional metadata with a default value, you should use that.

As a *nice-to-have* feature, we want to allow this type to be converted to another type – in our case, `Dictionary<string, object?>`.

One of the methods that `DynamicObject` provides that can be overridden is the `TryConvert` method. This method will be called if an explicit cast is done from the type to a different target type. Add the following method to the `JsonSchemaType` class:

```
public override bool TryConvert(ConvertBinder binder, out object?
result)
{
    if (binder.Type.Equals(typeof(Dictionary<string,
      object?>)))
    {
        var returnValue = new Dictionary<string,
          object?>(_values);
        var missingProperties =
        _schema.ActualProperties.Where(_ =>
        !_values.Any(kvp => _.Key == kvp.Key));
        foreach (var property in missingProperties)
        {
            object defaultValue = property.Value.Type
              switch
            {
                JsonObjectType.Array =>
                    Enumerable.Empty<object>(),
                JsonObjectType.Boolean => false,
```

```
                JsonObjectType.Integer => 0,
                JsonObjectType.Number => 0,
                _ => null!
            };


            returnValue[property.Key] = defaultValue;
        }
        result = returnValue;
        return true;
    }
    return base.TryConvert(binder, out result);
}
```

The code only allows conversion to `Dictionary<string, object?>`, so it checks for this first by looking at the `Type` property of the `ConvertBinder` type being passed in. It is a good practice to return values for all properties in the schema and not leave out any properties, and since all properties might be set, the code creates a new dictionary from the existing `_values` dictionary and then finds any properties that are missing. For every property that is missing, it sets a default value.

> **Important note**
>
> The default values have been simplified. As mentioned earlier, for production you should consider a more sophisticated approach to default values and look at possible additional metadata in the JSON schema.

The last piece of the puzzle we want to add is the ability for outsiders to reason about what members are available. The `DynamicObject` type gives us a method that can be overridden for this. Add the following method to the `JsonSchemaType` class:

```
public override IEnumerable<string> GetDynamicMemberNames() => _
schema.ActualProperties.Keys;
```

This method will be called by `DynamicMetaObject` that `DynamicObject` produces. `DynamicObject` is also `IDynamicMetaObjectProvider` and implements the `GetMetaObject()` method.

`DynamicObject` has more methods that can be overridden to invoke methods, perform binary operations, and so on. However, for this sample, we will focus on the data aspects with properties.

Using the schema infrastructure

What you've built so far is an infrastructure to work with JSON schemas, together with the DLR. Let's take `JsonSchemaType` out for a spin. Open the `Program.cs` file and take out all its content. Add the following:

```
using NJsonSchema;
using Chapter9;

var schema = await JsonSchema.FromFileAsync("person.json");
dynamic personInstance = new JsonSchemaType(schema);
var personMetaObject = personInstance.GetMetaObject(Expression.
Constant(personInstance));
var personProperties = personMetaObject.GetDynamicMemberNames();
Console.WriteLine(string.Join(',', personProperties));
```

The code reads the JSON schema from the `person.json` file you created earlier. Then, it creates an instance of `JsonSchemaType` and hands it the schema. Since `JsonSchemaType` is a dynamic object, it implements `IDynamicMetaObjectProvider`, and we can call the `GetMetaObject()` method with the instance of the object and then get its members.

When run, the code should produce the following:

```
FirstName,LastName
```

Setting and getting properties should work as expected:

```
personInstance.FirstName = "Jane";
Console.WriteLine($"FirstName : '{personInstance.FirstName}'");
```

Running the code should give you the following output:

```
FirstName : 'Jane'
```

Since the implementation of `JsonSchemaType` supports default values for properties that have not been set, you can get a valid property without any problems:

```
Console.WriteLine($"LastName : '{personInstance.LastName}'");
```

The result of this should be the following:

```
LastName : ''
```

Converting this property to a dictionary should also work out of the box through an explicit cast:

```
var dictionary = (Dictionary<string, object>)personInstance;
Console.WriteLine(JsonSerializer.Serialize(dictionary));
```

The result of this should be the following:

```
{"FirstName":"Jane","LastName":null}
```

To test the validation, you can try to set the `LastName` property to an unsupported type:

```
personInstance.LastName = 42;
```

The result of this should be the following:

```
Unhandled exception. Chapter9.InvalidTypeForProperty: Property
'LastName' on 'Person' is invalid.
```

The last thing we can do to verify that all is working as expected is to set a property that does not exist in the schema:

```
personInstance.FullName = "Jane Doe";
```

This should produce the following result:

```
Unhandled exception. Microsoft.CSharp.RuntimeBinder.
RuntimeBinderException: 'Chapter9.JsonSchemaType' does not contain a
definition for 'FullName'
```

Working with the `DynamicObject` helper type eases the development of dynamic objects, as you don't have to worry about the complexity of the moving parts and can focus on the actual shape and capabilities of the dynamic object you want to provide.

Summary

This chapter explored the dynamic realm of the .NET runtime and how you can take advantage of it to create dynamic types that have its types defined outside of C# code. When working with third parties through APIs, this approach can be very handy. If you look at REST APIs and the OpenAPI standard, you'll see extensive use of JSON schemas, and marrying the approach in this chapter with such standards can provide you a powerful mechanism to dynamically integrate with third parties, and at the same time, you can be strict about the shape.

The DLR can be a powerful tool in your toolbox. It provides another approach to dynamically create types and code. Compared to generating intermediate language code, it can come across as more intuitive.

One of the downsides of the DLR is that the types generated can be hard to work with in a modern IDE or code editor, as it does not know about the types and can't offer services such as IntelliSense for members.

Another aspect of using the DLR and a dynamic approach can be performance. It will not be as performant as generating intermediate language code. This is one of the trade-offs you will have to make, but for specific scenarios, that might not be an issue at all.

In the next chapter, we will shift gears a little bit and look at how we can take advantage of some of the techniques we've discussed so far in the book and start thinking in terms of **convention over configuration**.

Part 3:
Increasing Productivity, Consistency, and Quality

In this part, you will see how metaprogramming can be used to improve code quality and leave you with a more maintainable and consistent code base. At the same time, this part gives you ideas on how techniques can improve the productivity of you and your developers. The different chapters touch on principles and software design patterns and how they can be used in real life.

This part has the following chapters:

- *Chapter 10, Convention over Configuration*
- *Chapter 11, Applying the Open-Closed Principle*
- *Chapter 12, Go Beyond Inheritance*
- *Chapter 13, Applying Cross-Cutting Concerns*
- *Chapter 14, Aspect-Oriented Programming*

10

Convention over Configuration

Our programs need to be configured. Some of these configurations are things such as connection strings to a database or a URL for a REST API we are calling. These might change depending on the different environments our code is running in (e.g. development, testing, or production). On top of this, we often have to configure our code to be able to run as we expect. The type of configuration we do is often dictated by some third-party library or framework we're using. In growing solutions, this type of configuration tends to also grow, and since configuration is often done at a specific point during the startup of the program, it's not uncommon to end up with large files acting as dumping grounds for this type of thing.

In this chapter, we will look into how we can leverage the power of the metadata we already have in running code to make code automatically configure itself and become more consistent as a result.

We will cover the following topics:

- Inversion of control and its role

- Automatic ServiceCollection registrations by convention

By end the of the chapter, you will have an idea of what conventions can do for you and how they can make you more productive and also allow you to create more consistent code bases.

Technical requirements

The source code specific to the chapter can be found on GitHub (`https://github.com/PacktPublishing/Metaprogramming-in-C-Sharp/tree/main/Chapter10`) and it builds on top of the `Fundamentals` code that is found at `https://github.com/PacktPublishing/Metaprogramming-in-C-Sharp/tree/main/Fundamentals`.

You will need Docker Desktop installed (`https://www.docker.com/products/docker-desktop/`), Postman (`https://www.postman.com`), and a MongoDB editor such as Compass (`https://www.mongodb.com/try/download/compass`).

Inversion of control and its role

Software needs structure really fast when growing beyond one page of source code. Typically, you'd group things logically in types that have a specific purpose in your system. With your software being broken up for better maintainability, the different parts are then often dependent on each other to be able to perform the overall tasks you need it to do.

Building a module for registering users

Let's build a simple system that handles a user sign-up feature exposed as a REST API. Start by creating a folder called `Chapter10`. Change into this folder in your command line and create a new web-based project:

```
dotnet new web
```

The type of information you'd want to capture involves both personal information and also the user's credentials that we want to have as part of the body of our API. Add a file called `RegisterUser.cs` and add the following to it:

```
namespace Chapter10;

public record RegisterUser(string FirstName, string
  LastName, string SocialSecurityNumber, string UserName,
    string Password);
```

The `RegisterUser` type takes all the different properties you want to capture for the user for the API. This is not what you want to store directly in a database. When you store this, you want to store this as two separate things – the user credentials and the user details. Create a file called `User.cs` and add the following to it:

```
namespace Chapter10;

public record User(Guid Id, string UserName, string
  Password);
```

The `User` type only captures the actual user name and the password and has a unique identifier for the user. Then add a file called `UserDetails` and add the following to it:

```
namespace Chapter10;

public record UserDetails(Guid Id, Guid UserId, string
  FirstName, string LastName, string SocialSecurityNumber);
```

`UserDetails` holds the rest of the information we will be getting from the `RegisterUser` type.

The next thing we need is an API controller to take this and store the information in the database. We will be using MongoDB as a backing store.

We will be relying on a third-party library to access MongoDB. Add the package to the project by running the following in the terminal:

```
dotnet add package mongodb.driver
```

Create a file called UsersController and add the following to it:

```
using Microsoft.AspNetCore.Mvc;
using MongoDB.Driver;

namespace Chapter10;

[Route("/api/users")]
public class UsersController : Controller
{
    IMongoCollection<User> _userCollection;
    IMongoCollection<UserDetails> _userDetailsCollection;

    public UsersController()
    {
        var client = new MongoClient
          ("mongodb://localhost:27017");
        var database = client.GetDatabase("TheSystem");
        _userCollection = database.GetCollection<User>
          ("Users");
        _userDetailsCollection = database.GetCollection
          <UserDetails>("UserDetails");
    }

    [HttpPost("register")]
    public async Task Register([FromBody] RegisterUser
      userRegistration)
    {
        var user = new User(Guid.NewGuid(),
            userRegistration.UserName,
              userRegistration.Password);
        var userDetails = new UserDetails(Guid.NewGuid(),
            user.Id, userRegistration.FirstName,
              userRegistration.LastName, userRegistration
                .SocialSecurityNumber);
        await _userCollection.InsertOneAsync(user);
        await _userDetailsCollection.InsertOneAsync
```

```
                (userDetails);
        }
    }
```

The code sets up in its constructor the database and gets the two different collections in which we will be storing the user information coming in. The register API method then takes `RegisterUser` and splits it up into the two respective types and inserts them into each of their MongoDB collections.

> **Important note**
> In a real system, you would obviously encrypt the password with a strong (preferably one-way) encryption strategy and not just store the password as clear text.

Open your `Program.cs` file and make it look like the following:

```
var builder = WebApplication.CreateBuilder(args);
builder.Services.AddControllers();

var app = builder.Build();
app.UseRouting();
app.UseEndpoints(_ => _.MapControllers());
app.Run();
```

Before you run the solution so far, you need to start the MongoDB server. You do this by using Docker. In your terminal, run the following:

```
docker run -d -p 27017:27017 mongo
```

The command should start MongoDB as a background daemon and expose port `27017` so that you can connect to it. You should see something similar to the following line:

```
9fb4b3c16d7647bfbb69eabd7863a169f6f2e4218191cc69c7454978627
f75d5
```

This is the unique identifier of the running Docker image.

You can now run the code you've created so far from your terminal:

```
dotnet run
```

You should now see something similar to the following:

```
info: Microsoft.Hosting.Lifetime[14]
      Now listening on: http://localhost:5000
info: Microsoft.Hosting.Lifetime[0]
      Application started. Press Ctrl+C to shut down.
```

```
info: Microsoft.Hosting.Lifetime[0]
      Hosting environment: Development
info: Microsoft.Hosting.Lifetime[0]
      Content root path: /Users/einari/Projects/
        Metaprogramming-in-C/Chapter10/
```

Testing the API

With the code thus far, you now have an API that has a route of `/api/users/register` that accepts an HTTP POST.

You can test your API by using Postman with the following steps:

1. Select **POST**.

2. Enter the URL for the API – `http://localhost:5000/api/user/register`.

3. In the **Body** tab, select **Raw** as the input and then **JSON** as the type.

> **Important note**
>
> The port of the URL has to match the port in the output where it says `Now listening on:`
> `http://localhost:{your port}`.

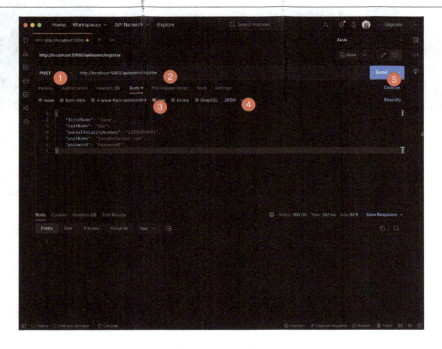

Figure 10.1 – Testing the API using Postman

Once you've clicked **Send**, you should get **200 OK** at the bottom. Then you can open the MongoDB editor – for instance, Compass, as suggested in the pre-requisites.

Create a new connection to the MongoDB server and perform the following steps:

1. Make sure the connection string is pointing to your MongoDB server. By default, it should say `mongodb://localhost:27017`, which matches the code.

2. Click the **Connect** button.

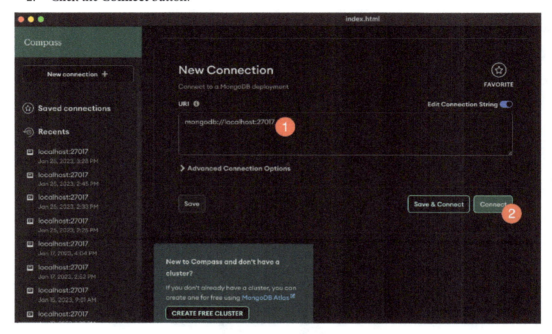

Figure 10.2 – Creating a new connection

Once connected, you should see the database **TheSystem** on the left-hand side and, within it, the collections. Clicking the **user** collection or **user-details**, you should see the data you registered on the right side.

Figure 10.3 – Registered data

This is all fine, and the code certainly does its job as expected. But the code could be improved.

Refactoring the code

There are a couple of challenges with this type of code:

- Firstly, the controller is taking on the responsibility for the infrastructure

- Secondly, it also takes on the responsibility for the actual domain logic and knowing exactly how to store things in a database

An API surface should instead just rely on other subsystems to do their specific job and then delegate to them rather and then become a composition.

For instance, we could go and isolate the user credential registration and the user details registration into two different services that we could use.

Creating services

Let's pull it apart a little bit and start putting in some structure. Create a file called `UsersService.cs` and make it look like the following:

```
using MongoDB.Driver;

namespace Chapter10;

public class UsersService
```

```
{
    readonly IMongoCollection<User> _usersCollection;

    public UserService()
    {
        var client = new MongoClient
            ("mongodb://localhost:27017");
        var database = client.GetDatabase("TheSystem");
        _usersCollection = database.GetCollection<User>
            ("Users");
    }

    public async Task<Guid> Register(string userName,
        string password)
    {
        var user = new User(Guid.NewGuid(),
            userRegistration.UserName, userRegistration
                .Password);
        await _usersCollection.InsertOneAsync(user);
        return user.Id;
    }
}
}
```

The code is doing exactly the same as it did in `UsersController` for registering the user, just that it is now formalized as a service. Let's do the same for the user details. Create a file called `UserDetailsService.cs` and make it look like the following:

```
namespace Chapter10;

public class UserDetailsService
{
    readonly IMongoCollection<User> _userDetailsCollection;

    public UserDetailsService(IDatabase database)
    {
        var client = new MongoClient
            ("mongodb://localhost:27017");
        var database = client.GetDatabase("TheSystem");
        _userDetailsCollection = database.GetCollection
            <User>("UserDetails");
    }

    public Task Register(string firstName, string lastName,
        string socialSecurityNumber, Guid userId)
```

```
        => _userDetailsCollection_.InsertOneAsync
            (new(Guid.NewGuid(), userId, firstName, lastName,
                socialSecurityNumber));
}
```

As with `UsersService`, the code does exactly the same as the original code in `UsersController`, only now separated out and focused.

This is a great step. Now the infrastructure details of the database are hidden from the outside world and anyone wanting to register a user only has to focus on the information needed to do so and not how it's done.

The next step is for you to change `UsersController` to leverage the new services.

Changing the controller

Go and change the controller to look like the following:

```
[Route("/api/users")]
public class UsersController : Controller
{
    readonly UsersService _usersService;
    readonly UserDetailsService _usersDetailsService;

    public UsersController()
    {
        _usersService = new UsersService();
        _userDetailsService = new UserDetailsService();
    }

    [HttpPost("register")]
    public async Task Register([FromBody] RegisterUser
        userRegistration)
    {
        await _usersService.Register(
            userRegistration.UserName,
            userRegistration.Password);
        await _userDetailsService.Register(
            userRegistration.FirstName,
            userRegistration.LastName,
            userRegistration.SocialSecurityNumber);
    }
}
```

The code creates an instance of the UsersService class in the constructor and uses the Register method directly in the Register API method.

If you run the sample at this point and perform the HTTP POST again, you will get the exact same result.

UsersService and UserDetailsService are now dependencies that UsersController have and it creates those dependencies as instances itself. There are a couple of downsides to this. The dependencies are basically now following the life cycle of the controller. Since controllers are created once per web request, it means UsersService and UserDetailsService will be created every time as well. This could be a performance issue, and is not really a problem the controller should be worried about. Its main job is just to provide an API surface for registering users.

It's also very hard to be able to write tests for UsersController, as the dependencies are now hard-wired and it brings in all the infrastructure with it and then makes it much harder to test the logic of UsersController in isolation.

This is where dependency inversion comes in, by reversing the relationship and saying that the system, in our case UsersController, is not responsible for creating the instance itself, but rather has it as an argument to the constructor, and letting whoever is instantiating the controller be responsible for providing the dependencies UsersController has.

Change UsersController to take the dependency on the constructor:

```
[Route("/api/users")]
public class UsersController : Controller
{
    readonly UsersService _usersService;
    readonly UserDetailsService _usersDetailsService;

    public UsersController(
        UsersService usersService,
        UserDetailsService userDetailsService)
    {
        _usersService = usersService;
        _userDetailsService = userDetailsService;
    }

    [HttpPost("register")]
    public async Task Register([FromBody] RegisterUser
userRegistration)
    {
        await _usersService.Register(
            userRegistration.UserName,
            userRegistration.Password);
        await _userDetailsService.Register(
```

```
                 userRegistration.FirstName,
                 userRegistration.LastName,
                 userRegistration.SocialSecurityNumber);
    }
}
```

The code now takes `UsersService` and `UserDetailsService` as arguments and uses those directly instead of creating an instance of them itself.

We now have the benefit of the dependencies being very clear to the outside world. The life cycle of `UsersService` can then be managed outside of the controller.

However, since the controller is taking the concrete instances, it is still tied to the infrastructure. This can be improved upon to decouple the infrastructure and make it more testable.

Contract oriented

To improve further on this, we could also extract the content of `UsersService` and `UserDetailsService` into interfaces and use those instead. The benefits of that are that you would decouple from the concrete implementation and its infrastructure needs and add flexibility in your code by allowing different implementations and, depending on the configuration or the system being in a specific state, switch out which implementation of the interface to use.

An additional benefit of extracting into an interface is that you make it easier to write tests that focus purely on the unit being tested and only the interaction with its dependencies, without having to bring in the entire infrastructure to write the automated test.

Create a file called `IUsersService.cs` and make it look like the following:

```
namespace Chapter10;

public interface IUsersService
{
    Task<Guid> Register(string userName, string password);
}
```

The code holds the `Register` method with the same signature as in the original `UsersService` class. Then the implementation of `UsersService` only changes by adding the `IUsersService` inheritance. Open the `UsersService` file and make it implement the `IUsersService` interface:

```
public class UsersService : IUsersService
{
    /*
    Same code as before within the UsersService
    */
}
```

For `UserDetailsService`, we want to do the same. Add a file called `IUserDetailsService.cs` and make it look like the following:

```
namespace Chapter10.Structured;

public interface IUserDetailsService
{
    Task Register(string firstName, string lastName, string
      socialSecurityNumber, Guid userId);
}
```

The code holds the `Register` method with the same signature as in the original `UserDetailsService` class. Then the implementation of `UserDetailsService` only changes by adding the `IUserDetailsService` inheritance. Open the `UserDetailsService` file and make it implement the `IUserDetailsService` interface:

```
public class UserDetailsService : IUserDetailsService
{
    /*
    Same code as before within the UserDetailsService
    */
}
```

With these two changes, we can now change how we express the dependencies. In `UsersController`, you then change from using `UsersService` to `IUsersService` and `UserDetailsService` to `IUserDetailsService`:

```
[Route("/api/users")]
public class UsersController : Controller
{
    readonly IUsersService _usersService;
    readonly IUserDetailsService _userDetailsService;

    public UsersController(
        IUsersService usersService,
        IUserDetailsService userDetailsService)
    {
        _usersService = usersService;
        _userDetailsService = userDetailsService;
    }

    // Same register API method as before would go here
}
```

The code now takes the two `IUsersService` and `IUserDetailsService` dependencies using their interfaces and the rest of the code remains unchanged.

So far, we've discussed dependencies and the benefits of the **dependency inversion principle**. Still, we need to be able to provide these dependencies. And it is very impractical if we have to manually provide these all around our system and maintain life cycles of them in different ways. It could lead to a very messy, unmaintainable code base and could also lead to unknown side effects.

What you really want is something that manages this for you. This is what is known as an **inversion of control container (IoC container)**. Its job is to hold information about all your services, which implementation is used for what interface, and also the life cycle of these. The IoC container is a centralized piece that you configure at the beginning of your application and after its configuration is done, you can ask it to provide instances of anything that is registered with it. It's very useful for registering any kind of dependencies, not just the ones where it is an interface to an implementation. You can register concrete types, delegate types, or pretty much anything.

The IoC container works recursively and will deal with dependencies of dependencies and resolve everything correctly.

In ASP.NET Core, the concept of an IoC container is already set up out of the box and is really easy to use with what is known as `ServiceCollection`, where you can set up all the service registrations.

Automatic ServiceCollection registrations by convention

We've now left the code in a non-functional state. This is because the built-in IoC container does not know how to resolve the `IUsersService` dependency and `IUserDetailsService`.

You need to explicitly tell ASP.NET which implementation it should use. Open your `Program.cs` file and put in the binding as follows:

```
var builder = WebApplication.CreateBuilder(args);
builder.Services.AddControllers();

// Add these two lines to bind the services
builder.Services.AddSingleton<IUsersService,
  UsersService>();
builder.Services.AddSingleton<IUserDetailsService,
  UserDetailsService>();

var app = builder.Build();
app.UseRouting();
app.UseEndpoints(_ => _.MapControllers());
app.Run();
```

The code adds a registration in the ASP.NET Core `ServiceCollection` for `IUsersService` to be resolved to `UsersService`, and it also explicitly says that it should add it as a **singleton**. This means that there will only be one instance of this service within the process.

You should now have a working program again, the only difference now is that the ASP.NET IoC container is resolving the instance for you, and it will be the same instance for every request.

> **Important note**
>
> Singletons can be dangerous. If the type being a singleton has a dependency on something that shouldn't be a singleton but should in fact be new on every request, the type being singleton will be a blocker for that. Use them wisely.

The code thus far is very contained and simple. In real systems, you tend to want to be even clearer about responsibilities by dividing up the code into more focused units.

Further refactoring

Too much responsibility lies on `UsersService` right now. The database part is not something it should own. Knowing how to create a database connection is something that should be extracted so that you do that in one place. Be conscious of the responsibilities of each unit in your system.

Let's introduce a unit representing the database. Start by creating an interface by adding a file called `IDatabase.cs` to the project, and make it look like the following:

```
using MongoDB.Driver;

namespace Chapter10;

public interface IDatabase
{
    IMongoCollection<T> GetCollectionFor<T>();
}
```

The interface gives us access to getting MongoDB collections for types specified using generics.

> **Important note**
>
> By creating an abstraction for the database, one could argue we could have gone further and created something that represented the database operations you typically do adhering to what is known as the repository pattern. If you did that, you would quickly find that you would not be able to work with the underlying database and its capabilities. Also, for the context of this book, we'll keep it at this level.

With the `IDatabase` interface in place, you now need an implementation of it. Create a file called `Database.cs` and add the following to it:

```
using MongoDB.Driver;

namespace Chapter10;

public class Database : IDatabase
{
    static readonly Dictionary<Type, string>
      _typeToCollectionName = new()
    {
        { typeof(User), "Users" },
        { typeof(UserDetails), "UserDetails" }
    };
    readonly IMongoDatabase _mongoDatabase;

    public Database()
    {
        var client = new MongoClient
          ("mongodb://localhost:27017");
        _mongoDatabase = client.GetDatabase("TheSystem");
    }

    public IMongoCollection<T> GetCollectionFor<T>() =>
      _mongoDatabase.GetCollection<T>(_typeToCollectionName
        [typeof(T)]);
}
```

The code contains most of the database access you had in `UsersService` but adds a dimension of mapping types to collection names.

As a little bit of a sidetrack, but still on the theme of convention over configuration, let's improve the `Database` class a little bit. At the top of the class, there is the map of `Type` to the collection name. This is something that would grow over time. If you look at the `User` type, it gets mapped to `Users` – a convention that I prefer, having the collection names as plural, indicating there is more than one user.

> **Important note**
>
> The concept of convention over configuration was coined by David Heinemeier Hansson to describe the philosophy of the Ruby on Rails web framework. You can read more about it here: https://rubyonrails.org/doctrine#convention-over-configuration.

This is something that can be automated and would truly be convention over configuration. Let's pull in a third-party library that deals with pluralization for us. Go to your terminal and run the following in the Chapter10 folder:

```
dotnet add package Humanizer
```

The Humanizer library knows how to pluralize English words by default, but it has support for other languages as well. I recommend reading more about it over on GitHub (https://github. com/Humanizr/Humanizer).

With the package installed, you can improve and simplify your Database code. Change the Database class to be like the following:

```
using Humanizer;
using MongoDB.Driver;

namespace Chapter10.Structured;

public class Database : IDatabase
{
    readonly IMongoDatabase _mongoDatabase;

    public Database()
    {
        var client = new MongoClient("mongodb://
          localhost:27017");
        _mongoDatabase = client.GetDatabase("TheSystem");
    }

    public IMongoCollection<T> GetCollectionFor<T>() =>
      _mongoDatabase.GetCollection<T>(typeof(T).Name
        .Pluralize());
}
```

The code is pretty much the same, except you now don't have Dictionary with the mapping between Type and collection names. Also, for the GetCollection() method, you no longer need to do a lookup but instead, just use the type name and use the .Pluralize() extension method on it. With this, you're leveraging the type metadata to your advantage in a very simple way.

With this fix, you've basically made your code future-proof and will not have to perform open-heart surgery on the code to add support for a new collection. It's a predictable convention.

Since you now have encapsulated the infrastructure part of the system into the Database class, you can now start fixing UserService and UserDetailsService to leverage this centerpiece.

Start by changing `UsersService` to the following:

```
namespace Chapter10;

public class UsersService : IUsersService
{
    readonly IDatabase _database;

    public UsersService(IDatabase database)
    {
        _database = database;
    }

    public async Task<Guid> Register(string userName,
        string password)
    {
        var user = new User(Guid.NewGuid(), userName,
            password);
        await _database.GetCollectionFor<User>()
            .InsertOneAsync(user);
        return user.Id;
    }
}
```

The code now completely gets rid of the management of the database connection and how to get a collection, and also not even the name of the collection, instead pulling in `IDatabase` as a dependency and letting the implementation of that interface take the full responsibility of the infrastructure. This is now just by convention, and you can trust that it will be a predictable collection name for the type you give it.

You need to do the same to `UserDetailsService`. Change it to the following:

```
namespace Chapter10.Structured;

public class UserDetailsService : IUserDetailsService
{
    readonly IDatabase _database;

    public UserDetailsService(IDatabase database)
    {
        _database = database;
    }

    public Task Register(string firstName, string lastName,
```

```
        string socialSecurityNumber, Guid userId)
          => _database.GetCollectionFor<UserDetails>()
            .InsertOneAsync(new(Guid.NewGuid(), userId,
              firstName, lastName, socialSecurityNumber));
}
```

As with `UsersService`, the code change is pretty much the same, bringing in the `IDatabase` infrastructure dependency and letting `UserDetailsService` focus on its primary job of registering user details.

The activity of refactoring the code has led to a more decoupled system and a more maintainable system, where each component is laser-focused on doing one thing, a single responsibility. It now needs to be brought together.

Composing

With the system broken up into focused components, we have to bring it together. Since the IoC container does not know how to resolve `IDatabase`, we need to add that binding. Change your `Program.cs` to look like the following:

```
var builder = WebApplication.CreateBuilder(args);
builder.Services.AddControllers();

builder.Services.AddSingleton<IUsersService,
  UsersService>();
builder.Services.AddSingleton<IUserDetailsService,
  UserDetailsService>();
// Add these two lines to bind the services
builder.Services.AddSingleton<IDatabase, Database>();

var app = builder.Build();
app.UseRouting();
app.UseEndpoints(_ => _.MapControllers());
app.Run();
```

The code adds the `.AddSingleton<IDatabase, Database>()` call to register the binding between `IDatabase` and `Database` and also say we only need it to be a singleton. You should, at this point, have a working system again. Running this and performing the API call using Postman should give you the same result as before.

However, already there is a bit of a code smell here. The fact that we have to go and manually add a registration to the IoC container for everything we add is again open-heart surgery we have to perform every time we create something. With just a couple of components, this not only becomes tedious but quickly also makes `Program.cs` a dumping ground for this type of configuration.

Luckily, there is a pattern we can turn into a convention. All the implementations have an interface representation that is named the same as the implementation, only prefixed with a capital *I*. This is a very common convention. We can make the code more future-proof by discovering the connections between the interfaces and implementations.

Even though we can discover the relationship between implementations and interfaces, we wouldn't know how to know which life cycle they should be. To do this, we shift the responsibility of knowing the life cycle onto the implementation. We do this by introducing metadata in the form of attributes. The default behavior should be that every binding we do is **transient**, meaning that we get a new instance every time we ask the IoC container. Then all we need is attributes for overriding that behavior. For this sample, we'll keep it to only one life cycle: singleton.

Add a file called `SingletonAttribute.cs` and make it look like the following:

```
namespace Chapter10;

[AttributeUsage(AttributeTargets.Class)]
public sealed class SingletonAttribute : Attribute
{
}
```

The code represents an attribute that is for classes and lets you look for during discovery and decide whether or not it is a singleton.

Let's take advantage of the **Fundamentals** project in the GitHub repository mentioned in the pre-requisites. You should add a project reference to it for this chapter by doing the following in your terminal:

```
dotnet add reference ../Fundamentals/Fundamentals.csproj
```

> **Important note**
> The path to the project might be different on your computer, depending on where you have the `Fundamentals` project from the GitHub repository.

What you now want to do is create an extension method for `IServiceCollection` that you've been calling to register bindings with.

Start by adding a file called `ServiceCollectionExtensions.cs` and make it look like the following:

```
using Fundamentals;

namespace Chapter10;

public static class ServiceCollectionExtensions
```

```
{
    public static IServiceCollection AddBindingsBy
      Convention(this IServiceCollection services, ITypes
        types)
    {
        return services;
    }
}
```

The code just sets up a new extension method called AddBindingsByConvention() that also takes the ITypes system from Fundamentals and returns services given to it to be able to chain calls when using the method.

Go and add the following to the top of the AddBindingsConvention() method:

```
Func<Type, Type, bool> convention = (i, t) => i.Namespace
  == t.Namespace && i.Name == $"I{t.Name}";
var conventionBasedTypes = types!.All.Where(_ =>
{
    var interfaces = _.GetInterfaces();
    if (interfaces.Length > 0)
    {
        var conventionInterface = interfaces
          .SingleOrDefault(i => convention(i, _));
        if (conventionInterface != default)
        {
            return types!.All.Count(type => type
              .HasInterface(conventionInterface)) == 1;
        }
    }
    return false;
});
```

The code uses ITypes to get all the discovered types in the system. For every type, it looks at whether the type implements any interfaces. If it does implement an interface, it will see whether any of the interfaces match the convention. The convention is that the interface type and the implementation type have to be in the same namespace and that the interface type has to match the name of the implementation, only prefixed with a capital *I*.

The result of this will be a collection of types that matches the convention. Next, you'll need to add code that registers the bindings. Add the following code after the previous code you added in the AddBindingsByConvention() method:

```
foreach (var conventionBasedType in conventionBasedTypes)
{
```

```
    var interfaceToBind = types.All.Single(_ =>
      _.IsInterface && convention(_, conventionBasedType));
    if (services.Any(_ => _.ServiceType == interfaceTo
      Bind))
    {
        continue;
    }

    _ = conventionBasedType.HasAttribute
        <SingletonAttribute>() ?
        services.AddSingleton(interfaceToBind,
          conventionBasedType) :
        services.AddTransient(interfaceToBind,
          conventionBasedType);
}
```

The code loops through all the types that adhere to the convention and gets the actual interface and then binds it either as a singleton or transient based on whether or not the implementation has SingletonAttribute or not.

Let's go and make all the services singleton using the attribute. Open the Database.cs file and add SingletonAttribute in front of the type declaration:

```
[Singleton]
public class Database : IDatabase
{
    // Keep your original code
}
```

Do the same for UserDetailsService:

```
[Singleton]
public class UserDetailsService : IUserDetailsService
{
    // Keep your original code
}
```

And then do the same for UsersService.

```
[Singleton]
public class UsersService : IUsersService
{
    // Keep your original code
}
```

All you now need to do is change the program startup. Open `Program.cs` and change it to look like the following:

```
using Chapter10;
using Fundamentals;

var builder = WebApplication.CreateBuilder(args);
builder.Services.AddControllers();

// Create an instance of Types and register it with the IoC
var types = new Types();
builder.Services.AddSingleton<ITypes>(types);

// Add all the bindings based on convention
builder.Services.AddBindingsByConvention(types);

var app = builder.Build();
app.UseRouting();
app.UseEndpoints(_ => _.MapControllers());
app.Run();
```

The code changes from all the explicit bindings of the different services to now leverage the `Types` class from **Fundamentals**, binding it as a singleton, and then adding all the bindings discovered by convention.

Running your application should still give you the same behavior and it should work in the exact same way. The only difference is that everything is now by convention, and you can just add things without having to configure anything.

Summary

In this chapter, you've tasted a little bit of how powerful conventions can be for concrete everyday C# coding, touching on how to improve the experience working with the IoC container in ASP.NET Core by optimizing a common scenario of registering services by their interface. We've also looked at how designing by contract helps you create a system that is more flexible and much easier to test.

The concept of *convention over configuration* is probably the thing that has impacted me personally the most in my career. It makes your code more consistent and if you fail to be consistent, it doesn't work, which is a good thing because then you will have to fix your code to be more consistent.

Having to not configure everything and just be able to add code is a true productivity boost, and anyone working on the project will thank you for it. However, you need to be clear with all team members about what the conventions are, otherwise, they will not thank you at all. There is nothing worse than having your code work or not work seemingly arbitrarily. Document it and be clear about how things work.

Also worth mentioning is that conventions are not for all projects and are not necessarily for all teams. For conventions to make sense, the team needs to accept that way of working. If the team prefers reading code and seeing everything explicitly set up, then conventions will only cause confusion. If the project is a very small one, it might not be worth the cognitive overhead.

Coming up in the next chapter, we'll get more into the open/closed principle, something we've touched on in this chapter, and see how it can benefit your code base.

11

Applying the Open-Closed Principle

The open-closed principle is credited to Bertrand Meyer, after its appearance in his 1988 book, *Object-Oriented Software Construction* (`https://en.wikipedia.org/wiki/Object-Oriented_Software_Construction`). This book describes the following principles that we can apply to our software:

- A type is open if it can be extended
- A type is closed when it is available to other types

Suppose we have a class called `Shape` that has a method called `area`, which in turn calculates the area of the shape. We want to be able to add new shapes to our program without modifying the `Shape` class, so we make the `Shape` class open for extension.

To do this, we create a new class called `Triangle` that inherits from `Shape` and overrides the `area` method to calculate the area of a triangle. We can also create a `Rectangle` class and any other new shapes we want.

Now, whenever we need to calculate the area of a shape, we can simply create a new instance of the appropriate shape class and call its `area` method. Because the `Shape` class is closed for modification, we don't need to modify it every time we add a new shape to our program.

Classes in C# are, by default, open for extension. We can inherit from any classes that are not sealed and add new meanings to them. But the base class we're inheriting from should be closed, meaning that there shouldn't be a need for any change in the base type for the new type to work.

This helps us to design our code for extensibility and keep responsibilities in the right place.

Taking a step back, we can apply some of this at the system level. What if we could simply expand on our systems, without the need to add configurations at the heart of a type for it to know about the additions?

This type of thinking is the type we used earlier in *Chapter 4, Reasoning about Types Using Reflection*, with the `ICommand` interface and its implementations. The two commands we added were not known by any parts of the system, but by implementing the `ICommand` interface, we could see both types through an introspective of our system.

In this chapter, we will cover the following topics:

- The goal of the open-closed principle
- Encapsulating type discovery
- Encapsulating the discovery of instances
- Hooking up with the service collection
- A practical use case

By the end of the chapter, you will understand how you can set your code and projects up for success in order to make them more flexible and extensible, and how to create code that welcomes changes and additions without having to perform open-heart surgery on your code every time.

Technical requirements

The source code specific to the chapter can be found on GitHub (`https://github.com/PacktPublishing/Metaprogramming-in-C-Sharp/tree/main/Chapter11`) and it builds on the `Fundamentals` code, which can be found at `https://github.com/PacktPublishing/Metaprogramming-in-C-Sharp/tree/main/Fundamentals`.

The goal of the open-closed principle

In a world with ever-changing and growing requirements, newly discovered business opportunities, or even pivots for your business, it's not very helpful if your software has to go through triple-bypass surgery for changes to be made. At the heart of an agile mindset sits the ability to be nimble and react to change in a timely fashion. From a business perspective, this is a type of elasticity that is very useful. The goal is to be cost-effective when changes come in. In projects or product developments that I've been part of, I've often noticed that this translates into an ad hoc mindset, and often a total disregard for writing code in a way that makes it possible to let the code have longevity and be understood by developers.

The initial phase of development, the exciting part of getting to the first version of a software product, is where we set the tone for the code future of the code base. In most cases, however, this only represents a small fraction of the lifecycle of the code. This is why I believe we should focus much more on how we can set ourselves up for success in the maintenance of code.

A very common idea I often also encounter is the strong belief that just getting the first version out the door is key and that after that, we can start fixing all the things we weren't proud of originally, such as all the shortcuts we had to take because we thought we didn't have time to do it *properly*. Chasing a **Minimum Viable Product** (**MVP**) is a very popular approach. The chase is driven by a desire to deliver products to the market and learn from them. Unfortunately, in my experience, we often don't get to create a viable product at all, but rather prototypes that prove what we want to build. They might feel like products on the surface, but they lack a proper foundation to stand on. From a non-technical viewpoint, it feels like this is exactly what the developers wanted, and that they want you to move on. And who can blame them? Customers who start using these products might also feel like they are using a product, but they have no idea what's going on under the surface. Pretty soon after getting the first version out there, the business, customers, and end users will come back with new things they'd like the software to do. I've yet to see a business prioritize fixing the foundation at this point. When this is combined with reported shortcomings or concrete faults in the software, you end up sprinting toward new goals. The excitement you had getting the first version out goes away, and the work becomes a chore.

We did the business a huge disservice by not putting design-based thinking into our code, which would have set the business up for success. The code might be in a worse state than it could've been, making it hard to make all these changes. This often leads to less satisfied developers, who might ultimately decide to leave in the hope that their next place of work will offer them a better working environment for writing better code.

Where am I going with all this? I do believe it is possible to deliver actual MVPs, lower the amount of technical debt in the code base dramatically, and make it possible to iterate on the MVP to deliver more, faster, and more accurately with a strong foundation. I'm pretty sure businesses would rather have the latter – something that won't die a slow death the second it hits the market.

At the heart of enabling this sits one of my favorite principles: **the open-closed principle**. As I mentioned previously, I see it as a strategic mindset: not just a tactical approach to writing classes, but a system-level method. How can we make sure we can just drop code in at any time, extending the capabilities of our software, with the confidence that it won't break the existing system? If we can avoid having to modify existing code to accomplish our new objectives, we lower the risk of regressions in our software dramatically.

We can leverage the building blocks we've built so far in this book to accomplish this and improve on them to make them more friendly.

Encapsulating type discovery

In *Chapter 4, Reasoning about Types Using Reflection*, we introduced a class called `Types`, which encapsulates the logic used in finding types. This is a very powerful construct for enabling software to be extensible. We can make it a little bit better and build a construct on top of it that simplifies its use.

In the `Types` class, we have a method called `FindMultiple()`, which allows us to find types that implement a specific type. A small improvement on this would be to allow us to represent the different types we want implementations of by taking a dependency in a constructor of a specific type that describes this.

> **Important note**
>
> You'll find the implementation of this in the **Fundamentals** part of the repository mentioned in the *Technical requirements* section.

The concept is basically to have the type represented as an interface, as follows:

```
public interface IImplementationsOf<T> : IEnumerable<Type>
    where T : class
{
}
```

The interface takes a generic type that describes the type whose implementations you're interested in. It then says it is an enumerable of `Type`, which makes it possible for you to iterate over it directly. The generic constraint of `class` is there to limit the scope of the types you can work with, since it wouldn't be useful to allow primitive types such as `int`, which aren't inheritable.

The implementation of the interface is straightforward and looks as follows:

```
public class ImplementationsOf<T> : IImplementationsOf<T>
    where T : class
{
    readonly IEnumerable<Type> _types;

    public ImplementationsOf(ITypes types)
    {
        _types = types.FindMultiple<T>();
    }

    public IEnumerator<Type> GetEnumerator()
    {
        return _types.GetEnumerator();
    }

    IEnumerator IEnumerable.GetEnumerator()
    {
        return _types.GetEnumerator();
    }
}
```

The code takes `ITypes` as dependencies, as it will use it to actually find the implementations.

Discovering types is one thing, and this makes the approach a little bit nicer by making the code more readable and clearer. But this only gives you the type. A more common method is to get not only the type but also its instances.

Encapsulating the discovery of instances

Another encapsulation we can perform, which is probably more suited to our current scenario, is to find the implementations and then get their instances directly.

> **Important note**
> You'll find the implementation of this in the **Fundamentals** part of the repository, in the *Technical requirements* section.

The concept is basically to represent the code similarly to the case in which `IImplementationsOf<T>` is used as the interface, as follows:

```
public interface IInstancesOf<T> : IEnumerable<T>
    where T : class
{
}
```

The interface in the code uses the generic parameter to determine the types for which it can provide instances. It then implements `IEnumerable<T>`, making it possible to enumerate its instances directly and get instances of the type.

The implementation of the interface is straightforward and is as follows:

```
public class InstancesOf<T> : IInstancesOf<T>
    where T : class
{
    readonly IEnumerable<Type> _types;
    readonly IServiceProvider _serviceProvider;

    public InstancesOf(ITypes types,
        IServiceProvider serviceProvider)
    {
        _types = types.FindMultiple<T>();
        _serviceProvider = serviceProvider;
    }

    public IEnumerator<T> GetEnumerator()
```

```
    {
        foreach (var type in _types) yield return
        (T)_serviceProvider.GetService(type)!;
    }


    IEnumerator IEnumerable.GetEnumerator()
    {
        foreach (var type in _types) yield return
        _serviceProvider.GetService(type);
    }
}
```

The code leverages `ITypes` and, as with `ImplementationsOf<T>`, it uses the `FindMultiple()` method to find the actual types. Since it will discover types it does not know anything about and, consequently, it does not know how to instantiate them if they don't have a default constructor without arguments, it needs support in order to do this. To this end, it leverages the `IServiceProvider` instance found in .NET. `IServiceProvider` is what gets set up when using the .NET dependency injection system. The `GetEnumerator()` implementation then iterates the types and provides the instance by calling the `GetService()` method on `IServiceProvider`.

Note that the implementation asks `IServiceProvider` only when enumerated instead of just doing this in the constructor. The reason for this is that you don't want to run the risk of something taking a dependency on `IInstancesOf<T>` that has a longer lifecycle than the implementations. For instance, if a class using `IInstancesOf<T>` is a **singleton**, all the instances in the class using it are themselves singletons.

The only caveat is that when calling `GetService()` for types that do not have a concrete registration on `IServiceProvider`, you'll get `null`. This is not very useful.

Hooking up with the service collection

Since we're leveraging `ServiceProvider` to create instances, and since its default behavior is to have everything explicitly registered with it, it might not have a registration for the concrete type we asked.

In *Chapter 10*, *Convention over Configuration*, you did an implementation for discovering the relationship between interfaces and implementations according to a convention. We can extend this thinking and say that it should be possible to resolve classes themselves according to their type.

To do this, we leverage more reflection metadata to filter out the different types we are not interested in.

In *Chapter 10*, *Convention over Configuration*, you created something called `Service CollectionExtensions`. We want to make use of this here as well, but we also want to add some additional functionality. Move the file into the shared `Fundamentals` project.

Open the `ServiceCollectionExtensions` class and add the following:

```
public static IServiceCollection AddSelfBinding(this
IServiceCollection services, ITypes types)
{
    const TypeAttributes staticType =
      TypeAttributes.Abstract | TypeAttributes.Sealed;

    types.All.Where(_ =>
        (_.Attributes & staticType) != staticType &&
        !_.IsInterface &&
        !_.IsAbstract &&
        services.Any(s => s.ServiceType !=
          _)).ToList().ForEach(_ =>
    {
        var __ = _.HasAttribute<SingletonAttribute>() ?
            services.AddSingleton(_, _) :
            services.AddTransient(_, _);
    });

    return services;
}
```

The code uses the `ITypes` system and filters down types by ignoring `static` classes, as they can't be instantiated. In addition, it also ignores interfaces and abstract types for the same reason. It then ignores any types that are already registered in the `services` collection. Any type that is left is then registered. If the type has the `[Singleton]` attribute, it registers as a singleton; otherwise, it uses a **transient** lifecycle, meaning you'll get a new instance every time you ask for one.

With this in place, we're getting ready to apply what we have in a more practical way.

Practical use case

Let's build something that leverages the new form of discovery but, more importantly, shows the concept of an elastic growing system that does not require changes at the core for new features to be added.

Let's revisit the concept of compliance, which is a very common scenario in software. We looked into GDPR in *Chapter 4, Reasoning about Types Using Reflection*, and *Chapter 5, Leveraging Attributes*. GDPR is just one type of compliance with which it is important to deal with.

The goal is to create a system in which the core "engine" does not know about the different types of compliance metadata that can exist and instead provides extensibility points, where developers can just add new compliance metadata types as they're needed.

We want the engine to be generalized and accessible to everyone. Following the GitHub repository mentioned in *Technical requirements*, you'll find that there is a **Fundamentals** project. All the code listed here can be found there.

Let's start by creating a record that represents the type of metadata that leverages the `ConceptAs<>` base record found in `Fundamentals`. Add a file called `ComplianceMetadataType.cs` and make it look as follows:

```
namespace Fundamentals.Compliance;

public record ComplianceMetadataType(Guid Value) :
ConceptAs<Guid>(Value)
{
    public static readonly ComplianceMetadataType PII = new(Guid.
Parse("cae5580e-83d6-44dc-9d7a-a72e8a2f17d7"));

    public static implicit operator
      ComplianceMetadataType(string value) =>
      new(Guid.Parse(value));

    public static implicit operator
      ComplianceMetadataType(Guid value) => new(value);
}
```

The code introduces a `record` instance inheriting `ConceptAs<>` and makes the value inside it a `Guid` instance. It then adds a well-known type for **personally identifiable information**, or **PII** for short. The type also adds implicit operators for converting from a `string` representation of a `Guid` instance, as well as directly from a `Guid` instance.

> **Important note**
>
> The `ConceptAs<>` type is explained in *Chapter 4, Reasoning about Types Using Reflection*.

Next, we want a type that will represent the actual metadata. Add a file called `ComplianceMetadata.cs` and make it look as follows:

```
namespace Fundamentals.Compliance;

public record ComplianceMetadata(ComplianceMetadataType MetadataType,
string Details);
```

The code represents the metadata as a reference to the type of metadata, followed by a `Details` string.

In order for us to be able to discover the metadata, we need something that can provide this metadata. We represent this as an interface that is discoverable for us on its own.

Add a file called `ICanProvideComplianceMetadataForType.cs` and make it look as follows:

```
namespace Fundamentals.Compliance;

public interface ICanProvideComplianceMetadataForType
{
    bool CanProvide(Type type);

    ComplianceMetadata Provide(Type type);
}
```

The code represents a provider that decides whether it's capable of providing using the `CanProvide()` method, followed by a method for actually providing the metadata. The key to the extensibility lies with this pattern, which enables us to drop in any implementations that can be called for any type, and the implementation itself decides whether it can provide the metadata.

Since `ICanProvideComplianceMetadataForType` is only focused on providing metadata for `Type`, we need another provider for the properties of a type.

Add a file called `ICanProvideComplianceMetadataForProperty.cs` and make it look as follows:

```
namespace Fundamentals.Compliance;

public interface ICanProvideComplianceMetadataForProperty
{
    bool CanProvide(PropertyInfo property);

    ComplianceMetadata Provide(PropertyInfo property);
}
```

As with `ICanProvideComplianceMetadataForType`, you'll see that `ICanProvideComplianceMetadataForProperty` has the `CanProvide()` method and a `Provide()` method; the only difference is that it is focused on `PropertyInfo`.

With the discoverable interfaces in place, we can start to build the engine that discovers these things and combines them into something that can be leveraged as a system.

Let's start by defining the contract for the compliance engine by adding an interface for it. Add a file called `IComplianceMetadataResolver.cs` and make it look as follows:

```
namespace Fundamentals.Compliance;

public interface IComplianceMetadataResolver
{
    bool HasMetadataFor(Type type);
```

```
    bool HasMetadataFor(PropertyInfo property);
    IEnumerable<ComplianceMetadata> GetMetadataFor(Type
      type);
    IEnumerable<ComplianceMetadata>
      GetMetadataFor(PropertyInfo property);
}
```

The code adds methods for asking whether `Type` or `PropertyInfo` has metadata associated with it and getting the associated metadata.

Helping the developer

It's good practice to be clear on whether calling code skips calling the `Has*()` methods and goes directly for the `Get*()` method, and whether there is no metadata. If there is no metadata, the `Get*()` methods can't really do anything except throw an exception.

Add a file called `NoComplianceMetadataForType.cs` and make it look as follows:

```
namespace Fundamentals.Compliance;

public class NoComplianceMetadataForType : Exception
{
    public NoComplianceMetadataForType(Type type)
        : base($"Types '{type.FullName}' does not have any
        compliance metadata.")
    {
    }
}
```

The code represents an exception with a clear name and a clear message saying that the type does not have any metadata.

Let's do the same for the properties without metadata. Add a file called `NoCompliance MetadataForProperty.cs` and make it look like the following:

```
namespace Fundamentals.Compliance;

public class NoComplianceMetadataForProperty : Exception
{
    public NoComplianceMetadataForProperty(PropertyInfo
      property)
        : base($"Property '{property.Name}' on type
        '{property.DeclaringType?.FullName}' does not
        have any compliance metadata.")
    {
```

Now you need to implement the methods from the interface. 'd the following code to the end of
the CompilanceMetadataResolver class:

```
public bool HasMetadataFor(Type type) => _type!
_.CanProvide(type));
                                           lers.Any(_ =>

public IEnumerable<ComplianceMetadata> GetMetadata
{                                                  e type)
    ThrowIfNoComplianceMetadataForType(type);
    return _typeProviders
        .Where(_ => _.CanProvide(type))
        .Select(_ => _.Provide(type))
        .ToArray();
}

void ThrowIfNoComplianceMetadataForType(Type type)
{
    if (!HasMetadataFor(type))
    {
        throw new NoComplianceMetadataForType(type);
    }
}
```

The code uses _typeProviders discovered in the constructor to determine whether the type
to it is something for which the provider can provide metadata. If it can, it will return true; if not, it
return false. The GetMetadataFor() method checks whether it can provide; if it can't, it will thr.
the NoComplianceMetadataForType exception. If it can, it will filter down to the provider.
that can provide and then ask them to provide. It then combines all the metadata into one collection.

Supporting properties

You now want to do the same for the properties. Add the following code to the end of the
ComplianceMetadataResolver class:

```
public bool HasMetadataFor(PropertyInfo property) => _
propertyProviders.Any(_ => _.CanProvide(property));

public IEnumerable<ComplianceMetadata> GetMetadataFor(PropertyInfo
property)
{
    ThrowIfNoComplianceMetadataForProperty(property);
    return _propertyProviders
        .Where(_ => _.CanProvide(property))
        .Select(_ => _.Provide(property))
        .ToArray();
```

```
}

void ThrowIfNoComplianceMetadataForProperty(PropertyInfo property)
{
    if (!HasMetadataFor(property))
    {
        throw new
          NoComplianceMetadataForProperty(property);
    }
}
```

As for types, the code asks _propertyProviders whether they can provide and then uses this to filter for the properties using the GetMetadataFor() method. The same behavior as that of the types throwing an exception will occur if there is no metadata when it is requested.

With the engine in place, we now need to make use of it and create the first implementation.

In Fundamentals, you should already have an attribute called PersonalIdentifiable InformationAttribute. You now want to create a provider that can provide metadata for this on a property level.

Add a file called PersonalIdentifiableInformationMetadataProvider.cs in a sub-folder called GDPR, in the Compliance folder, inside Fundamentals, and make it look as follows:

```
namespace Fundamentals.Compliance.GDPR;

public class PersonalIdentifiableInformationMetadataProvider
  : ICanProvideComplianceMetadataForProperty
{
    public bool CanProvide(PropertyInfo property) =>
        property.
GetCustomAttribute<PersonalIdentifiableInformationAttribute>() !=
default ||
        property.DeclaringType?.
GetCustomAttribute<PersonalIdentifiableInformationAttribute>() !=
default;

    public ComplianceMetadata Provide(PropertyInfo
      property)
    {
        if (!CanProvide(property))
        {
            throw new
              NoComplianceMetadataForProperty(property);
        }
```

```
        var details = property.GetCustomAttribute<
          PersonalIdentifiableInformationAttribute>()!
          .ReasonForCollecting;
        return new
          ComplianceMetadata(ComplianceMetadataType.PII,
          details);
    }
}
```

The code looks for `PersonalIdentifiableInformationAttribute` in the property given; if it's present in the property or the declaring type, it can provide `ComplianceMetadata`. This method provides `ComplianceMetadata` if it is present and uses `ReasonForCollecting` for the details.

Using the GDPR infrastructure

With your first GDPR provider in place, you can start to create a system that leverages it.

Let's now create a folder, called `Chapter11`, at the root of your repository. Change into this folder in your command-line interface and create a new console project, as follows:

```
dotnet new console
```

You're going to make use of the Microsoft hosting model to get the .NET default service provider without spinning up a web application. To achieve this, you'll need the package called `Microsoft.Extensions.Hosting`. In the terminal, you'll add the reference by doing the following:

```
dotnet add package Microsoft.Extensions.Hosting
```

The next thing you'll need to do is to reference the `Fundamentals` project. In the terminal, do the following:

```
dotnet add reference ../Fundamentals/Fundamentals.csproj
```

Now you can start modeling a simple domain model for a patient system. Start by adding a file called `JournalEntry.cs` and make it look like the following:

```
namespace Chapter11;

public class JournalEntry
{
    public string Title { get; set; } = string.Empty;

    public string Content { get; set; } = string.Empty;
}
```

The code adds a type that represents an entry in a patient's journal with a title and a content property.

Add a file called `Patient.cs` and make it look like the following:

```
using Fundamentals.Compliance.GDPR;

namespace Chapter11;

public class Patient
{
    [PersonalIdentifiableInformation("Employment records")]
    public string FirstName { get; set; } = string.Empty;

    [PersonalIdentifiableInformation("Employment records")]
    public string LastName { get; set; } = string.Empty;

    [PersonalIdentifiableInformation("Uniquely identifies
      the employee")]
    public string SocialSecurityNumber { get; set; } =
      string.Empty;

    public IEnumerable<JournalEntry> JournalEntries { get;
      set; } = Enumerable.Empty<JournalEntry>();
}
```

The code adds a definition of a patient with their first name, last name, and social security number, as well as all the journal entries for the patient. For the personal information, metadata is used in the form of `[PersonalIdentifiableInformation]`.

Open the `Program.cs` file and make it look as follows:

```
using Chapter11;
using Fundamentals;
using Fundamentals.Compliance;
using Microsoft.Extensions.DependencyInjection;
using Microsoft.Extensions.Hosting;

var host = Host.CreateDefaultBuilder()
    .ConfigureServices((context, services) =>
    {
        var types = new Types();
        services.AddSingleton<ITypes>(types);
        services.AddBindingsByConvention(types);
        services.AddSelfBinding(types);
```

```
        })
        .Build();
```

The code sets up a generic host builder, registers `Types` as a singleton, and then leverages `AddBindingsByConvention()`, which you created in *Chapter 10, Convention over Configuration*, to hook up the services by convention. It then calls the `AddSelfBinding()`, which you introduced earlier in this chapter. It ends by building the host instance.

With the host instance, we get the `Services` property, which is the build service provider. You use this to get an instance of `IComplianceMetadataResolver`.

Add the following code at the end of `Program.cs`:

```
var complianceMetadataResolver = host.Services.
  GetRequiredService<IComplianceMetadataResolver>();

var typeToCheck = typeof(Patient);
Console.WriteLine($"Checking type for compliance rules: {typeToCheck.
  FullName}");

if (complianceMetadataResolver.HasMetadataFor(typeToCheck))
{
    var metadata =
      complianceMetadataResolver.GetMetadataFor(
      typeToCheck);
    foreach (var item in metadata)
    {
        Console.WriteLine($"Type level - {item.Details}");
    }
}
```

The code uses `IComplianceMetadataResolver` to get the metadata for the types. In your case, for now, it's hardcoded to `Patient`.

To get the metadata from the properties, add the following code at the end of `Program.cs`:

```
foreach (var property in typeToCheck.GetProperties())
{
    if (complianceMetadataResolver
      .HasMetadataFor(property))
    {
        var metadata = complianceMetadataResolver
          .GetMetadataFor(property);
        foreach (var item in metadata)
        {
```

```
                Console.WriteLine($"Property: {property.Name} -
                  {item.Details}");
            }
        }
        else if (property.PropertyType.IsGenericType &&
          property.PropertyType.GetGenericTypeDefinition()
          .IsAssignableTo(typeof(IEnumerable<>)))
        {
            var type = property.PropertyType
              .GetGenericArguments().First();
            if (complianceMetadataResolver
              .HasMetadataFor(type))
            {
                Console.WriteLine($"\nProperty {property.Name}
                  is a collection of type {type.FullName} with
                  type level metadata");

                var metadata = complianceMetadataResolver.
                  GetMetadataFor(type);
                foreach (var item in metadata)
                {
                    Console.WriteLine($"{property.Name} -
                      {item.Details}");
                }
            }
        }
    }
}
```

The code loops through the properties of typeToCheck and then prints out any details on the metadata from the properties. It also looks for any properties that have a generic argument and happen to implement IEnumerable<>, and it prints out any metadata associated with the item type.

Running your program should give you the following output:

```
Checking type for compliance rules: Chapter11.Patient

Property: FirstName - Employment records
Property: LastName - Employment records
Property: SocialSecurityNumber - Uniquely identifies the employee

Property JournalEntries is a collection of type Chapter11.JournalEntry
with type level metadata
```

Adding more providers

With the engine in place, you can now start adding to it by simply dropping in new providers. Let's add one for `JournalEntry`. Add a file called `JournalEntryMetadataProvider.cs` and make it look like the following:

```
using Fundamentals.Compliance;

namespace Chapter11;

public class JournalEntryMetadataProvider :
ICanProvideComplianceMetadataForType
{
    public bool CanProvide(Type type) => type == typeof(JournalEntry);

    public ComplianceMetadata Provide(Type type) => new("7242aed8-
        8d70-49df-8713-eea45e2764d4", "Journal entry");
}
```

The code uses the `JournalEntry` type to decide whether it can provide or not. Every `JournalEntry` should be treated specially as that holds critical information that shouldn't be shared. The `Provide()` method creates a new entry with a unique identifier for the `JournalEntry` type.

Running the program should now give you more information; notice the journal entries that have been added to your output:

```
Checking type for compliance rules: Chapter11.Patient

Property: FirstName - Employment records
Property: LastName - Employment records
Property: SocialSecurityNumber - Uniquely identifies the employee

Property JournalEntries is a collection of type Chapter11.JournalEntry
  with type level metadata
JournalEntries - Journal entry
```

To continue to add things to your system, let's add something that lets you mark a type as **confidential**.

Add a file called `ConfidentialAttribute.cs` and make it look like the following:

```
namespace Chapter11;

[AttributeUsage(AttributeTargets.Class, AllowMultiple = false,
  Inherited = true)]
public sealed class ConfidentialAttribute : Attribute
{
}
```

The attribute is targeting classes.

Next, you need a provider that can provide metadata for the new attribute. Add a file called `ConfidentialMetadataProvider.cs` and make it look like the following:

```
using System.Reflection;
using Fundamentals.Compliance;

namespace Chapter11;

public class ConfidentialMetadataProvider :
    ICanProvideComplianceMetadataForType
{
    public bool CanProvide(Type type) =>
        type.GetCustomAttribute<ConfidentialAttribute>() !=
        null;

    public ComplianceMetadata Provide(Type type) =>
        new("8dd1709a-bbe1-4b98-84e1-9e7be2fd4912", "The data
        is confidential");
}
```

The provider looks for `ConfidentialAttribute` to decide whether it can provide. If it can, the `Provide()` method creates a new instance of `ComplianceMetadata` with a unique identifier for the type it represents.

Open the `Patient.cs` file and add the `[Confidential]` attribute in front of the `Patient` class, making the class look as follows:

```
using Fundamentals.Compliance.GDPR;

namespace Chapter11;

[Confidential]
public class Patient
{
    [PersonalIdentifiableInformation("Employment records")]
    public string FirstName { get; set; } = string.Empty;

    [PersonalIdentifiableInformation("Employment records")]
    public string LastName { get; set; } = string.Empty;

    [PersonalIdentifiableInformation("Uniquely identifies
      the employee")]
    public string SocialSecurityNumber { get; set; } =
```

```
        string.Empty;

    public IEnumerable<JournalEntry> JournalEntries { get;
        set; } = Enumerable.Empty<JournalEntry>();
}
```

Running the program now should give you an output that includes the type-level information at the very top:

```
Checking type for compliance rules: Chapter11.Patient
Type level - The data is confidential

Property: FirstName - Employment records
Property: LastName - Employment records
Property: SocialSecurityNumber - Uniquely identifies the employee

Property JournalEntries is a collection of type Chapter11.JournalEntry
with type level metadata
JournalEntries - Journal entry
```

You've now created a system that is flexible and extensible. You don't have to go into the "engine" to perform any changes to introduce new capabilities. This is a powerful feature and a trait of a healthy system.

Summary

Building software that is **evergreen** is hard. Software that stands the test of time, does not lose its maintainability, and has the ability to allow development of new capabilities in a reasonable time frame is even harder. Keeping the time it takes to develop new business value close to constant is what we're aiming for. This makes it much easier for businesses to determine the impact of new functionalities. It also makes this impact more predictable for developers.

To this end, there are techniques, patterns, practices, and principles that can help. Thinking in extensible terms and designing the code to not become locked down is key, in my opinion. In this way, most of the time, it's possible to focus on additions, rather than having to perform open-heart surgery just to add new capabilities.

In the next chapter, we're going to look at combining what we looked at in this chapter with what you started doing with conventions in *Chapter 10*, *Convention over Configuration*. Conventions can take many forms, and they can help you go beyond the inheritance model of C# and .NET.

12

Go Beyond Inheritance

With object-oriented languages such as C#, we can derive our types from other types and we can also implement contracts (interfaces) and make them fulfill that contract. Implementing interfaces and making an implementation fulfill these is really one of the great things about a type-safe language. With the compiler, we get everything checked to make sure we implement the contract, while at runtime, we can leverage the interface type to be a representation rather than having to know the actual implementor.

Sometimes, however, the verbosity of having to implement an interface can be too much. It can also be limited to what you're trying to achieve.

In this chapter, we will cover the following topics:

- Method signature conventions
- By the end of the chapter, you will have an idea of how conventions can let you go beyond having to inherit from a base type or an interface and how that sometimes caters to a cleaner code base.

Technical requirements

The source code specific to the chapter can be found on GitHub (https://github.com/PacktPublishing/Metaprogramming-in-C-Sharp/tree/main/Chapter12) and it builds on top of the Fundamentals code that is found at https://github.com/PacktPublishing/Metaprogramming-in-C-Sharp/tree/main/Fundamentals.

Method signature conventions

Coming up with good examples to do a home run on a topic for a book can be very hard. For this chapter, I've decided to go with something that is part of my day-to-day job.

I work with a platform that is centered around event-driven architecture, or more specifically, with event sourcing. This topic might be unfamiliar to you, so let's dive into what this specifically is, to give you the context.

In traditional **CRUD** (short for **Create, Read, Update, Delete**) systems, the primary focus is on the concrete data that is commonly stored in a relational or document database. These systems revolve around the four fundamental operations – creating new records, retrieving existing records, updating records, and deleting records.

The data in such systems represents the outcome of a user's actions, and the system's flow typically follows a one-to-one mapping from the user's input form to the database. However, this approach to software development has a significant drawback – it only captures the effect and not the cause.

With event sourcing, the effect is less important, and it's all about capturing what caused the effect. The cause captures how we got to the conclusion, as shown in the following diagram:

Figure 12.1 – Capturing the cause

The cause is what is known as an event – something that happened in the system. We capture these by giving them a clear name, and we store them in the sequence in which they occur. The events are never deleted. All events are stored in what is referred to as an **event store**. There are technologies out there that specialize in this, such as the platform I'm working on, called Cratis (`https://cratis.io`), but you could also use any database and do this yourself.

By prioritizing the capturing of events, we gain the ability to control how the effects are presented. This is achieved by extracting relevant information from various event types as they occur and then converting it into specialized objects for easy access. These objects are typically stored in conventional data stores such as relational or document databases, which allow for the efficient querying of the end result.

One major advantage of this approach is that the event store becomes the source of truth in the system rather than relying solely on traditional data stores. This means that modifying how data is represented becomes significantly easier, as you can simply replay the relevant events when implementing changes. You can also decide to have multiple representations, catering to special needs within a system. This could then have a huge performance benefit, as well as clarity in code, and avoiding tension often seen in developing systems where one shares the same data and objects.

The following figure shows an imaginary bank system with events being produced and how they are projected down to materialized objects, referred to as read models. It also shows the relationship with other systems or other microservices in a microservice-centric architecture by projecting to events that can be communicated outside of the bounds of the system-producing events.

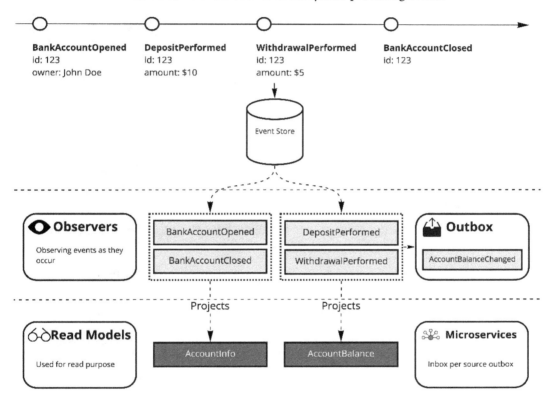

Figure 12.2 – Imaginary bank system with events produced

The observer is a key element of this architecture. They are the ones responsible for observing the events as they occur and creating an effect. For the most part, the effect comes in the form of a projection to a read model that is stored, but it could also perform other tasks such as sending emails or, in fact, append new events as the consequence of an analysis the observer performs.

It's these observers that we want to bring forward as an example in this chapter. Let's narrow it down to a pipeline that looks like the following figure:

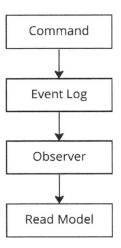

Figure 12.3 – Logical pipeline

A command represents something the user desires, an action to be performed. The action typically would then decide what event, or possibly multiple events, it should generate. This is appended to the main event log within the event store. The event log is the event sequence that holds all the events in the order they occurred, with an incremental sequence number.

Once the event is in the event log, we want to notify all the interested observers that the event has been appended and they should react.

The following figure shows more concretely what we want to accomplish and will be the basis of the example in this chapter.

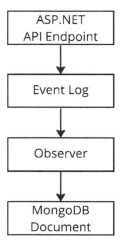

Figure 12.4 – Concrete pipeline

In order to be able to do this, you're going to need some infrastructure that will give you the conventions.

Infrastructure

Let's create a bare foundation of what's needed for having observers that can respond to events being appended.

Let's create a folder called `Chapter12` at the root of your repository. Change into this folder in your command-line interface and create a new console project:

```
dotnet new console
```

You're going to make use of the Microsoft hosting model to get the .NET default service provider without spinning up a web application. To achieve this, you'll need the package called `Microsoft.Extensions.Hosting`. In the terminal, you'd add the reference by doing the following:

```
dotnet add package Microsoft.Extensions.Hosting
```

The next thing you'll need to do is to reference the `Fundamentals` project. In the terminal, do the following:

```
dotnet add reference ../Fundamentals/Fundamentals.csproj
```

As I discussed in *Chapter 4, Reasoning about Types Using Reflection*, one of the things I do in all my code is to formalize types rather than use primitives. This makes the APIs much clearer and also helps avoid mistakes.

You're going to be using `ConceptAs<>` to formalize the types.

Inside the `Chapter12` folder, create a folder dedicated to the `EventSourcing` infrastructure, and call this folder `EventSourcing`.

Within the `EventSourcing` folder, create a file called `EventSourceId.cs` and make it look like the following:

```
using Fundamentals;

namespace EventSourcing;

public record EventSourceId(string Value) :
  ConceptAs<string>(Value)
{
    public static EventSourceId New() =>
      new(Guid.NewGuid().ToString());
}
```

The `EventSourceId` concept represents the unique identifier of the source of events. In domain modeling, this is typically the identifier of an object, a noun, in your domain. An example of this could be the unique identifier of a bank account or the unique identifier of a person in the system. The `EventSourceId` code sets up `ConceptAs<>` for this and makes the inner value a string, enabling basically any representation of a unique identifier. It adds a convenient method for creating a new `EventSourceId` by leveraging `Guid`, which can then generate a unique identifier on the fly. You'll be using `EventSourceId` later and it should become clearer why it's needed.

When appending an event to a sequence of events, as we discussed earlier, every event gets a sequence number. This is an incremental number that increases by 1 for every event added. Let's formalize a type that represents this number.

Within the `EventSourcing` folder, create a file called `EventSequenceNumber.cs` and make it look like the following:

```
using Fundamentals;

namespace EventSourcing;

public record EventSequenceNumber(ulong Value) :
  ConceptAs<ulong>(Value)
{
    public static implicit operator
      EventSequenceNumber(ulong value) => new(value);
}
```

The code introduces a concrete type for `EventSequenceNumber` that is `ConceptAs<>` with its inner value of the `ulong` type. With `ulong`, you get a full 64-bit value and this should most likely be more than sufficient as an incremental sequence number. For convenience, there is also an implicit operator that can convert `ulong` to the encapsulated `EventSequenceNumber` type.

For the observers that you'll be adding later, you'll be marking them with an attribute to indicate they are an observer. An alternative to this would be to use an empty interface. The point of this is just to be able to mark a type, making it possible to discover.

Within the `EventSourcing` folder, create a file called `ObserverAttribute.cs` and make it look like the following:

```
namespace EventSourcing;

[AttributeUsage(AttributeTargets.Class, AllowMultiple =
  false)]
public sealed class ObserverAttribute : Attribute
{
}
```

The code introduces an attribute that can be added to classes.

For the observer methods, you typically find the information related to the event in addition to the actual event itself. The type of information you want to know is the `EventSourceId`, `EventSequenceNumber`, and when the event occurred. We call this `EventContext`.

Within the `EventSourcing` folder, create a file called `EventContext.cs` and make it look like the following:

```
namespace EventSourcing;

public record EventContext(
    EventSourceId EventSourceId,
    EventSequenceNumber SequenceNumber,
    DateTimeOffset Occurred);
```

The code holds `EventSourceId`, `SequenceNumber`, and `Occurred` in the form of `DateTimeOffset`. In a full event-sourced system, we would typically hold more details, but this will suffice for this example.

For the events to be discoverable and classified as events, you're going to need a building block in the infrastructure.

Within the `EventSourcing` folder, create a file called `IEvent.cs` and make it look like the following:

```
namespace EventSourcing;

public interface IEvent { }
```

Now comes the juicy part: the code that will discover methods on a type that matches certain criteria.

The convention we're looking for is one that allows for two base method signatures and two variants of these, supporting both synchronous and asynchronous models.

The synchronous signatures are as follows:

```
void <name-of-method>(YourEventType @event);
void <name-of-method>(YourEventType @event, EventContext
    context);
```

And then the asynchronous signatures are as follows:

```
Task <name-of-method>(YourEventType @event);
Task <name-of-method>(YourEventType @event, EventContext
    context);
```

As you can see, the convention does not care about the name of the method but only the parameters and return types. This gives flexibility to the developer in creating more precise named methods and increases the readability and maintainability of the code, something regular inheritance wouldn't allow for.

Let's create a system that enables calling the methods by convention.

Within the `EventSourcing` folder, create a file called `ObserverHandler.cs` and make it look like the following:

```
using System.Reflection;

namespace EventSourcing;

public class ObserverHandler
{
    readonly Dictionary<Type, IEnumerable<MethodInfo>>
      _methodsByEventType;
    readonly IServiceProvider _serviceProvider;
    readonly Type _targetType;

    public IEnumerable<Type> EventTypes =>
      _methodsByEventType.Keys;

    public ObserverHandler(IServiceProvider
      serviceProvider, Type targetType)
    {
        _serviceProvider = serviceProvider;
        _targetType = targetType;

        _methodsByEventType =
          targetType.GetMethods(BindingFlags.Instance |
          BindingFlags.NonPublic | BindingFlags.Public)
                              .Where(_ =>
                              IsObservingMethod(_))
                              .GroupBy(_ =>
                              _.GetParameters()[0].
                              ParameterType)
                              .ToDictionary(_ =>
                              _.Key, _ =>
                              _.ToArray()
                              .AsEnumerable());
    }
}
```

The code sets up the basis for the `ObserverHandler` class. The constructor takes two parameters, `serviceProvider` and `targetType`. The `serviceProvider` parameter will be used to get instances of `targetType` representing the observer when an event needs to be handled. Within the constructor, the code uses reflection to look for instance methods, both public and non-public methods.

It then filters down the methods by those matching the signature with a method called `IsObservingMethod()`, which you'll be adding next. Then it groups it by the first parameter on the method, which is the event type, and creates a dictionary enabling fast lookup.

> **Important note**
>
> Notice the `EventTypes` property that is added; this exposes what event types the handler supports, and this will come in handy later.

In the LINQ query, it uses the `IsObservingMethod()` method, which is a method that should be inside the `ObserverHandler` class. Add the following private method at the bottom of the `ObserverHandler` class:

```
bool IsObservingMethod(MethodInfo methodInfo)
{
    var isObservingMethod =
      methodInfo.ReturnType.IsAssignableTo(typeof(Task)) ||
                         methodInfo.ReturnType ==
                            typeof(void);

    if (!isObservingMethod) return false;
    var parameters = methodInfo.GetParameters();
    if (parameters.Length >= 1)
    {
        isObservingMethod = parameters[0]
          .ParameterType.IsAssignableTo(typeof(IEvent));
        if (parameters.Length == 2)
        {
            isObservingMethod &= parameters[1]
              .ParameterType == typeof(EventContext);
        }
        else if (parameters.Length > 2)
        {
            isObservingMethod = false;
        }
        return isObservingMethod;
    }

    return false;
}
```

To identify allowed signatures, the code examines `MethodInfo` and begins by recognizing the permitted return types, which are `Task` or `void`. If the return type is anything other than a valid observing method, it will be considered invalid. The code then proceeds to examine the parameters of the method. If the method has one parameter and its type implements the `IEvent` interface, it qualifies as an observing method. Alternatively, if the method has two parameters and the first parameter type implements `IEvent`, and the second parameter type is `EventContext`, then it is also classified as an observing method.

With the discovery part in place, all you need is a method that understands the convention and can invoke the method on the observer.

In the `ObserverHandler` class, add the following code:

```
public async Task OnNext(IEvent @event, EventContext
  context)
{
    var eventType = @event.GetType();

    if (_methodsByEventType.ContainsKey(eventType))
    {
        var actualObserver =
          _serviceProvider.GetService(_targetType);
        Task returnValue;
        foreach (var method in
          _methodsByEventType[eventType])
        {
            var parameters = method.GetParameters();

            if (parameters.Length == 2)
            {
                returnValue =
                  (Task)method.Invoke(actualObserver, new
                  object[] { @event, context })!;
            }
            else
            {
                returnValue =
                  (Task)method.Invoke(actualObserver, new
                  object[] { @event })!;
            }

            if (returnValue is not null) await returnValue;
        }
    }
}
```

The OnNext() method is responsible for doing the call to the observer; it does so by taking an event of any type implementing the IEvent interface and EventContext for the event. From this, it finds the method in _methodsByEventType populated in the constructor based on the type of event supported by the observer. If it is supported, it goes on to get an instance of the observer type by using the service provider. For each method, it invokes based on the correct signature for the method and if the method is asynchronous, it will await Task returned.

With the concrete handler that handles the invocation, you're going to need a service that knows about all the observers and can call the correct ones when an event occurs.

Within the EventSourcing folder, create a file called IObservers.cs and make it look like the following:

```
namespace EventSourcing;

public interface IObservers
{
    Task OnNext(IEvent @event, EventContext context);
}
```

The code represents the contract for IObservers. The OnNext() method will be the method called by the system that knows when events have occurred.

You're going to need an implementation of this interface.

Within the EventSourcing folder, create a file called Observers.cs and make it look like the following:

```
using System.Reflection;
using Fundamentals;

namespace EventSourcing;

[Singleton]
public class Observers : IObservers
{
    readonly IEnumerable<ObserverHandler> _handlers;

    public Observers(ITypes types, IServiceProvider
      serviceProvider)
    {
        _handlers = types.All.Where(_ =>
          _.HasAttribute<ObserverAttribute>())
                        .Select(_ =>
                        {
```

```
                              var observer =
                                  _.GetCustomAttribute
                                  <ObserverAttribute>()!;
                              return new
                                  ObserverHandler(
                                  serviceProvider, _);
                          });
        }
}
```

The code leverages ITypes from fundamentals for discovery. The code scans through all the types and filters out those that do not have ObserverAttribute, leaving only the types that do have it. For every type that has the ObserverAttribute, it then creates an instance of ObserverHandler by passing in serviceProvider and the target type, which is the observer itself.

For invoking the handler, you need an implementation of the OnNext() method. In the Observers class, add the following method at the bottom:

```
public Task OnNext(IEvent @event, EventContext context)
{
    var tasks = _handlers.Where(_ =>
        _.EventTypes.Contains(@event.GetType()))
                    .Select(_ => _.OnNext(@event,
                        context));
    return Task.WhenAll(tasks);
}
```

The code filters down to only the handlers that are capable by looking at the EventTypes property of the handler, and whether it contains the type of the @event argument. It then calls the OnNext() method of the handler and collects all the Task instances for all the calls it made, so that it can wait for them all to finish.

With the observer infrastructure in place, you'll need something that triggers this. We're not going to implement a fully working event sourcing system, as that would be too involved. Instead, we're going to make a few shortcuts and not save the events anywhere.

In an event-sourced system, you need a place to append the events to a sequence; the main place you append to is called an event log. Let's introduce this concept.

Within the EventSourcing folder, create a file called IEventLog.cs and make it look like the following:

```
namespace EventSourcing;

public interface IEventLog
```

```
{
    Task Append(EventSourceId eventSourceId, IEvent
      @event);
}
```

The code represents the contract for the event log with only one method in this version, which enables you to append an event for a specific EventSourceId.

You'll need an implementation of the IEventLog interface.

Within the EventSourcing folder, create a file called EventLog.cs and make it look like the following:

```
namespace EventSourcing;

public class EventLog : IEventLog
{
    readonly IObservers _observers;
    EventSequenceNumber _sequenceNumber = 0;

    public EventLog(IObservers observers)
    {
        _observers = observers;
    }

    public async Task Append(EventSourceId eventSourceId,
      IEvent @event)
    {
        // TODO: persist the event

        await _observers.OnNext(
            @event,
            new EventContext(eventSourceId,
              _sequenceNumber, DateTimeOffset.UtcNow));

        _sequenceNumber++;
    }
}
```

The code represents a very simplistic implementation that takes a direct dependency on IObservers for it to call when an event has been appended. It manages internally the _sequenceNumber. As you can see, there is no persistence and the whole implementation is naive at best. But it serves the purpose of this chapter.

Now that you have built all this nice infrastructure for invoking methods by the convention on observers, you're probably eager to take it out for a spin.

Using the infrastructure

Going with the bank theme of the chapter, let's create something that represents that domain. In a bank, you can open an account, deposit and withdraw money from it, and then possibly, and ultimately, close an account. All of these are very important events that happen in the lifespan of an account.

Within the root folder of the chapter code, create a file called `Events.cs` and make it look like the following:

```
using EventSourcing;

namespace Chapter12;

public record BankAccountOpened(string CustomerName) :
  IEvent;
public record BankAccountClosed() : IEvent;
public record DepositPerformed(decimal Amount) : IEvent;
public record WithdrawalPerformed(decimal Amount) : IEvent;
```

The code holds all the events we want for now as `record` types and they all implement the `IEvent` interface.

> **Important note**
>
> In a production environment, I would recommend keeping one file per type, as that makes it easier to navigate and discover events in your system.

With the events in place, you can now go ahead and create observers that will react to the events occurring.

Within the root folder of the chapter code, create a file called `AccountLifecycle.cs` and make it look like the following:

```
using EventSourcing;

namespace Chapter12;

[Observer]
public class AccountLifecycle
{
    public Task Opened(BankAccountOpened @event)
    {
```

```
        Console.WriteLine($"Account opened for
          {@event.CustomerName}");
        return Task.CompletedTask;
    }

    public Task Closed(BankAccountClosed @event,
      EventContext context)
    {
        Console.WriteLine($"Account with id
          {context.EventSourceId} closed");
        return Task.CompletedTask;
    }
}
```

The code adds a class called `AccountLifecycle` and adorns it with the `[Observer]` attribute. Its purpose is to only deal with the life cycle events of `BankAccountOpened` and `BankAccountClosed`. Notice that it uses the convention fully with custom names of the methods and also the different signatures.

For the events that affect the balance of an account, you could then separate that particular logic into its own observer.

Within the root folder of the chapter code, create a file called `AccountBalance.cs` and make it look like the following:

```
using EventSourcing;

namespace Chapter12;

[Observer]
public class AccountBalance
{
    public Task DepositPerformed(DepositPerformed @event,
      EventContext context)
    {
        Console.WriteLine($"Deposit of {@event.Amount}
          performed on {context.EventSourceId}");
        return Task.CompletedTask;
    }

    public Task WithdrawalPerformed(WithdrawalPerformed
      @event, EventContext context)
    {
        Console.WriteLine($"Withdrawal of {@event.Amount}
          performed on {context.EventSourceId}");
```

```
        return Task.CompletedTask;
    }
}
```

The code adds a class called `AccountBalance` and adorns it with the [Observer] attribute. Its purpose is to only deal with the balance events of `DepositPerformed` and `WithdrawalPerformed`.

Both observers are just logging what has happened to the console. In a real implementation of these, you'd probably want to store the data somewhere. The benefit here is that you could store the data in two different locations. For life cycle events, you're only interested in the ownership and any details related to the account, while with the balance events, you're only interested in what affects the balance and not interested in anything else. Breaking these things up makes it easier to choose the right technology for the job and also model each of these independently and create a less coupled system.

Now you want to do the last hookup and throw some events at it and verify that it does the job.

Open the `Program.cs` file and make it look like the following:

```
using Chapter12;
using EventSourcing;
using Fundamentals;
using Microsoft.Extensions.DependencyInjection;
using Microsoft.Extensions.Hosting;

var host = Host.CreateDefaultBuilder()
    .ConfigureServices((context, services) =>
    {
        var types = new Types();
        services.AddSingleton<ITypes>(types);
        services.AddBindingsByConvention(types);
        services.AddSelfBinding(types);
    })
    .Build();
```

The code sets up the necessary plumbing code to get the default .NET inversion of the control container going; it leverages `AddBindingsByConvention()` that you created in *Chapter 10, Convention over Configuration*, to hook up services by convention, and `AddSelfBinding()` that you created in *Chapter 11, Applying the Open-Closed Principle*.

With the basic infrastructure in place, you can now ask for an instance of `IEventLog` and start appending events to it.

Add the following code at the bottom of `Program.cs`:

```
var eventLog = host.Services
    .GetRequiredService<IEventLog>();
```

```
var bankAccountId = EventSourceId.New();
eventLog.Append(bankAccountId, new BankAccountOpened("Jane
  Doe"));
eventLog.Append(bankAccountId, new DepositPerformed(100));
eventLog.Append(bankAccountId, new
  WithdrawalPerformed(32));
eventLog.Append(bankAccountId, new BankAccountClosed());
```

Running your program should give you a similar output:

```
Account opened for Jane Doe
Deposit of 100 performed on a3d7dbae-9e2a-4d2d-a070-
ead70e48f87a
Withdrawal of 32 performed on a3d7dbae-9e2a-4d2d-a070-
ead70e48f87a
Account with id a3d7dbae-9e2a-4d2d-a070-ead70e48f87a closed
```

You now have the beginning of an event-sourcing component. But more importantly, it should give you an idea of what could be done dynamically without having to be tied to the strictness of inheritance.

As an illustration of the implication of doing this with inheritance instead, we would need something like an interface that defines the method for the event; it could look something like the following:

```
public interface IObserveEvent<TEvent> where TEvent :
  IEvent
{
    Task Handle(TEvent @event, EventContext context);
}
```

With this interface, we could take the `AccountLifecycle` observer and do the following:

```
public class AccountLifecycle :
    IObserveEvent<BankAccountOpened>,
    IObserveEvent<BankAccountClosed>
{
    public Task Handle(BankAccountOpened @event,
      EventContext context)
    {
        Console.WriteLine($"Account opened for
          {@event.CustomerName}");
        return Task.CompletedTask;
    }

    public Task Handle(BankAccountClosed @event,
```

```
    EventContext context)
{
    Console.WriteLine($"Account with id
        {context.EventSourceId} closed");
    return Task.CompletedTask;
}
}
```

While using this approach can provide compile-time safety, there are several downsides to consider. Firstly, naming every method `Handle` can lead to ambiguity and confusion, both in terms of tooling and readability. It may be difficult to determine which method to work with without carefully examining the parameters. Additionally, this approach limits you to only one method handling one event, while the convention-based approach allows for multiple individual methods with specific purposes to handle different aspects of the event.

If you have an observer handling numerous events, you'd end up having to implement `IObserveEvent<>` for every type it handles. This can easily make your code less readable and maintainable.

There are pros and cons to both approaches, but hopefully, the takeaway is the potential this gives and, hopefully, it is useful and applicable to the code bases you work on.

Summary

Conventions, like those explained in this chapter with the discovery of well-known signatures, can be very powerful and help clean up your code. Forcing the developer to implement an interface for every class supported can be tedious and make the code look a little strange.

The downside of using a convention for method signatures is obviously that you are now at the mercy of runtime checks; there is no compiler that will help you. If you happen to make a little error, it won't be noticed until you're at runtime, which can be very annoying while in the zone and developing. In *Chapter 17, Static Code Analysis*, we will look at how we can detect errors at compile time.

In the next chapter, we're going to look at how automation can go further with conventions to put developers in the pit of success and avoid a recipe-driven development.

13

Applying Cross-Cutting Concerns

As software projects evolve, they gain a certain structure, and if the team is disciplined, it will be somewhat consistent. When you get more team members, you might even document the structure. In addition to structure, you might also have ways of doing things and clear recipes of what needs to be done when creating different types of functionalities for the different parts of the stack. For global ownership, you might have these written down as well.

This is where cross-cutting concerns can come to the rescue. In this chapter, we will look at how to increase productivity for you as a developer by removing mundane tasks and improving consistency, and reducing risks. We will also look at how cross-cutting concerns can improve the maintainability of your software.

We will cover the following topics in this chapter:

- What are cross-cutting concerns?
- Leveraging the ASP.NET pipeline
- Authorization based on metadata or structure

Technical requirements

The source code specific to the chapter can be found on GitHub (https://github.com/PacktPublishing/Metaprogramming-in-C-Sharp/tree/main/Chapter13), and it builds on top of the Fundamentals code that is found on GitHub (https://github.com/PacktPublishing/Metaprogramming-in-C-Sharp/tree/main/Fundamentals).

You will need Postman (https://www.postman.com) for testing the APIs created in this chapter.

What are cross-cutting concerns?

As the lead-in to the chapter suggests, you might find yourself in your project with guidelines, formalized or not, that give you recipes for how to do things. For instance, to write a **representational state transfer (REST)** API that performs actions in your application, you might have a list of things defined that is there to help you remember what to do:

- Check authorization

- Check whether the input is valid

- Check whether the action is allowed as per business rules

- Add logging for the action

- Perform the action by calling the domain logic

- Translate the result from the domain to something digestible for REST consumption

- Remember to wrap the call to the domain in `try {} catch {}` and return the correct error

For each of these steps, there is always the risk that the developer will forget. This can pose a risk, cause security issues, data consistency, or other problems.

Personally, I'm a huge fan of automating anything that is repetitive. Computers are really good at doing repetitive tasks, so why not let the human in front focus on delivering the business value?

Cross-cutting concerns are basically those things that are applied once and henceforth continue to be there. Some cross-cutting concerns can be entirely automatic and need no extra intervention from the developer once applied, while others tend to be more configurable and context-based.

Logging is probably the most canonical example of a cross-cutting concern. If you, for instance, know what to add in a log statement for every call to a Web API controller in your ASP.NET application, you can quite easily do so by adding an action filter.

I tend to focus a lot on how we can boost the productivity of a team. With that in mind, you can do quite a bit of automation. To understand this better, we can use an example from ASP.NET Web APIs. Let's say you're building an application that has a frontend, and you need to provide an API for the frontend. Typically, your domain logic shouldn't be in the API layer, as that is just a transport mechanism. An opportunity here is to automatically generate the API layer from the domain layer based on a convention. The convention could be derived from the namespace that could then automatically create the correct route. This would then remove an entire layer.

One of the possible benefits of applying cross-cutting concerns is that you end up writing less code in the implementations where you'd normally add the things it automates. This is also a good thing from a maintenance perspective. It makes it easier to maintain. For instance, if you want to change the behavior of your system rather than having to change it in multiple places, you'd have a single place to change it.

One of my favorite cross-cutting concerns is for Web APIs to have a consistent result and also not just rely on the HTTP status codes but rather consistently include all needed information to the consumer about the call.

Leveraging the ASP.NET pipeline

REST APIs are based on the HTTP standard. The standard is a protocol standard and will not necessarily reflect in a good way what really happened when you performed an operation.

One way to do this would be to create a common result object that all Web API controller actions need to return. But that would then become one of these recipes that could be forgotten and leave the solution in an inconsistent state.

The idea of having a common result object is undoubtedly desirable, but we should work towards returning it automatically for all Web API calls. However, there is a difference between performing an operation and getting data. Basically, in HTTP, that is what the different verbs are for, HTTP GET represents getting data, while verbs such as POST, PUT, or DELETE represent the operations you want to perform.

These types of operations are typically what you tend to perform as operations on a database in a data-driven application. You'll often use the same model for all the operations, and you're basically just modifying data.

I'm an advocate for the **Command Query Responsibility Segregation (CQRS)** principle, coined by Greg Young (`https://www.martinfowler.com/bliki/CQRS.html`), which is a further formalization of Bertrand Meyers' **Command Query Separation (CQS)** principle (`https://www.martinfowler.com/bliki/CommandQuerySeparation.html`).

The CQRS principle challenges the common approach of treating everything as data in a **Create, Read, Update, and Delete** (**CRUD**) manner. It focuses on explicitly modeling the state change in a system and represents the intention of changing with a **command**, while retrieving data is represented as **queries**. Since CQRS is an evolution of CQS, it also implies that commands represent a changing state and do not return a value, while queries return a value but do not change any state.

We're not going to dive any deeper into CQRS or CQS, but we want to utilize the concept of command and, with that, limit the surface area for what we want to support in the sample in this chapter. The sample here has nothing to do with CQRS, but being an advocate for it, I figured I'd slip it into the conversation, hoping it triggers some curiosity…haha.

Building consistent result objects

Let's build a simple system that registers employees exposed as a REST API. The goal is to provide a consistent result object for all commands being performed. We define a command in this context to be an HTTP POST call to any Web API controller.

Start by creating a folder called `Chapter13`. Change into this folder in your command line and create a new web-based project:

```
dotnet new web
```

Let's take advantage of the **Fundamentals** project in the GitHub repository mentioned in the *Technical requirements* section. You should add a project reference to it for this chapter by doing the following in your terminal:

```
dotnet add reference ../Fundamentals/Fundamentals.csproj
```

We will leverage the concept of an **action filter**, a building block provided by ASP.NET Core. In *Chapter 3, Demystifying through Existing Real-World Examples*, we touched on this building block for changing the default behavior related to validation—a good example of a cross-cutting concern.

In ASP.NET Core, you, as a developer, have 100% flexibility on the behavior of your Web API controllers. That means that you decide what to return to the client, and you also decide whether or not you really care about the validation result. As we did in *Chapter 3, Demystifying through Existing Real-World Examples*, we will be a bit more opinionated and not let the controller's actions decide whether or not something is valid, but handle this in a cross-cutting manner. In addition to this, we want to wrap this up in a nice way for the consumer to get the result consistently.

Create a subfolder in `Chapter13` called `Commands`. This is where you'll create the necessary infrastructure.

Let's start by adding a consistent representation of a validation result. ASP.NET Core has the concept of `ModelError`; you could use this directly if you'd like. But `ModelError` represents both `Exception` and a validation error. Those are different concerns that I personally would like to separate and make clearer. Being in an invalid state is different from having an exceptional non-recoverable state.

Add a file in the `Commands` folder called `ValidationResult.cs`. You can make it look like the following:

```
namespace Chapter13.Commands;

public record ValidationResult(string Message, string Member);
```

The code introduces a type called `ValidationResult`, which holds an error and the member the error is for. With the member clearly in the result, the consumer can map the error back to the object it sent. As a user interface, this is very useful as you can then easily show the error directly for the user input field that is invalid.

Since ASP.NET Core has its `ModelError` and you've now introduced a type representing just the validation result, you would want something that converts to your type. Add a file called `ModelErrorExtensions.cs` to the `Commands` folder and make it look like the following:

```
using Fundamentals;
using Microsoft.AspNetCore.Mvc.ModelBinding;

namespace Chapter13.Commands;

public static class ModelErrorExtensions
{
    public static ValidationResult ToValidationResult(this
      ModelError error, string member)
    {
        member = string.Join('.',
          member.Split('.').Select(_ => _.ToCamelCase()));
        return new ValidationResult(error.ErrorMessage,
          member);
    }
}
```

The code introduces an extension method for the `ModelError` type and takes a specific member as a string to associate the error. By default, all JSON serialization in ASP.NET Core will be camel cased; the code, therefore, converts the member to camel case. It even supports deeply nested members by its navigational path represented with a dot for each level in the nested hierarchy. The `ToCamelCase()` method call comes from `StringExtensions` found in the `Fundamentals` project referenced previously.

CommandResult

With a representation of validation, you can now create the common result type for all operations or commands. We call this `CommandResult`. It will encapsulate all the different aspects of an API call in a structured manner. To do this, add a file called `CommandResult.cs` to the `Commands` folder and make it look like the following:

```
namespace Chapter13.Commands;

public class CommandResult
{
    public Guid CorrelationId { get; init; }
    public bool IsSuccess => IsAuthorized && IsValid &&
      !HasExceptions;
    public bool IsAuthorized { get; init; } = true;
    public bool IsValid => !ValidationResults.Any();
    public bool HasExceptions => ExceptionMessages.Any();
    public IEnumerable<ValidationResult> ValidationResults
      {get; init;} = Enumerable.Empty<ValidationResult>();
```

```
public IEnumerable<string> ExceptionMessages { get;
    init; } = Enumerable.Empty<string>();
public string ExceptionStackTrace { get; init; } =
    string.Empty;
public object? Response { get; init; }
}
```

The code introduces a CommandResult type that holds the concrete information related to validation results and whether there was an exception that might have occurred. In addition, it contains properties that allow you to easily conclude whether or not the result represents success. If the result is not a success, you can dive into whether or not it is related to authorization, validity, or an exception. It also introduces the CorrelationId property, which identifies the call that was performed and could be used for tracing back in logs or tracing systems to understand whether an exception occurred and why it happened.

With the formalized CommandResult in place, you'll need something that will produce this. This is where the ASP.NET Core action filter mechanism comes in handy.

Add a file called CommandActionFilter.cs to the Commands folder and make it look like the following:

```
using Microsoft.AspNetCore.Mvc;
using Microsoft.AspNetCore.Mvc.Filters;

namespace Chapter13.Commands;

public class CommandActionFilter : IAsyncActionFilter
{
    public async Task OnActionExecutionAsync(
        ActionExecutingContext context,
        ActionExecutionDelegate next)
    {
        if (context.HttpContext.Request.Method ==
            HttpMethod.Post.Method)
        {
        }
        else
        {
            await next();
        }
    }
}
```

The code gives you a bare-bones action filter by implementing the `IAsyncActionFilter` interface. The action filter is only interested in HTTP POST methods, as discussed earlier, and the rest of the implementation will take place within that clause. If it is not an HTTP POST method, it just forwards the request to the next middleware using the `next ()` method.

Let's start filling in the blanks. Inside the scope of the HTTP POST method clause, add the following code:

```
var exceptionMessages = new List<string>();
var exceptionStackTrace = string.Empty;
ActionExecutedContext? result = null;
object? response = null;
if (context.ModelState.IsValid)
{
    result = await next();

    if (result.Exception is not null)
    {
        var exception = result.Exception;
        exceptionStackTrace = exception.StackTrace;

        do
        {
            exceptionMessages.Add(exception.Message);
            exception = exception.InnerException;
        }
        while (exception is not null);

        result.Exception = null!;
    }

    if (result.Result is ObjectResult objectResult)
    {
        response = objectResult.Value;
    }
}
```

The code handles whether `ModelState` is valid, meaning that all validators have run successfully and thus didn't report anything invalid. This can mean one of two things:

- There is an exception
- It's all OK, and the action was performed

Within the `IsValid` clause, the code calls `next ()`, which invokes the rest of the ASP.NET Core pipeline, ultimately calling the Web API controller action. The `result` object is of the

`ActionExecutedContext` type, which holds information about the call to the action. On it, you'll find `Exception` and `Result`. If there is an exception, the code unwinds all the messages recursively through `InnerException` of each exception and then resets the `Exception` property on the `result` object to `null` to avoid the default output of exceptions of ASP.NET Core from kicking in. If there are no exceptions, the code looks to capture the actual result if it is `ObjectResult` from the action.

> **Important note**
>
> Even though we said commands should only perform a state change and not return a result, there are cases where you need to return something to the client. This could be important information, such as the key of an object created, which could then be leveraged directly by the consumer.

The next thing you will need is to create an instance of `CommandResult` and populate validation results and exceptions. Add the following code after the previous code:

```
var commandResult = new CommandResult
{
    CorrelationId = Guid.NewGuid(),
    ValidationResults = context.ModelState.SelectMany(_ =>
      _.Value!.Errors.Select(e => e.ToValidationResult(
      _.Key))),
    ExceptionMessages = exceptionMessages.ToArray(),
    ExceptionStackTrace = exceptionStackTrace ??
      string.Empty,
    Response = response
};
```

The code creates an instance of the `CommandResult` type and sets the properties on it. `CorrelationId` is generated as a new `Guid`, `ValidationResults` is derived from `ModelState` using the extension method you put in earlier for converting, and `ExceptionMessages` comes from the code you put in for unwinding the exceptions. Then it puts in `ExceptionStackTrace` if there is any or just `string.Empty` if not. Finally, it forwards the response from the controller action directly, if any.

Even though you've now encapsulated the result in something that is more readable and consistent for the consumer, it is still good practice to set the correct HTTP status code. Add the following code after the instantiation of `CommandResult`:

```
if (!commandResult.IsAuthorized)
{
    context.HttpContext.Response.StatusCode = 401;
}
else if (!commandResult.IsValid)
```

```
{
    context.HttpContext.Response.StatusCode = 409;
}
else if (commandResult.HasExceptions)
{
    context.HttpContext.Response.StatusCode = 500;
}
```

The code says that when we're not authorized, it is an HTTP 401 status code, while if not valid, it is a 409 status code, and if there is an exception, it is 500.

For CommandResult to be the actual result you get as output, you'll need to explicitly set the Result property on ActionExecutedContext if we were validly authorized, or directly on ActionExecutingContext, which is passed as the first parameter of the method of the action filter. Add the following code right after the previous block:

```
var actualResult = new ObjectResult(commandResult);

if (result is not null)
{
    result.Result = actualResult;
}
else
{
    context.Result = actualResult;
}
```

The code creates a new ObjectResult with CommandResult as content and sets it on either the ActionExecutedContext object or ActionExecutingContext. This will guarantee that you consistently get the same structure whether you've called the controller action or not.

Let's create a concrete sample that will make use of this new and improved pipeline. Add a file called Employee.cs in the root of the Chapter13 project and make it look like the following:

```
using System.ComponentModel.DataAnnotations;

namespace Chapter13;

public record Employee(
    [Required]
    string FirstName,

    [Required]
    string LastName);
```

The code introduces a `record` type that represents an employee with only two properties: `FirstName` and `LastName`. It instructs that these properties are both required by leveraging the `[Required]` attribute.

For the API to work you'll need a controller. Add a file called `EmployeesController` in the root of the `Chapter13` project and make it look like the following:

```
using Microsoft.AspNetCore.Mvc;

namespace Chapter13;

[Route("/api/employees")]
public class EmployeesController : Controller
{
    [HttpPost]
    public int Register([FromBody] Employee employee)
    {
        // Todo: Implement logic for actually
        // registering...
        return 1;
    }
}
```

The code introduces a controller with an action for registering an employee. The `[FromBody]` attribute in front of the `employee` argument says that the content of `employee` is found in the HTTP request body. The action returns an integer and is hardcoded to return 1. Keep in mind that this is more of an example of where you could return your key if needed. It would be perfectly fine not to return anything and make the method return `void`. With the `[Route]` attribute in front of the class, the route for the API will be `/api/employees`.

Open up the `Program.cs` file and make it look like the following:

```
using Chapter13.Commands;

var builder = WebApplication.CreateBuilder(args);
builder.Services.AddControllers(mvcOptions => mvcOptions.Filters.
  Add<CommandActionFilter>());
var app = builder.Build();
app.MapControllers();

app.Run();
```

The code adds all controllers by convention and maps the routes of these. When adding controllers, the code adds `CommandActionFilter` as a filter to the pipeline.

That should be enough to take it for a spin. Run the project using the following command:

```
dotnet run
```

You should see a similar output to the following:

```
Building...
info: Microsoft.Hosting.Lifetime[14]
      Now listening on: https://localhost:7126
info: Microsoft.Hosting.Lifetime[14]
      Now listening on: http://localhost:5234
info: Microsoft.Hosting.Lifetime[0]
      Application started. Press Ctrl+C to shut down.
info: Microsoft.Hosting.Lifetime[0]
      Hosting environment: Development
info: Microsoft.Hosting.Lifetime[0]
      Content root path: /Users/einari/Projects/Metaprogramming-in-C/
         Chapter13/
```

You can now test the API using Postman:

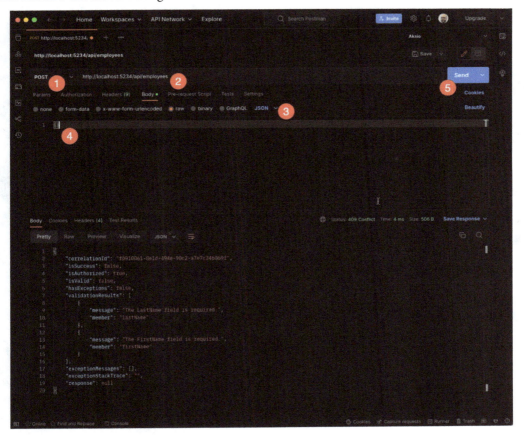

Figure 13.1 – Posting with Postman

Set the verb to be **POST**, and then use the URL from the output of your run and add /api/employees to the URL. Then select **JSON** in the **Body** tab, add an empty JSON document, and click **Send**.

The response should be similar to the following:

```
{
    "correlationId": "f0910061-0e1d-494e-90c2-a7e7c246069f",
    "isSuccess": false,
    "isAuthorized": true,
    "isValid": false,
    "hasExceptions": false,
    "validationResults": [
        {
            "message": "The LastName field is required.",
            "member": "lastName"
        },
        {
            "message": "The FirstName field is required.",
            "member": "firstName"
        }
    ],
    "exceptionMessages": [],
    "exceptionStackTrace": "",
    "response": null
}
```

Use POST for a valid object:

```
{
    "firstName": "Jane",
    "lastName": "Doe"
}
```

In Postman, you should then get a successful result back:

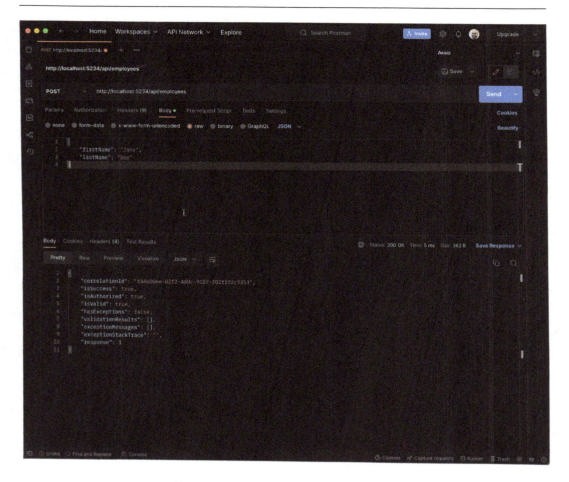

Figure 13.2 – A successful posting in Postman

You should see a response similar to the following:

```
{
    "correlationId": "f44600ee-02f2-4d0c-9187-f02ff02c9353",
    "isSuccess": true,
    "isAuthorized": true,
    "isValid": true,
    "hasExceptions": false,
    "validationResults": [],
    "exceptionMessages": [],
    "exceptionStackTrace": "",
    "response": 1
}
```

You now have a clear, consistent result object for all POST actions. ASP.NET Core is very extensible and flexible, and most of the parts can be extended to perform cross-cutting concerns; authorization is a good example.

Authorization based on metadata or structure

By default, the approach for setting authorization for controllers in ASP.NET Core uses the [Authorize] attribute or the fluent interface when registering controllers or endpoints. For some scenarios, this can be very explicit, and in applications with a large number of controller endpoints, you might want to consider securing them in a cross-cutting manner.

If sections of your application are just meant to be used by users with a given role, this could be a great candidate for applying security policies for all of these based on namespace. Through structure, we get the implicit metadata that follows the types, and we can use that as a way to make decisions for us.

To do this, we need to put in a few things. First of all, we need to have a mechanism for authenticating users. For this sample, we will use hardcoded users to avoid the complexity of having to set up proper authentication with an identity provider.

You'll need a file called HardCodedAuthenticationOptions.cs in the root of Chapter13 and then add the following:

```
using Microsoft.AspNetCore.Authentication;

namespace Chapter13;

public class HardCodedAuthenticationOptions :
    AuthenticationSchemeOptions
{
}
```

The code introduces an option type that will be used by the custom hardcoded identity provider. It doesn't have any options since the provider will be completely hardcoded.

Next, add a file called HardCodedAuthenticationHandler.cs in the root of Chapter13 and make it look like the following:

```
using System.Security.Claims;
using System.Text.Encodings.Web;
using Microsoft.AspNetCore.Authentication;
using Microsoft.Extensions.Options;

namespace Chapter13;

public class HardCodedAuthenticationHandler :
```

```
AuthenticationHandler<HardCodedAuthenticationOptions>
{
    public const string SchemeName =
      "HardCodedAuthenticationHandler";

    public HardCodedAuthenticationHandler(
        IOptionsMonitor<HardCodedAuthenticationOptions>
          options,
        ILoggerFactory logger,
        UrlEncoder encoder,
        ISystemClock clock)  : base(options, logger,
          encoder, clock)
    {
    }

    protected override Task<AuthenticateResult>
      HandleAuthenticateAsync() => Task.FromResult(
        AuthenticateResult.Success(
            new AuthenticationTicket(
                new ClaimsPrincipal(
                    new ClaimsIdentity(
                        new[]
                        {
                            new Claim(ClaimTypes.Name,
                              "Bob"),
                            new Claim(ClaimTypes.Role,
                              "User")
                        },
                        SchemeName)), SchemeName)));
}
```

The code implements `AuthenticationHandler<>` and takes the dependencies the base class needs into the constructor and passes these down. The `HandleAuthenticateAsync()` method will always return a successful authentication with a hardcoded principal with an identity on it. For the time being, the identity has the role of `User`.

You will need an authorization policy that is specific to this sample. It should say you have to be an `Admin` within namespaces starting with a specific string. In ASP.NET, this is done by implementing a requirement, which is basically the configuration object for the policy, and then a handler that is capable of handling the requirement.

Add a file called `AdminForNamespace.cs` in the root of `Chapter13` and make it look like the following:

```
using Microsoft.AspNetCore.Authorization;

namespace Chapter13;

public class AdminForNamespace : IAuthorizationRequirement
{
    public AdminForNamespace(string @namespace)
    {
        Namespace = @namespace;
    }

    public string Namespace { get; }
}
```

The code holds the configuration in the form of a namespace string that will be used in the code that checks the policy. IAuthorizationRequirement is an empty marker interface with nothing to implement.

Next, you need the handler. Add a file called AdminForNamespaceHandler.cs in the root of Chapter13 and make it look like the following:

```
using Microsoft.AspNetCore.Authorization;
using Microsoft.AspNetCore.Mvc.Controllers;

namespace Chapter13;

public class AdminForNamespaceHandler :
AuthorizationHandler<AdminForNamespace>
{
    protected override Task HandleRequirementAsync(
      AuthorizationHandlerContext context,
      AdminForNamespace requirement)
    {
        if (context.Resource is HttpContext httpContext)
        {
            var endpoint = httpContext.GetEndpoint();
            if (endpoint is not null)
            {
                var controllerActionDescriptor =
                  endpoint!.Metadata.GetMetadata<Controller
                  ActionDescriptor>();
                if (controllerActionDescriptor?
                        .MethodInfo
                        .DeclaringType?
```

```
                        .Namespace?
                        .StartsWith(requirement.Namespace,
                           StringComparison.InvariantCulture
                           ) == true &&
                      !httpContext.User.IsInRole("Admin"))
                {

                    context.Fail();
                }
                else
                {

                    context.Succeed(requirement);
                }
            }
        }
        return Task.CompletedTask;
    }
}
```

This overrides the abstract HandleRequirementAsync() method from the base class. In the context argument, there is a property called Resource. For Web API controller actions, this is typical of type HttpContext. The code, therefore, checks whether it is HttpContext and then has the implementation of the policy within that clause. In HttpContext, you can get the endpoint information. In the endpoint, there is metadata associated with it, and for our purpose, we're looking for the specific controller information. The ControllerActionDescriptor metadata contains the actual method that is supposed to be called on your controller. On this, the code gets DeclaringType and uses its namespace to see whether the namespace requirement matches. If the type has a namespace that starts with the requirement and the user does not have the Admin role, it fails the context, meaning that the user is not authorized. You can provide reasons and more details for failing, but for this sample, we're just keeping it clean.

> **Tip**
> If the user is Admin, it will succeed. It will also succeed if the namespace does not start with the requirement.

With the policy handler in place, you need it to be hooked up so that it actually gets called. The default approach in ASP.NET Core is to add policies during the setup of the authorization. This approach, however, takes away the cross-cutting opportunity as you would then need to be explicit regarding the controllers whose policies should be applied. Instead, you'll implement IAuthorizationPolicyProvider and set up the policies in this.

Add a file called CrossCuttingPoliciesProvider.cs in the root of Chapter13. It should be made to look like the following:

```
using Microsoft.AspNetCore.Authorization;

namespace Chapter13;

public class CrossCuttingPoliciesProvider :
IAuthorizationPolicyProvider
{
    readonly AuthorizationPolicy _policy;

    public CrossCuttingPoliciesProvider()
    {
        _policy = new AuthorizationPolicyBuilder()
                .AddRequirements(new
                AdminForNamespace("Chapter13")
            ).Build();
    }

    public Task<AuthorizationPolicy>
        GetDefaultPolicyAsync() => Task.FromResult(_policy);
    public Task<AuthorizationPolicy?>
        GetFallbackPolicyAsync() =>
        Task.FromResult<AuthorizationPolicy?>(_policy);
    public Task<AuthorizationPolicy?> GetPolicyAsync(string
        policyName) =>
        Task.FromResult<AuthorizationPolicy?>(_policy);
}
```

The code sets up `AuthorizationPolicy` that includes the `AdminForNamespace` policy. `IAuthorizationPolicyProvider` requires you to implement methods for getting policies for different scenarios; all of these return the same policy.

> **Important note**
> Returning the same policy for `GetDefaultPolicyAsync()`, `GetFallbackPolicyAsync()`, and `GetPolicyAsync()` might not be the desired behavior. This is done for the simplicity of the sample.

Next, you will be tying the authorization back into `CommandActionFilter` you created earlier, and to do that, we have to communicate the authorization results that are returned. Unfortunately, this information is not easily accessible in the following stages of the ASP.NET Core pipeline.

Add a file called `HttpContextExtensions.cs` in the root of `Chapter13` and make it look like the following:

```
using Microsoft.AspNetCore.Authorization.Policy;
```

```
namespace Chapter13;

public static class HttpContextExtensions
{
    const string AuthorizeResultKey = "_AuthorizeResult";

    public static PolicyAuthorizationResult?
      GetAuthorizationResult(this HttpContext context) =>
      (context.Items[AuthorizeResultKey] as
      PolicyAuthorizationResult)!;

    public static void SetAuthorizationResult(this
      HttpContext context, PolicyAuthorizationResult
      result) => context.Items[AuthorizeResultKey] =
      result;
}
```

The code uses the `Items` dictionary on `HttpContext` and provides both a set method and a get method for working with `PolicyAuthorizationResult`. `Items` is a key/value store that can hold anything as part of the current Web request. This is perfect for when you want to make something available to other stages.

ASP.NET Core provides specific middleware for dealing with the result of authorization. Add a file called `CrossCuttingAuthorizationMiddlewareResultHandler.cs` and make it look like the following:

```
using Microsoft.AspNetCore.Authorization;
using Microsoft.AspNetCore.Authorization.Policy;

namespace Chapter13;

public class CrossCuttingAuthorizationMiddlewareResultHandler :
  IAuthorizationMiddlewareResultHandler
{
    readonly AuthorizationMiddlewareResultHandler
      _defaultHandler = new();

    public async Task HandleAsync(RequestDelegate next,
      HttpContext context, AuthorizationPolicy policy,
      PolicyAuthorizationResult authorizeResult)
    {
        context.SetAuthorizationResult(authorizeResult);
        await _defaultHandler.HandleAsync(next, context,
```

```
            policy, PolicyAuthorizationResult.Success());
    }
}
```

The code implements the IAuthorizationMiddlewareResultHandler interface, which holds a HandleAsync() method. This method gets called after all policies have been handled but before the action filters. The implementation of HandleAsync() puts authorizationResult on HttpContext for the availability of later stages. It then uses the default implementation of the interface called AuthorizationMiddlewareResultHandler to invoke the rest of the pipeline, only now simulating a success. The reason it simulates success is to trick the handler to perform the action filters. We want CommandActionFilter to add support for authorization and return the CommandResult structure consistently.

Open the CommandActionFilter.cs file in the Commands folder within Chapter13 and make the top of the method look like the following:

```
if (context.HttpContext.Request.Method == HttpMethod.Post.Method)
    // Adding call to get authorization result and setting
    // authorized variable
    var authorizationResult =
      context.HttpContext.GetAuthorizationResult();
    var isAuthorized = authorizationResult?.Succeeded ??
      true;

    var exceptionMessages = new List<string>();
    var exceptionStackTrace = string.Empty;
    ActionExecutedContext? result = null;
    object? response = null;

    // Using authorized variable, we don't want to call the
    // controller if we are
    if (context.ModelState.IsValid && isAuthorized)
```

The change you're performing is making use of the authorization result. If the authorization result has not succeeded, you don't want to call the rest of the pipeline, but you want to capture it in the command result.

In the same file and method, change how you create CommandResult to include the IsAuthorized property:

```
var commandResult = new CommandResult
{
    CorrelationId = Guid.NewGuid(),

    // Adding isAuthorized
```

```
    IsAuthorized = isAuthorized,
    ValidationResults = context.ModelState.SelectMany(_ =>
      _.Value!.Errors.Select(e =>
      e.ToValidationResult(_.Key))),
    ExceptionMessages = exceptionMessages.ToArray(),
    ExceptionStackTrace = exceptionStackTrace ??
      string.Empty,
    Response = response
};
```

The code now has `CommandResult` that includes `IsAuthorized`. Since the rest of the action filter takes this into consideration, you should also be getting the correct HTTP status codes.

Open the `Program.cs` file in the root of the `Chapter13` project and change it to look like the following:

```
using Chapter13;
using Chapter13.Commands;
using Microsoft.AspNetCore.Authorization;

var builder = WebApplication.CreateBuilder(args);
builder.Services.AddControllers(mvcOptions => mvcOptions.Filters.
  Add<CommandActionFilter>());

// Adding authorization and the handlers
builder.Services.AddAuthorization(options => options.
  AddPolicy("Chapter13Admins", policy => policy.Requirements.Add(new
AdminForNamespace("Chapter13"))));
builder.Services.AddSingleton<IAuthorizationHandler,
  AdminForNamespaceHandler>();
builder.Services.AddSingleton<IAuthorizationMiddlewareResultHandler,
  CrossCuttingAuthorizationMiddlewareResultHandler>();
builder.Services.AddSingleton<IAuthorizationPolicyProvider,
  CrossCuttingPoliciesProvider>();

// Adding authentication with our hardcoded handler
builder.Services
    .AddAuthentication(options => options.DefaultScheme =
      HardCodedAuthenticationHandler.SchemeName)
    .AddScheme<HardCodedAuthenticationOptions,
      HardCodedAuthenticationHandler>(
      HardCodedAuthenticationHandler.SchemeName, _ => {});

var app = builder.Build();
```

```
app.MapControllers();

// Use authentication and authorization
app.UseAuthentication();
app.UseAuthorization();

app.Run();
```

The changes introduce both authentication and authorization and hooks `Services` into the different handlers and providers you have created. For the authentication, it sets up the hardcoded handler as the default authentication schema and configures the scheme to use the handler type you created.

Running the application and performing the same operation as before using Postman should yield the following result:

Figure 13.3 – An unauthorized result in Postman

The output should have isAuthorized set to false:

```
{
    "correlationId": "eb26b553-45f3-43a4-9d92-9860b2fe541e",
    "isSuccess": false,
    "isAuthorized": false,
    "isValid": true,
    "hasExceptions": false,
    "validationResults": [],
    "exceptionMessages": [],
    "exceptionStackTrace": "",
    "response": null
}
```

Let's try to change the role of the user to **Admin**. Open the HardCodedAuthenticationHandler.cs file in the root of Chapter13 and change the role from User to Admin. To do this, find the line that says the following:

```
new Claim(ClaimTypes.Role, "User")
```

Then make it look like the following:

```
new Claim(ClaimTypes.Role, "Admin")
```

Running the application now and performing the same operation again should give you a result where you're authorized:

Figure 13.4 – An authorized result in Postman

The JSON output should look like the following:

```
{
    "correlationId": "80191dbc-8908-4c89-9dfb-7bce8b4b9e44",
    "isSuccess": true,
    "isAuthorized": true,
    "isValid": true,
    "hasExceptions": false,
    "validationResults": [],
    "exceptionMessages": [],
    "exceptionStackTrace": "",
    "response": 1
}
```

This should give you an idea of what is possible. With ASP.NET Core, you can go deep into replacing default behavior and customizing it to your needs, which is fabulous when you're looking to apply some cross-cutting concerns.

Summary

Recipes are pieces of code that clearly specify, in a linear manner, what they do, are a great tool for new developers. The developer can really see what's going on, reason about the code, and find errors. As the developer, team, and project mature, the recipes start to feel like unnecessary chores or at least become very repetitive. Not only is this something that potentially affects productivity, but these kinds of repetitive tasks are easy to get wrong. Getting it wrong could pose multiple risks to the system:

- Security risks
- The risk of persisting invalid data
- The risk of allowing operations that are not allowed
- The risk of losing operational insight due to a lack of logging

The tradeoff between imperative procedural code that a developer can quickly reason about and the need for a consistent system is one you should consider. In smaller projects, it might not be worth the cognitive load of being "different" in applying things cross-cuttingly, while in larger systems, it might be completely crucial. There could be a correlation with the size of the team as well—the bigger the team, the more things you want to automate and standardize.

Applying cross-cutting concerns can be extremely powerful, but it can feel like a black box if the developers don't know about it and can't understand why something is happening. My advice on that is to make sure all developers are educated on how cross-cutting concerns are handled and ensure that it is possible to follow code paths. Rather than documenting the recipes, my suggestion would be to document how they are automated and how developers can, for instance, debug things.

In the next chapter, we'll dive into how you can go deeper by leveraging aspect-oriented programming.

14

Aspect-Oriented Programming

Throughout the book, you should have noticed a theme: automation. This means writing code that makes your code easier, more maintainable, and takes away repetitive work. In *Chapter 13, Applying Cross-Cutting Concerns*, we talked about code that could be created for a specific concern and be automatically applied. In this chapter, we will take this concept to the next level and dive into a formalization that is designed for this purpose; **aspect-oriented programming (AOP)**.

In this chapter, we will cover the following topics:

- What is AOP?
- Logging
- Mixins
- Authorization

By the end of this chapter, you should have a solid understanding of AOP and how it can be used in C# to create more modular, maintainable, and scalable applications.

Technical requirements

The source code specific to the chapter can be found on GitHub (https://github.com/PacktPublishing/Metaprogramming-in-C-Sharp/tree/main/Chapter14) and it builds on top of the Fundamentals code that is found on GitHub (https://github.com/PacktPublishing/Metaprogramming-in-C-Sharp/tree/main/Fundamentals).

What is AOP?

In traditional programming, developers write code to implement the desired behavior of their applications. This code is organized into functions, classes, and modules that implement specific functionalities. However, many applications require additional functionality that spans multiple parts of the codebase, such as logging, error handling, and security. These functionalities, often referred to as cross-cutting concerns, can be difficult to manage and maintain when scattered throughout the codebase.

AOP is a programming paradigm that aims to address this problem by separating cross-cutting concerns from the rest of the code. In AOP, developers define aspects, which encapsulate the behavior of cross-cutting concerns, and apply them to specific parts of the codebase using join points and pointcuts.

AOP is very well suited in combination with other programming paradigms, such as **object-oriented programming** (**OOP**) and **functional programming** (**FP**), to create more modular, maintainable, and scalable applications. AOP has become increasingly popular in recent years, and there are many AOP frameworks available for various programming languages and platforms.

In this chapter, we will explore how AOP can be used in C# to address cross-cutting concerns and improve code maintainability and reusability. We will cover the key concepts of AOP, such as aspects, pointcuts, and join points, and show how they can be applied to specific use cases, such as security and logging. We will do so using a framework called Castle Windsor (`https://www.castleproject.org/projects/windsor/`), and show how you use it to implement AOP in your C# applications.

Aspects

In AOP, an aspect is a modular unit of behavior that can be selectively applied to different parts of a program. An aspect is essentially a set of instructions that describe how to modify the behavior of a program in a particular way.

Aspects are used to address cross-cutting concerns, which are concerns that span multiple parts of a program and cannot be encapsulated in a single module or class. Examples of cross-cutting concerns include logging, security, caching, and error handling.

An aspect can be thought of as a reusable, modular piece of code that can be applied to multiple parts of a program. Aspects can be designed to be composable so that different aspects can be combined to achieve more complex behavior.

Aspects are typically implemented as classes or modules that define the behavior to be added to the program. In AOP frameworks such as Castle Windsor, aspects are often implemented as interceptors, which are classes that intercept calls to methods or properties and modify their behavior.

Pointcuts

Pointcuts are the mechanism used in AOP to specify the places in the code where an aspect should be applied. A pointcut is a set of join points, which are specific locations in the code where the aspect can be applied.

A join point is a point in the execution of a program where an aspect can be applied. Examples of join points include method calls, method executions, field accesses, and exception handlers.

To define a pointcut, you need to specify the join points that the pointcut includes. This can be done using a variety of criteria, such as method name, method signature, class name, or annotations.

Join points

In AOP, join points are specific points in the execution of a program where an aspect can be applied. Join points represent specific events, or method calls in the program, that can be intercepted by an aspect. For example, a join point could be a method call, field access, or an exception being thrown.

Join points are defined using pointcuts, which specify the criteria for selecting the join points where an aspect should be applied. Pointcuts can be defined using various criteria, such as method signatures, class names, or annotations. For example, a pointcut could select all methods that have a specific attribute or all methods in a specific namespace.

Once a pointcut has been defined, it can be used to apply an aspect to the selected join points. Aspects can modify the behavior of the join points they intercept by adding, modifying, or removing functionality. For example, an aspect could add logging or caching functionality to a method call or validate user input before allowing it to be processed.

Join points are an essential concept in AOP, as they allow aspects to be applied selectively to specific parts of the codebase rather than having to modify the entire codebase to implement cross-cutting concerns. Join points also enable the modularization of cross-cutting concerns, making them easier to manage and maintain.

Some common examples of join points in C# include the following:

- **Method calls**: These are join points that intercept method calls, either before the method is called (using a before advice) or after the method is called (using an after advice)
- **Field access**: These are join points that intercept read or write access to a field, either before the field is accessed (using a before advice) or after the field is accessed (using an after advice)
- **Exception handling**: Join points that intercept the throwing of an exception, allowing the aspect to handle the exception or modify its behavior

The following diagram summarizes **Aspect**, **Pointcuts**, and **Join Points**:

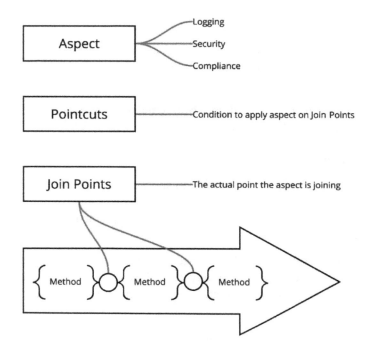

Figure 14.1 – AOP terminology visualization

With the terminology in place, we should now be ready to take a first dive into AOP and use it in some canonical examples.

Logging

Logging is often cited as the canonical example of how AOP can be used to improve the modularity and maintainability of software. Logging is a common cross-cutting concern, meaning that it affects multiple parts of a software system and cannot be easily encapsulated within a single module or class.

AOP provides a way to encapsulate the logging behavior and apply it consistently throughout the system without the need to modify each module or class individually. This allows developers to focus on the core functionality of their modules while still providing a consistent and coherent way to log system behavior.

In this section, we will explore the role of logging in software systems and how AOP can be used to implement logging behavior in a modular and maintainable way. We will look at the benefits and drawbacks of different logging approaches and how AOP can help to address some of the challenges associated with logging in complex software systems.

Creating a logging sample

Let's start by creating a new project for the chapter. Create a folder called `Chapter14`, change into this folder in your command line and create a new console project:

```
dotnet new console
```

For this chapter, as discussed, we will use a framework called Castle Windsor. It's one of many frameworks coming out of **The Castle Project**, which you can read more about it here (`http://www.castleproject.org/`). Castle Windsor is an **Inversion of Control** (**IoC**), a container that provides extensive capabilities performing AOP.

To make all the AOP magic possible, Castle Windsor is built on top of a project called Castle Core, which provides a convenient way to create dynamic runtime proxy objects, as we did in *Chapter 6, Dynamic Proxy Generation*. This could be a natural step up from having to do everything yourself.

It is all open source, and the concrete framework you will be using here is the **Windsor** part and can be found on GitHub (`https://github.com/castleproject/Windsor`).

Add the package to dependency of the project:

```
dotnet add package Castle.Windsor
```

To get started with the Windsor container, you can simply replace the content of `Program.cs` with the following:

```
using System.Reflection;
using Castle.Windsor;
using Castle.Windsor.Installer;

var container = new WindsorContainer();
container.Install(FromAssembly.InThisApplication(Assembly.
  GetEntryAssembly()));
```

The code creates an instance of `WindsorContainer` and instructs it to install any implementations of `IWindsorInstaller` from the running application. An installer is a way to configure the container. They are discovered in the `.Install()` call, and you can have multiple installers for specific use cases.

We want to create `DefaultInstaller` that will set up a default behavior for the container. Add a file called `DefaultInstaller.cs` and make it look like the following:

```
using System.Reflection;
using Castle.MicroKernel.Registration;
using Castle.MicroKernel.SubSystems.Configuration;
using Castle.Windsor;
```

```
namespace Chapter14;

public class DefaultInstaller : IWindsorInstaller
{
    public void Install(IWindsorContainer container,
      IConfigurationStore store)
    {
        container.Register(Classes
          .FromAssemblyInThisApplication(Assembly
          .GetEntryAssembly())
            .Pick()
            .WithService.DefaultInterfaces()
            .LifestyleTransient());
    }
}
```

The code implements the `IWindsorInstaller` interface and implements the `Install()` method. Within it, the code instructs `container` to register all classes from the application by associating it with a service represented by what is referred to as `DefaultInterfaces`. This means that it will establish a convention as we did in *Chapter 10, Convention over Configuration*, that says any class with a matching interface with a name prefixed by `I` will be bound together (`IFoo -> Foo`). Finally, it tells it that the lifestyle should be transient. Castle Windsor has a default life cycle of singleton, which could be dangerous and have undesired side effects, so my recommendation is to stay with transient as default and then override it when needed.

An installer is just a tool to help you structure your code and help you with keeping things focused on a single responsibility and enable a more cohesive codebase. You can, in fact, work directly with the container right after instantiating it, as we will see later. Some things make sense to do right away, while others should be separated.

`Console.WriteLine()` is not optimal for logging, so let's use the Microsoft logger instead.

Adding the Microsoft logger

By writing to the console using `Console.WriteLine()`, you don't get any structure to your logging. Log messages just become text, and the format is what you put into it. You often also want a different output for your local development than in production. Using a structured logging approach captures any values used in a log statement that could then be forwarded to a centralized log database, indexing them and making them searchable. There are many such tools out there, and I recommend looking at Seq (`https://datalust.co/seq`), which provides a tool that is free for local development.

For this sample, we will use a library from Microsoft for structured logging. It is the same one used by Microsoft for everything they build. It provides extension points and can also be used with other popular logging libraries, such as Serilog (`https://serilog.net`).

Start by adding package references to the core logging package and also to the `Console` output:

```
dotnet add package Microsoft.Extensions.Logging
dotnet add package Microsoft.Extensions.Logging.Console
```

Then in the `Program.cs` file, add the following code at the end:

```
var loggerFactory = LoggerFactory.Create(builder => builder.
  AddConsole());
container.Register(Component.For<ILoggerFactory>().
  Instance(loggerFactory));
```

The code creates `LoggerFactory` and configures it to output to the console. It then goes on to register the `ILoggerFactory` interface with the concrete instance you just configured into the Windsor IoC container. Any constructors with a dependency to `ILoggerFactory` will now get this instance. `ILoggerFactory` provides a way to create concrete `ILogger` instances, which is what will be used for logging.

In ASP.NET Core, `ILoggerFactory` is being used internally in some cases to create logger instances. While in other cases, constructors have a dependency to `ILogger` and, even more specifically, on the generic `ILogger<>` version. The generic version of `ILogger` allows you to get a scoped logger that is for your specific type. In the log output, you'll see the source of the log messages, which is important metadata.

Let's configure the IoC container to support both of these scenarios. In the `Program.cs` file, add the following code at the end:

```
var createLoggerMethod = typeof(LoggerFactoryExtensions)
    .GetMethods(BindingFlags.Public | BindingFlags.Static)
    .First(_ => _.Name == nameof(
      LoggerFactory.CreateLogger) && _.IsGenericMethod);

container.Register(Component.For<ILogger>().
  UsingFactoryMethod((kernel, context) =>
{
    var loggerFactory = kernel.Resolve<ILoggerFactory>();
    return loggerFactory.CreateLogger(
      context.Handler.ComponentModel.Implementation);
}).LifestyleTransient());
container.Register(Component.For(typeof(ILogger<>)).
  UsingFactoryMethod((kernel, context) =>
{
    var loggerFactory = kernel.Resolve<ILoggerFactory>();
    var logger = createLoggerMethod
      .MakeGenericMethod(context.RequestedType
```

```
            .GenericTypeArguments[0]).Invoke(null, new[] {
            loggerFactory });
        return logger;
}));
```

The code starts by using reflection to get the `CreateLogger<>()` extension method from `LoggerFactoryExtensions`. This is because `ILoggerFactory` only has a non-typed way of creating a logger, and the generic one is an extension method. Next, the code registers the untyped non-generic `ILogger` with the container using a factory method that will create the instance dynamically when asked. It then leverages the container to get `ILoggerFactory` and then creates a logger by giving it the type `Ilogger` is being injected into. Since the default behavior of Windsor is to make everything a singleton, we explicitly configure `Ilogger` to be transient. This way, we get different logger instances for the types using it. Otherwise, you would be sharing the same logger across all types. Lastly, the code configures the generic `ILogger<>` using a factory method that uses the `CreateLogger<>()` extension method from `LoggerFactoryExtensions` by creating a generic method for the requested type and its generic type argument.

With the basic logging infrastructure in place, we're now ready to apply cross-cutting logging.

Interceptors

In Castle Windsor, there is the concept of interceptors. They represent how you can implement the actual aspect and perform the cross-cutting operation.

Let's create one for handling logging for all method calls. In the root of `Chapter14`, add a file called `LoggingInterceptor.cs` and make it look like the following:

```
using Castle.DynamicProxy;

namespace Chapter14;

public class LoggingInterceptor : IInterceptor
{
    public void Intercept(IInvocation invocation)
    {
        // Do something before
        invocation.Proceed();
        // Do something after
    }
}
```

The code sets up an implementation of `IInterceptor` from Castle Windsor. In the `Intercept()` method, the code calls the `Proceed()` method on the invocation object, which will perform the actual call it is intercepting. Before and after this call is where we can do our cross-cutting operations.

With .NET 6, Microsoft introduced an approach to logging that helps you become even more structured by encapsulating log messages into its own code file. This helps you with the maintenance of log messages and makes it easier for those scenarios when you want to output the same log message for different scenarios.

Create a new file called `LoggingInterceptorLogMessages.cs` and add the following code to it:

```
using Microsoft.Extensions.Logging;

namespace Chapter14;

internal static partial class LoggingInterceptorLogMessages
{
    [LoggerMessage(1, LogLevel.Information, "Before
      invoking {Method}", EventName = "BeforeInvocation")]
    internal static partial void BeforeInvocation(this
      ILogger logger, string method);

    [LoggerMessage(2, LogLevel.Error, "Error invoking
      {Method}", EventName = "InvocationError")]
    internal static partial void InvocationError(this
      ILogger logger, string method, Exception exception);

    [LoggerMessage(3, LogLevel.Information, "Before
      invoking {Method}", EventName = "AfterInvocation")]
    internal static partial void AfterInvocation(this
      ILogger logger, string method);
}
```

The code sets up a static partial class with extension methods for each log statement and leverages `[LoggerMessage]` to configure the log message, its severity, a unique identifier within the file or globally, and optionally, an event name. Since all the methods are also partial and do not have any implementations, the C# compiler will generate the necessary code for this.

> **Important note**
>
> I find it to be good practice to make logger messages like this internal, for both the class and the methods. That way, you isolate them for their module and do not run the risk of making them an extension method that will show up as IntelliSense in your editor globally across different projects. Normally you should also use the generic `ILogger<>` as the type to extend for the extension method makes it specific to your concrete type. But since the log messages we have here are cross-cutting, we don't know the type they will be used in.

With the log messages in place for what we want to log, we can modify `LoggingInterceptor` to do the logging. Open the `LoggingInterceptor` file and change it to look like the following:

```
using Castle.DynamicProxy;
using Microsoft.Extensions.Logging;

namespace Chapter14;

public class LoggingInterceptor : IInterceptor
{
    readonly ILoggerFactory _loggerFactory;

    public LoggingInterceptor(ILoggerFactory loggerFactory)
    {
        _loggerFactory = loggerFactory;
    }

    public void Intercept(IInvocation invocation)
    {
        var logger = _loggerFactory.CreateLogger(
          invocation.TargetType)!;
        logger.BeforeInvocation(invocation.Method.Name);
        invocation.Proceed();
        logger.AfterInvocation(invocation.Method.Name);
    }
}
```

The code gets changed to take `ILoggerFactory` as a dependency in the constructor. In the `Intercept()` method, you now use the logger factory to create a logger for the target type. It then uses structured logging calling `BeforeInvocation()` and `AfterInvocation()` and passing the name of the method being invoked.

> **Important note**
>
> Just seeing the method being invoked in your logs by name might not be enough information. The `IInvocation` type has details about the parameters being passed, and you could be logging them as well. The only thing to keep in mind would be to redact values that are sensitive, such as **General Data Protection Regulation** (**GDPR**)-related information or security information. Luckily, if you follow the advice in *Chapter 4, Reasoning about Types Using Reflection*, and use the `ConceptAs<>` encapsulation for types, you could easily identify the types you need to redact and automatically do so.

With the interceptor in place, the next step is to hook it up to Castle Windsor. Open the `DefaultInstaller.cs` file and change it to the following:

```
using System.Reflection;
using Castle.MicroKernel.Registration;
using Castle.MicroKernel.SubSystems.Configuration;
using Castle.Windsor;

namespace Chapter14;

public class DefaultInstaller : IWindsorInstaller
{
    public void Install(IWindsorContainer container,
      IConfigurationStore store)
    {
        // Added
        container.Register(Component.For<
          LoggingInterceptor>());
        container.Register(Classes
          .FromAssemblyInThisApplication(Assembly
          .GetEntryAssembly())
            .Pick()
            .WithService.DefaultInterfaces()

            // Added
            .Configure(_ =>
              _.Interceptors<LoggingInterceptor>())
            .LifestyleTransient());
    }
}
```

The only change made to the installer is the registration of LoggingInterceptor. Castle Windsor does not know how to resolve concrete types automatically, so we register it manually. The second addition is to configure the registration for the default convention to include LoggingInterceptor.

Now that you have all the infrastructure in place, you need something to test it with. Let's create a user service for registering users, not focusing on implementing it, just something to test the interceptor with.

Trying out the interceptor

Create a file called IUsersService.cs in the root of Chapter14 and make it look like the following:

```
namespace Chapter14;

public interface IUsersService
{
    Task<Guid> Register(string userName, string password);
```

```
}
```

The interface holds a single method for registering a user.

For the interface, you'll need an implementation. Add a file called `UsersService.cs` and add the following code to it:

```
using Microsoft.Extensions.Logging;

namespace Chapter14;

public class UsersService : IUsersService
{
    readonly ILogger<UsersService> _logger;

    public UsersService(ILogger<UsersService> logger)
    {
        _logger = logger;
    }

    public Task<Guid> Register(string userName,
        string password)
    {
        _logger.LogInformation("Inside register method");
        var id = Guid.NewGuid();
        return Task.FromResult(id);
    }
}
```

The code represents an implementation of `IUsersService`. It takes `ILogger<UsersService>` as a dependency so that we can log from within it. For the `Register()` method, it only logs it, creates a new `Guid`, and returns this as a result.

With a sample in place, you now need to get an instance of it and see that the interceptor works. Open the `Program.cs` file and add the following to the very end:

```
var usersService = container.Resolve<IUsersService>();
var result = await usersService.Register("jane@doe.io", "Password1");

Console.ReadLine();
```

The code asks the Castle Windsor container for an instance of `IUsersService` and then calls the `Register()` method. We put in `Console.ReadLine()` due to the use of async; if we didn't, it would exit without any of the log messages being printed.

You can now run this using `dotnet run` or your preferred approach in your editor, and you should see the following output:

```
info: Chapter14.UsersService[1]
      Before invoking Register
info: Chapter14.UsersService[0]
      Inside register method
info: Chapter14.UsersService[3]
      Before invoking Register
```

The calling code has no concept of the interceptor; it is configured once and will be weaved into the running code automatically.

However, the implementation of the `Intercept()` method in `LoggingInterceptor` is a bit naïve. It should support errors, and it also needs to support asynchronous method calls properly. Open the `LoggingInterceptor.cs` file and change the `Intercept()` method as follows:

```
public void Intercept(IInvocation invocation)
{
    var logger = _loggerFactory
      .CreateLogger(invocation.TargetType)!;
    logger.BeforeInvocation(invocation.Method.Name);

    try
    {
        invocation.Proceed();

        if (invocation.ReturnValue is Task task)
        {
            task.ContinueWith(t =>
            {
                if (t.IsFaulted)
                {
                    logger.InvocationError(
                        invocation.Method.Name,
                        t.Exception!);
                }
                else
                {
                    logger.AfterInvocation(
                        invocation.Method.Name);
                }
            });
        }
```

```
        else
        {
            logger.AfterInvocation(invocation.Method.Name);
        }
    }
    catch (Exception ex)
    {
        logger.InvocationError(invocation.Method.Name, ex);
        throw;
    }
}
```

The code wraps the `Proceed()` call in `try {} catch {}` to be able to log the error, but rethrows it as the logging shouldn't swallow the exception; it should bubble up to the original caller. For handling asynchronous calls, it looks at `ReturnValue` of the `invocation` instance if it is a `Task`. If it is a task, it will continue, and get notified when it is completed. Tasks can have a faulty state, which would be if the call results in an exception.

Mixins

In C++, multiple inheritances provide a powerful way to combine behaviors from multiple base classes. However, this can lead to complexity and the diamond problem. Mixins provide a simpler alternative to multiple inheritances that avoids these issues and are particularly useful for implementing cross-cutting concerns in your code.

In the .NET **common language runtime (CLR)**, however, multiple inheritance is not supported, as it uses a single inheritance model. This means that there is no built-in mechanism for combining behaviors from multiple classes. Mixins can be used to achieve this, providing a way to add functionality to a class without needing to modify its inheritance hierarchy. In this section, we'll explore what mixins are, how they work, and why you might want to use them in your C# applications to overcome the limitations of the .NET CLR's single inheritance model.

One of the key features of Castle Core is its support for dynamic proxies, which allow you to intercept method calls and add behavior at runtime.

Castle Windsor's approach to mixins builds on this support for dynamic proxies to provide a way to compose behavior from multiple sources into a single object. Mixins allow you to define a set of behaviors as independent components, which can be combined with the behavior of another object to create a new object with the combined behavior.

In Castle Windsor, mixins are implemented using a combination of dynamic proxies and an interception. When you register a component with mixins, Castle Windsor creates a dynamic proxy object that intercepts method calls to the component and delegates them to the mixins. The mixins can then modify the behavior of the component by adding new functionality or modifying the behavior of existing methods.

To register a component with mixins in Castle Windsor, you typically define one or more interfaces that represent the mixins and register them as separate components with the container. You then register the component to which you want to add the mixins to and specify the mixins as dependencies. When the component is resolved from the container, Castle Windsor creates a dynamic proxy object that implements the component interface and the mixin interfaces and delegates method calls to the appropriate objects.

Mixing it up

The UserService you created earlier could be a candidate for mixins. In a system, you typically need a way to authenticate users and a way to ask whether they are authorized to perform an action. Obviously, .NET provides building blocks and great support for both authentication and authorization, but let's say you want your abstraction on top of what .NET provides for specific use where you need to be able to authenticate a user by its username and password and then be able to ask whether the user is authorized to perform an action.

In the folder for the Chapter14 code, add a file called IAuthenticator.cs and put the following into it:

```
namespace Chapter14;

public interface IAuthenticator
{
    bool Authenticate(string username, string password);
}
```

The IAuthenticator interface defines a method for performing authentication with a username and a password. It would typically return true if it could successfully authenticate the user and false if not.

An implementation of IAuthenticator can be put in a file called Authenticator.cs, which looks like the following:

```
namespace Chapter14;

public class Authenticator : IAuthenticator
{
    public bool Authenticate(string username, string password)
    {
        return true;
    }
}
```

The code implements the `IAuthenticator` interface, and for demo purposes, it only returns `true`. Since we won't be building anything specifically and are just demonstrating the power of mixins, this is OK for now.

For the authorization part, you're going to need another interface. Add a file called `IAuthorizer.cs` and make it look like the following:

```
namespace Chapter14;

public interface IAuthorizer
{
    bool IsAuthorized(string username, string action);
}
```

Checking for authorization is done by giving it a username and an action. The method will then return `true` if the user is authorized to perform the action and `false` if not.

For the authorizer, you'll also need an implementation, so create a file called `Authorizer.cs` and put the following into it:

```
namespace Chapter14;

public class Authorizer : IAuthorizer
{
    public bool IsAuthorized(string username, string action)
    {
        return true;
    }
}
```

As with the `Authenticator` implementation, it will just return `true` for demonstration purposes. This is where you'd have your logic for checking whether the user is authorized for a specific action.

he `IAuthenticator` and `IAuthorizer`, with their respective implementations, are separate, they're also separate from `IUsersService`. This is great as they represent different aspects of king with a user. They serve specific responsibilities of the system, and it's logical to keep them ite, which leads to a more maintainable codebase.

r, it might be desirable to be able to access them all as one at runtime. This is where mixins nd can make it look as if it is one implementation.

do so, you need to configure Castle Windsor correctly. Open the `DefaultInstaller`. t the top of the `Install()` method, add the following:

```
.Register(
ent.For<IAuthenticator>()
```

```
        .ImplementedBy<Authenticator>()
        .LifestyleTransient());

container.Register(
    Component.For<IAuthorizer>()
        .ImplementedBy<Authorizer>()
        .LifestyleTransient());
```

The code adds explicit container registrations for the IAuthenticator and IAuthorizer services. The reason for adding this explicitly is that we have to add an explicit registration for IUsersService, and this has to happen prior to the automatic registrations that are already set up in DefaultInstaller. If you were to register IUsersService after the automatic registrations, you would get an exception saying there are duplicate registrations.

For the mixin, you're going to need another explicit registration. Add the following code right after the IAuthenticator and IAuthorize registrations and before the automatic registrations:

```
container.Register(
    Component.For<IUsersService>()
        .ImplementedBy<UsersService>()
        .Proxy.AdditionalInterfaces(typeof(IAuthorizer),
          typeof(IAuthenticator))
        .Proxy.MixIns(_ => _
            .Component<Authorizer>()
            .Component<Authenticator>())
        .Interceptors<LoggingInterceptor>()
        .LifestyleTransient());
```

The registration for IUsersService is slightly different from what you've done before. First, it instructs Castle Windsor that IUsersService is implemented by UsersService, then it instructs it to implement some additional interfaces: IAuthorizer and IAuthenticator. The additional interfaces are then instructed to be implemented using the .Mixins() call that tells it that they're implemented by their respective Authorizer and Authenticator components. Since this is an explicit registration, the automatic one will not kick in, and LoggingInterceptor you previously hooked up won't kick in for this. For it to do so, you need to add an explicit .Interceptors<>() call for the interceptor. Lastly, you set the lifestyle to be transient.

If you run this with the debugger attached, you can investigate what has happened to UserService. In the Program.cs file, you can put a breakpoint right after you call container. Resolve<IUserService>(). Run the debugger to this point:

```
   31     var usersService = container.Resolve<IUsersService>();
 ▷ 32     var result = await usersService.Register("jane@doe.io", "Password1");
   33     🌸
```

Figure 14.2 – The debug breakpoint

In the `Debug` console (immediate window) of your editor/**integrated development environment (IDE)**, you should be able to write the following:

```
usersService.GetType().GetInterfaces()
```

The output of this should be something like the following:

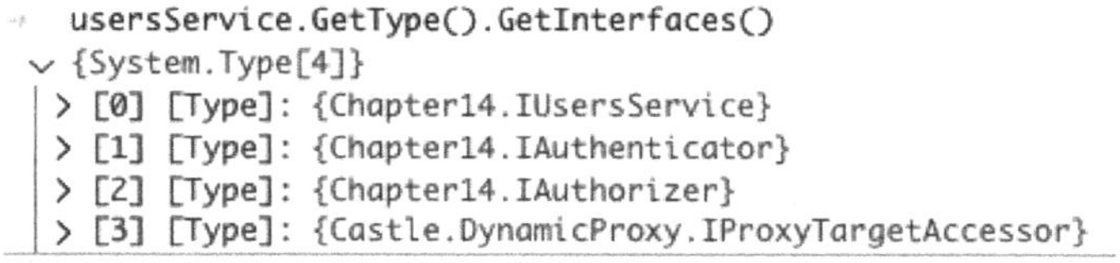

```
⟶   usersService.GetType().GetInterfaces()
  ∨ {System.Type[4]}
  | > [0] [Type]: {Chapter14.IUsersService}
  | > [1] [Type]: {Chapter14.IAuthenticator}
  | > [2] [Type]: {Chapter14.IAuthorizer}
  | > [3] [Type]: {Castle.DynamicProxy.IProxyTargetAccessor}
```

Figure 14.3 – The implemented interfaces

To prove the calls are going to the mixins, you can add the following to the `Program.cs` file before `Console.ReadLine();`:

```
var authenticated = (usersService as IAuthenticator)!.
  Authenticate("jane@doe.io", "Password1");
var authorized = (usersService as IAuthorizer)!.IsAuthorized("jane@
  doe.io", "Some Action");
Console.WriteLine($"Authenticated: {authenticated}");
Console.WriteLine($"Authorized: {authorized}");
```

The code assumes that `UserService` also implements the `IAuthenticator` and `IAuthorizer` interfaces and uses casting to get to them and calls the `Authenticate()` and `IsAuthorized()` methods, respectively. It then prints out the results of these.

If you run your application now, you should see an output similar to the following:

```
info:  Chapter14.UsersService[1]
       Before invoking Register
info:  Chapter14.UsersService[0]
       Inside register method
info:  Chapter14.Authenticator[1]
       Before invoking Authenticate
info:  Chapter14.UsersService[3]
       Before invoking Register
info:  Chapter14.Authenticator[3]
       Before invoking Authenticate
info:  Chapter14.Authorizer[1]
       Before invoking IsAuthorized
info:  Chapter14.Authorizer[3]
       Before invoking IsAuthorized
```

```
Authenticated: True
Authorized: True
```

The downside to this approach is that it is not clear in the contract of `IUsersService` that it will also implement the `IAuthenticator` and `IAuthorizer` interfaces. However, this can be overcome by different techniques.

One approach is to have an interface that represents the composition without an implementation, for instance, something such as the following:

```
public interface IUsersServiceComposition : IUsersService,
IAuthenticator, IAuthorizer
{
}
```

The `IUsersServiceComposition` interface is just for composition; it shouldn't have any direct members on it as the goal is to combine implementations of `IUsersService`, `IAuthenticator`, and `IAuthorizer`. We can then leverage the underlying `ProxyGenerator` in the Castle `DynamicProxy` library to create a proxy that represents this with the implementations in the different components.

In the `DefaultInstaller.cs` file, you can now create a new type of registration for the new `IUsersServiceComposition` interface. At the end of the method, you can add the following code:

```
container.Register(
    Component.For<IUsersServiceComposition>()
        .UsingFactoryMethod((kernel, context) =>
        {
            var proxyGenerator = new ProxyGenerator();
            var proxyGenerationOptions = new ProxyGenerationOptions();
            proxyGenerationOptions.AddMixinInstance(container.
            Resolve<IAuthorizer>());
            proxyGenerationOptions.AddMixinInstance(container.
            Resolve<IAuthenticator>());
            var logger = container.Resolve<ILogger<UsersService>>();
            proxyGenerationOptions.AddMixinInstance(new
            UsersService(logger));
            var usersServiceComposition = (proxyGenerator.
            CreateClassProxyWithTarget(
                typeof(object),
                new[] { typeof(IUsersServiceComposition) },
                new object(),
                proxyGenerationOptions) as IUsersServiceComposition)!;
            return usersServiceComposition;
        }));;a
```

The code sets up a registration that uses a method to create the instance. With the `UsingFactoryMethod()` instruction, you're giving Castle Windsor a method that will be called when it needs to resolve the instance. The factory method uses `ProxyGenerator` from the Castle `DynamicProxy` and adds the different mixins for the `IAuthorizer` and `IAuthenticator` interfaces by using the container to provide an instance of these. For `IUsersService`, we have to create an instance of it ourselves for this sample, providing the logger that uses the container to get an instance. The reason for this is that you already have a registration for `IUsersService` that adds mixins for the `IAuthorizer` and `IAuthenticator` interfaces, which would throw an exception when creating a proxy.

Once all the mixins are configured, the code creates a class proxy with a target based on the `object` type and tells it that it should implement the `IUsersServiceComposition` interface.

With all that, you now get an instance that implements all the interfaces and delegates the implementation of them to the mixed-in instances. Kind of neat.

Using `IUserServiceComposition` is now much more intuitive and very clear for the consumer, as you don't have to know what other interfaces it might implement. Open up the `Program.cs` file and add the following code before `Console.ReadLine()`:

```
var composition = container.Resolve<IUsersServiceComposition>();
authenticated = composition.Authenticate("jane@doe.io", "Password1");
authorized = composition.IsAuthorized("jane@doe.io", "Some Action");
Console.WriteLine($"Authenticated: {authenticated}");
Console.WriteLine($"Authorized: {authorized}");
```

Running the program should now give you a result similar to the following:

```
info: Chapter14.UsersService[1]
      Before invoking Register
info: Chapter14.UsersService[0]
      Inside register method
info: Chapter14.Authenticator[1]
      Before invoking Authenticate
info: Chapter14.UsersService[3]
      Before invoking Register
info: Chapter14.Authenticator[3]
      Before invoking Authenticate
info: Chapter14.Authorizer[1]
      Before invoking IsAuthorized
info: Chapter14.Authorizer[3]
      Before invoking IsAuthorized
Authenticated: True
Authorized: True
```

```
Authenticated: True
Authorized: True
```

Mixins provide a powerful way to add behavior to an object by combining it with behavior from other objects. Some of the benefits of using mixins include the following:

- **Composition**: Mixins allow you to compose complex behavior from simple, reusable components. This makes it easier to maintain and modify your code over time.

- **Separation of concerns**: Mixins enable you to separate the concerns of an object by breaking it down into smaller, more focused pieces of functionality. This makes it easier to understand and reason about your code.

- **Reusability**: Mixins allow you to reuse behavior across multiple objects, which reduces code duplication and makes it easier to maintain and modify your code over time.

- **Flexibility**: Mixins provide a flexible way to modify the behavior of an object by allowing you to selectively apply behavior as needed. This gives you greater control over the behavior of your code and makes it easier to customize for specific use cases.

- **Testability**: Mixins allow you to test individual pieces of functionality in isolation, which makes it easier to write tests and ensure the correctness of your code.

Mixins are often used in conjunction with techniques such as pointcuts, which allow you to apply behavior to specific points in your code. Pointcuts provide a way to selectively apply mixins to specific parts of your code, which gives you even greater flexibility and control over the behavior of your code.

In summary, mixins are a powerful tool for adding behavior to objects in a flexible, maintainable, and reusable way. When used in conjunction with pointcuts and other AOP techniques, they provide a powerful way to customize the behavior of your code and achieve greater modularity, flexibility, and testability.

Authorization

Authorization is a critical concern for many software systems, as it is important to ensure that users and applications only have access to the resources and functionality that they are authorized to use. AOP can be a powerful tool for implementing authorization behavior, as it allows developers to encapsulate authorization logic and apply it consistently throughout the system.

One approach to implementing authorization with AOP is to use join points to filter down to specific namespaces in C# code. Join points are points in the code where an aspect can be applied, such as method calls, field accesses, or object creation. By using join points to filter down specific namespaces, developers can apply authorization logic only to the relevant parts of the system, reducing the risk of errors or inconsistencies.

In AOP, a pointcut is a specific location in the source code where an aspect should be applied. In other words, it's a way to define the set of join points (i.e., specific points in a program's execution flow) where an aspect should be executed.

Pointcuts are often defined using a combination of different criteria, such as method names, method signatures, class names, package names, annotations, and more. The criteria used to define a pointcut are typically expressed using a syntax known as a "pointcut expression" or "pointcut language."

The pointcut language used may vary depending on the AOP framework being used. For example, in C#, with the help of libraries such as PostSharp, you can define pointcuts using a combination of attribute annotations and method signatures.

Once a pointcut is defined, it can be used to "weave" one or more aspects into the code at the specified join points. This means that the aspect's behavior is inserted into the code at the specified join points without requiring any modification to the original source code.

Overall, pointcuts provide a powerful way to apply cross-cutting concerns, such as logging, caching, or security, to specific parts of a program's execution flow.

Using pointcuts

With interceptors, you might not want them applied to everything. This could especially be true for authorization. You could have parts of your application that do not require authorization, such as infrastructure, and possibly also concrete parts that are open to all users. With Castle Windsor, we can create pointcuts by leveraging selectors for the interceptors. This is a way to provide the actual interceptors to be applied dynamically based on type and method information.

Let's create a service for adding to-do items to a list, represented with an `ITodoService` interface. Create a folder called `Todo` in the root of the `Chapter14` project, add a file called `ITodoService.cs`, and add the following to it:

```
namespace Chapter14.Todo;

public interface ITodoService
{
    void Add(string item);
}
```

The interface only exposes a simple `Add()` method for adding an item in the form of a string. Its implementation should be added to a file called `TodoService.cs` within the `Todo` folder and look like the following:

```
namespace Chapter14.Todo;

public class TodoService : ITodoService
```

```
{
    public void Add(string item)
    {
        Console.WriteLine($"Adding '{item}' to the todo list");
    }
}
```

Since we're not focused on building something that creates a todo item in a datastore, we just print what is added in the implementation. This is just to prove how you can leverage interceptors and selectors to filter what calls are made.

The next thing you will need is an interceptor that checks whether the user is authorized.

Add a file called AuthorizationInterceptor.cs to the root of the Chapter14 project and add the following code to it:

```
using Castle.DynamicProxy;

namespace Chapter14;

public class AuthorizationInterceptor : IInterceptor
{
    readonly IUsersServiceComposition _usersService;

    public AuthorizationInterceptor(IUsersServiceComposition
      usersService)
    {
        _usersService = usersService;
    }

    public void Intercept(IInvocation invocation)
    {
        if (_usersService.IsAuthorized("jane@doe.io", invocation.
          Method.Name))
        {
            invocation.Proceed();
        }
    }
}
```

The code implements the Castle DynamicProxy IInterceptor interface, and the constructor has a dependency on the IUsersServiceComposition service you created for the mixins section. The Intercept() method leverages the composed user service to check whether the user is authorized. If the user is authorized, it lets the invocation carry on.

> **Important note:**
> The user is hardcoded to jane@doe.io, you would obviously need to get the currently
> logged-in user in a production system. Also, the implementation does not do anything if it's
> not authorized. One approach could be to throw UnauthorizedException() and let
> that bubble up.

For the actual pointcut that will be filtering down which interceptors to apply when, you must implement
the IInterceptorSelector interface found in Castle DynamicProxy. Add a file in the root
of the project called InterceptorSelector.cs and add the following code to it:

```
using System.Reflection;
using Castle.DynamicProxy;

namespace Chapter14;

public class InterceptorSelector : IInterceptorSelector
{
    public IInterceptor[] SelectInterceptors(Type type, MethodInfo
      method, IInterceptor[] interceptors)
    {
        if (type.Namespace?.StartsWith("Chapter14.Todo",
          StringComparison.InvariantCulture) ?? false)
        {
            return interceptors;
        }

        return interceptors.Where(_ => _.GetType() !=
        typeof(AuthorizationInterceptor)).ToArray();
    }
}
```

The SelectInterceptors() method gets called with the target type and the method being called,
and you're given the configured interceptors. You can, at this stage, decide which interceptors should
be applied to the method call. The code makes this decision by looking at the namespace of the type
and anything that starts with Chapter14.Todo should have all interceptors, while anything else
gets all interceptors except AuthorizationInterceptor.

With the interceptor and the selector in place, you will have to register them both in the Castle Windsor
container and hook them up for use in existing registrations. Open the DefaultInstaller.cs
file and add the following to the top of the Install() method:

```
container.Register(Component.For<InterceptorSelector>());
container.Register(Component.For<AuthorizationInterceptor>());
```

The code registers both `InterceptorSelector` and `AuthorizationInterceptor` with the container, making them possible to be injected into services needing it. In the `Install()` method, there are two places where you've already added `LoggingInterceptor`; in both these places, we want to add the new `AuthorizationInterceptor` and also a statement telling Castle Windsor to use the new `InterceptorSelector` to select the correct interceptors.

The following lines add the interceptor and selector:

```
.Interceptors<AuthorizationInterceptor>()
.SelectInterceptorsWith(s => s.Service<InterceptorSelector>())
```

For reference, the block that configures `IUsersService` needs these two lines:

```
container.Register(
    Component.For<IUsersService>()
        .ImplementedBy<UsersService>()
        .Proxy.AdditionalInterfaces(typeof(IAuthorizer),
        typeof(IAuthenticator))
        .Proxy.MixIns(_ => _
            .Component<Authorizer>()
            .Component<Authenticator>())
        .Interceptors<LoggingInterceptor>()

        // Add the interceptor and the selector
        .Interceptors<AuthorizationInterceptor>()
        .SelectInterceptorsWith(s => s.Service<InterceptorSelector>())

        .LifestyleTransient());
```

And the second block that needs the two lines is generally, by convention, the automatic hookup:

```
container.Register(Classes.FromAssemblyInThisApplication(Assembly.
    GetEntryAssembly())
    .Pick()
    .WithService.DefaultInterfaces()
    .Configure(_ => _
        .Interceptors<LoggingInterceptor>()
        .Interceptors<AuthorizationInterceptor>()

        // Add the interceptor and the selector
        .Interceptors<AuthorizationInterceptor>()
        .SelectInterceptorsWith(s =>
          s.Service<InterceptorSelector>()))

    .LifestyleTransient());
```

Now that everything is registered, it's time to try it out. Open the `Program.cs` file and add the following before `Console.ReadLine()`:

```
var todo = container.Resolve<ITodoService>();
todo.Add("Buy milk");
```

By running your application now, you should see the following output:

```
info: Chapter14.UsersService[1]
      Before invoking Register
info: Chapter14.UsersService[0]
      Inside register method
info: Chapter14.UsersService[3]
      Before invoking Register
info: Chapter14.Authenticator[1]
      Before invoking Authenticate
info: Chapter14.Authenticator[3]
      Before invoking Authenticate
info: Chapter14.Authorizer[1]
      Before invoking IsAuthorized
info: Chapter14.Authorizer[3]
      Before invoking IsAuthorized
Authenticated: True
Authorized: True
Authenticated: True
Authorized: True
info: Chapter14.Todo.TodoService[1]
      Before invoking Add
Adding 'Buy milk' to the todo list
info: Chapter14.Todo.TodoService[3]
      Before invoking Add
```

As expected, you should be allowed to buy the milk. Let's alter the authorizer to not permit this. Open the `Authorizer.cs` file and return `false` instead:

```
namespace Chapter14;

public class Authorizer : IAuthorizer
{
    public bool IsAuthorized(string username, string action)
    {
        return false;
    }
}
```

Running the program again should produce a different result with the `Adding 'Buy milk' to the todo list` output being removed. You'll still see that the method invocation from the logger happens, but the actual invocation is filtered out:

```
info: Chapter14.UsersService[1]
      Before invoking Register
info: Chapter14.UsersService[0]
      Inside register method
Authenticated: True
info: Chapter14.UsersService[3]
      Before invoking Register
Authorized: False
info: Chapter14.Authenticator[1]
      Before invoking Authenticate
info: Chapter14.Authenticator[3]
      Before invoking Authenticate
info: Chapter14.Authorizer[1]
      Before invoking IsAuthorized
info: Chapter14.Authorizer[3]
      Before invoking IsAuthorized
Authenticated: True
Authorized: False
info: Chapter14.Todo.TodoService[1]
      Before invoking Add
info: Chapter14.Todo.TodoService[3]
      Before invoking Add
```

Windsor Castle provides a flexible and powerful pointcut mechanism, based on Castle `DynamicProxy`, that allows you to select join points based on the metadata found on the type and method. For example, you can create pointcuts based on the following criteria:

- The name of the method
- The return type of the method
- The parameters of the method
- The presence of attributes on the type or method
- The accessibility of the method (e.g., public, private, and so on)

By combining multiple criteria, you can create complex pointcuts that match very specific sets of join points. For example, you could create a pointcut that matches all public methods with a specific attribute or all non-public methods with a specific name.

Pointcuts are a powerful mechanism for filtering calls and applying aspects only to specific parts of the code. By using pointcuts, you can avoid the overhead of applying aspects to every single method call and, instead, selectively apply aspects only where they are needed. This can result in faster and more efficient code, with better separation of concerns.

Overall, pointcuts are a key feature of AOP, and Windsor Castle provides a rich and flexible pointcut mechanism that can be used to create complex and powerful aspect-based solutions.

Summary

Although we've used Castle Windsor throughout, there are other tools, frameworks, or libraries that could also be used, such as PostSharp (`https://www.postsharp.net`), Autofac (`https://autofac.org`), or just use the underlying Castle Core `DynamicProxy` to achieve the same without buying into a full-blown framework. You could be hand-rolling this yourself using reflection emit as well.

Overall, AOP and Castle Windsor provide a powerful mechanism for separating concerns in your code and making them more modular and reusable. By selectively applying aspects to specific parts of your code, you can achieve a high degree of flexibility and control over the behavior of your application.

In *Chapter 13, Applying Cross-Cutting Concerns*, we discussed the importance of reducing risk in your codebase, which is perhaps the most critical use case. Since security is the most vulnerable aspect of our software, it is essential to adopt a zero-trust mindset when it comes to this and take all necessary steps to prevent security vulnerabilities.

Moving onto the next chapter, we will dive into the power of the C# compiler, also known as Roslyn. With Roslyn, you get a whole new set of metadata to play with and new capabilities for metaprogramming.

Part 4:
Compiler Magic Using Roslyn

In this part, you will get a glimpse into the C# compiler's capabilities and the different extension points it provides through the .NET Compiler SDK. It dives into how the compiler has become an ecosystem and how you can do metaprogramming on a compile-time level rather than just the runtime. This part concludes the book with an overview of what the book has covered, thoughts on when to use what, and some closing words.

This part has the following chapters:

- *Chapter 15, Roslyn Compiler Extensions*
- *Chapter 16, Generating Code*
- *Chapter 17, Static Code Analysis*
- *Chapter 18, Caveats and Final Words*

15

Roslyn Compiler Extensions

Roslyn compiler extensions offer a powerful way to modify and extend the behavior of the C# compiler. With the Roslyn compiler, developers can write code that analyzes and modifies C# code at compile-time, opening new possibilities for code generation, code transformation, and optimization.

In this chapter, we will explore the technical setup of a Roslyn compiler extension project. The chapter itself is not focused on metaprogramming, but rather, on the technical setup for the two following chapters. We'll delve into the process of packaging a Roslyn compiler extension for reuse. We'll explore the different packaging options available, such as NuGet packages, and discuss best practices for making your extension easy to consume by other developers.

We will cover the following topics in this chapter:

- How to set up a project and its moving parts
- How to package your extension for reuse

By the end of this chapter, you will have a solid understanding of how to set up a Roslyn compiler extension project and package it for reuse. You'll be equipped with the knowledge and tools needed to start building powerful and flexible extensions that can significantly enhance the functionality of the C# compiler.

Technical requirements

The source code specific to the chapter can be found on GitHub, (`https://github.com/PacktPublishing/Metaprogramming-in-C-Sharp/tree/main/Chapter15`) and it builds on top of the `Fundamentals` code that is found on GitHub (`https://github.com/PacktPublishing/Metaprogramming-in-C-Sharp/tree/main/Fundamentals`).

How to set up a project and its moving parts

The C# compiler, powered by the Roslyn framework (`https://learn.microsoft.com/en-us/dotnet/csharp/roslyn-sdk/`), provides a mechanism to load and use custom extensions in the form of analyzer and code fix providers. These extensions can be packaged as NuGet packages or included as project references, and they are loaded into the compilation process to analyze or modify the source code being compiled.

When the C# compiler encounters a project that includes a reference to a Roslyn extension, it uses .NET's `AssemblyLoadContext` to load the extension's assembly into the compilation process. This allows the extension's code to be executed during the compilation process and participate in the analysis and transformation of the source code.

The Roslyn extensions are loaded into the compiler as analyzers, or source generators. Analyzers are responsible for examining the source code and reporting diagnostics, which are warnings, errors, or suggestions about potential issues in the code. Code fix providers provide suggestions or automated fixes to resolve the reported issues and are used by your code editor. Source generators, on the other hand, generate additional source code during compilation based on specific rules or templates.

The C# compiler scans the loaded assemblies for types that implement interfaces defined by the Roslyn framework for different extension points. It then creates instances of these types and invokes their methods to perform the analysis and transformation of the source code.

The loading of Roslyn extensions occurs dynamically at compile-time, allowing for flexibility in adding or removing extensions without modifying the compiler itself, a great example of how the open / closed principle can be applied.. This dynamic loading also enables the reuse of extensions across different projects and solutions, as they can be packaged and distributed as NuGet packages or shared as project references.

What can they do?

Roslyn compiler extensions provide a robust and flexible platform for metaprogramming in C#. With Roslyn, you have full access to the syntax tree and semantic model of the code being compiled, giving you deep insights into the structure, syntax, and semantics of the code. This allows you to perform sophisticated code analysis, generate code based on patterns or conventions, and apply transformations to the code to achieve various goals.

Here are some ways in which Roslyn compiler extensions can be powerful tools for metaprogramming:

- **Code generation**: Roslyn compiler extensions allow you to generate code during compilation. This can be used to automatically generate repetitive code patterns, such as data access layers, serialization code, or boilerplate code for repetitive tasks. You can also generate code based on conventions, configuration, or metadata, making it easy to create reusable and customizable code-generation tools.

- **Code analysis**: Roslyn compiler extensions enable you to perform custom code analysis during compilation. This can help you catch potential issues, enforce coding standards, and provide automated code review feedback. For example, you can use a Roslyn extension to identify and flag code smells, security vulnerabilities, or other code quality issues early in the development process, helping you maintain a high level of code quality in your projects.

- **Domain-Specific Language (DSL)**: Roslyn compiler extensions can be used to create DSLs that provide specialized syntax and semantics tailored to specific problem domains. This allows you to define your own DSL and use it in your projects to improve expressiveness and maintainability. With a Roslyn extension, you can create custom syntax, create custom semantic rules, and enforce domain-specific conventions, making it easier to work with complex domain-specific concepts.

- **Tooling and productivity**: Roslyn compiler extensions can be used to create custom tools and productivity features for development environments such as Visual Studio or VSCode. For example, you can create code refactoring tools, code completion providers, or diagnostics and quick fixes to streamline development workflows and catch common mistakes. With a Roslyn extension, you can create tailored tooling that fits your team's specific needs and development practices, enhancing productivity and code quality.

- **Experimentation and innovation**: Roslyn compiler extensions provide a platform for experimentation and innovation in the field of programming languages and compilers. You can use a Roslyn extension to prototype new language features, experiment with different programming paradigms, or implement novel programming techniques. This allows you to push the boundaries of what's possible with C# and explore new ideas in the field of software development.

Roslyn compiler extensions are a valuable tool in the toolbox of any C# developer interested in metaprogramming and pushing the boundaries of what's possible with C#.

Setting it up

In Visual Studio and other IDEs, you have project templates that allow you to create a Roslyn compiler extension easily. An extension is nothing more than a class library with the correct package references, depending on what type of extension you are creating.

Since we're not targeting a specific IDE, we'll be doing this from scratch with the .NET CLI and configuring the different files manually.

The first thing we'll need is a project folder. Since we're going to be reusing the extension project for the following chapters, let's create a folder called `Roslyn.Extensions`.

Within the `Roslyn.Extensions` folder, run the following:

```
dotnet new classlib
```

You should now get two files called `Roslyn.Extensions.csproj` and `Class1.cs`. Delete the `Class1.cs` file, as you won't be needing it.

Open the `Roslyn.Extensions.csproj` file in your editor. It should look something like the following:

```
<Project Sdk="Microsoft.NET.Sdk">
```

```
<PropertyGroup>
  <TargetFramework>net7.0</TargetFramework>
  <ImplicitUsings>enable</ImplicitUsings>
  <Nullable>enable</Nullable>
</PropertyGroup>

</Project>
```

You need to change this up a little bit for it to work with the compiler:

```
<Project Sdk="Microsoft.NET.Sdk">

  <PropertyGroup>
    <TargetFramework>netstandard2.0</TargetFramework>
    <LangVersion>11.0</LangVersion>
    <ImplicitUsings>enable</ImplicitUsings>
    <Nullable>enable</Nullable>
    <EnforceExtendedAnalyzerRules>true</EnforceExtendedAnalyzerRules>
  </PropertyGroup>

</Project>
```

The change of TargetFramework is necessary for it to work. The C# compiler won't be able to load it otherwise. However, you might still want to write your extension using the latest C# edition, so you set LangVersion to reflect the version of C# you want. You keep ImplicitUsings and Nullable if that is desirable. A project containing analyzers or source generators needs also to set EnforceExtendedAnalyzerRules to true.

For developing analyzers or source code generators, we're going to have to add a couple of NuGet package references. As mentioned earlier, the goal of this chapter is to set up a common package for the chapters following this one, so we'll be including what we want for those and a little bit more.

Within the <Project> tag of the Roslyn.Extensions.csproj file, after the initial <PropertyGroup> add the following <ItemGroup> block:

```
<ItemGroup>
    <PackageReference
      Include="Microsoft.CodeAnalysis.CSharp"
      Version="4.5.0" PrivateAssets="all" />
    <PackageReference
      Include="Microsoft.CodeAnalysis.Analyzers"
      Version="3.3.4" PrivateAssets="all" />
    <PackageReference
      Include="Microsoft.CodeAnalysis.CSharp.CodeStyle"
      Version="4.5.0" PrivateAssets="all"/>
```

```
    <PackageReference
      Include="Microsoft.CodeAnalysis.NetAnalyzers"
      Version="7.0.1" PrivateAssets="all"/>
    <PackageReference Include="StyleCop.Analyzers"
      Version="1.1.118" PrivateAssets="all"/>
  </ItemGroup>
```

The first three packages are for the development of analyzers and source code generators. While the next two packages are analyzers, we want to be used to making sure our code adheres to standards.

> **Important note**
> The `PrivateAssets` attribute used in the packages is for dependencies for the project they're added to, and anyone referencing this will not inherit these dependencies directly. This is important for when we package this project as a NuGet package.

If you want all the package references to be private to this package, you can do a neat little MSBuild trick by adding the following `ItemGroup` code:

```
<ItemGroup>
    <PackageReference Update="@(PackageReference)"
      PrivateAssets="All" />
</ItemGroup>
```

By doing that, you don't have to have the `PrivateAssets="All"` attribute for all your references.

Depending on the version of your .NET installation, the version numbers of referenced packages might be different. You can read more about which version is right for you here: `https://github.com/dotnet/roslyn/blob/main/docs/wiki/NuGet-packages.md`.

Adding common rules

One of the great things about how the .NET compiler and the underlying MSBuild engine that handles all the building works is that you can have a project with all your rules for how you want things. Every project that references it will then inherit this.

EditorConfig (`https://editorconfig.org`) is one of these items that can be reused among projects. Most IDEs and code editors out there honor the configuration of EditorConfig, which is great, because you can have a team using all kinds of editors, and they all adhere to the same settings.

At the root of a repository, you can place a file called `.editorconfig`, which contains the common setup of rules that apply to every file within your project. The rules can be anything from formatting, tabs versus spaces, indentation levels, and specific rules picked up by compilers such as the C# compiler.

This is great to get consistency in your codebase, avoid potential problems, and increase the maintainability of the source code. With .NET, we can go one further by packaging it in a project and making it so that every project that references it will get these rules. The benefit of this is that you can then reuse it outside the realms of your repository, which we'll come back to a little bit later in this chapter.

Let's create a file called `.globalconfig` in the `Roslyn.Extensions` folder. Add the following code to it:

```
is_global = true
end_of_line = lf
indent_style = space
indent_size = 4
charset = utf-8
```

This configuration sets `is_global` to `true` to indicate it should be a global settings file. It then goes on to specify how the end of the line is, the indentation style, and size, and then the charset used.

You can then go on and specify different rules specific to .NET. There are quite a few settings and rules you can configure, and I recommend reading more about it all here: `https://learn.microsoft.com/en-us/dotnet/fundamentals/code-analysis/code-style-rule-options`.

> **Important note**
>
> In the GitHub repository for this book, you'll find a more complete `.globalconfig` file with a lot of .NET and C#-specific rules specified. Be aware that the rules put in place are a reflection of how I personally like the code to be.

Since you added a dependency to `StyleCop`, we can also configure global options for it. Add a file called `stylecop.json` in the `Roslyn.Extensions` folder and add the following code to it:

```
{
    "$schema": "https://raw.githubusercontent.com/DotNetAnalyzers/
    StyleCopAnalyzers/master/StyleCop.Analyzers/StyleCop.Analyzers/
    Settings/stylecop.schema.json",
    "settings": {
        "indentation": {
            "useTabs": false,
            "indentationSize": 4,
            "tabSize": 4
        },
        "orderingRules": {
            "systemUsingDirectivesFirst": true,
            "usingDirectivesPlacement": "outsideNamespace",
            "blankLinesBetweenUsingGroups": "omit"
        }
```

```
        }
    }
```

As you can see, it duplicates the indentation style, which is recommended. It then goes on to specify specific rules for how you want the code to look. In this case, it specifies that the `using` directives should be sorted with those prefixed with `System` first. Then, it says that the using directives should be outside the namespace blocks and then omit any blank lines between using groups. These and more options can be found here: `https://github.com/DotNetAnalyzers/StyleCopAnalyzers/blob/master/documentation/Configuration.md`.

Common project settings

If you have a set of configuration properties you want for all your projects, you can create a common `.props` file that will automatically be picked up and used. All you need is a file called the same as the project with a `.props` extension. In our case, the project name is `Roslyn.Extensions`, so the file needed would be called `Roslyn.Extensions.props`.

A props file is basically just an MSBuild project file as the `.csproj` file. MSBuild has a convention of automatically importing this file from a common extension project like this into consumers of the extension package.

Within a common project settings file, you can do more than just add properties. You can include files, add package references, or do anything that you can do in a regular `.csproj` file. That is super powerful when you want to apply and enforce common settings.

Add a file called `Roslyn.Extensions.props` to the `Roslyn.Extensions` project and put the following code into it:

```
<Project>
    <PropertyGroup>
        <!-- Compiler settings -->
        <Nullable>enable</Nullable>
        <TreatWarningsAsErrors>True</TreatWarningsAsErrors>
        <MSBuildTreatWarningsAsErrors>true
            </MSBuildTreatWarningsAsErrors>

        <!-- Code Analysis -->
        <CodeAnalysisTreatWarningsAsErrors>True
            </CodeAnalysisTreatWarningsAsErrors>
        <RunAnalyzersDuringBuild>True
            </RunAnalyzersDuringBuild>
        <RunAnalyzersDuringLiveAnalysis>True
            </RunAnalyzersDuringLiveAnalysis>
        <RunAnalyzers>True</RunAnalyzers>
```

```
        <AnalysisMode>AllEnabledByDefault</AnalysisMode>

        <!-- Code Style -->
        <StyleCopTreatErrorsAsWarnings>false
            </StyleCopTreatErrorsAsWarnings>
        <EnforceCodeStyleInBuild>true
            </EnforceCodeStyleInBuild>
    </PropertyGroup>
</Project>
```

The properties added configure first a couple of standard C# compiler settings. It enables `Nullable` and then tells the compiler to be strict and treat any warnings as errors. Then, it tells the MSBuild engine to do the same.

Since we included code analysis, the next section configures it to force the compiler to run analyzers during the build and enable them all.

Lastly, it sets up the style cop analyzers to specifically not treat errors as warnings and enforces it during build.

The last thing you're going to need is to make sure the `.globalconfig` file and `stylecop.json` file get used in any projects referencing this one. This is done by adding `ItemGroup` after `PropertyGroup` in the `Roslyn.Extensions.props` file, and it looks like this:

```
<ItemGroup>
    <GlobalAnalyzerConfigFiles
        Include="$(MSBuildThisFileDirectory).globalconfig"/>
    <AdditionalFiles
        Include="$(MSBuildThisFileDirectory)stylecop.json"
        Link="stylecop.json" />
</ItemGroup>
```

This lets the compiler know about the two files for configuring static code analysis and code styles. It uses a variable called `MSBuildThisFileDirectory`, which is a well-known MSBuild variable that gets set to the folder of the file it is processing. Omitting this would make it look for this file relative to the current directory, which would be different for every project referencing this common project.

To this point, all you've done is wrap up common things in a common project that can, within a repository, be referenced and automatically configure all projects referencing it. Sometimes, you want to go beyond the boundaries of a single repository and publish the common project as a package that can then be reused by other projects and get the same benefits.

How to package your extension for reuse

One of the key advantages of Roslyn compiler extensions is their potential for reuse across different projects and solutions. Once you have developed a Roslyn extension, you can package it for reuse and share it with other developers or teams, providing a number of benefits and advantages:

- **Code consistency**: Reusing Roslyn extensions can help enforce consistent coding practices across different projects and solutions. You can create Roslyn extensions that encapsulate coding standards, conventions, or best practices, and share them across your organization. This ensures that all projects adhere to the same coding guidelines, reducing inconsistencies and improving code quality.

- **Productivity**: Reusing Roslyn extensions can enhance developer productivity by automating repetitive tasks and providing productivity features. For example, you can create Roslyn extensions that generate boilerplate code, automate code refactoring, or provide custom code completion providers. By reusing such extensions, you can save time and effort, and improve overall development productivity.

- **Maintainability**: Reusing Roslyn extensions can improve code maintainability by encapsulating complex logic or code generation patterns. You can create Roslyn extensions that encapsulate DSLs, custom syntax, or semantic rules, and share them across projects. This makes it easier to maintain and update the codebase, as changes can be made in a central location and propagated to all projects using the shared extension.

- **Extensibility**: Reusing Roslyn extensions can make your codebase more extensible by providing hooks or extension points for other developers. You can create Roslyn extensions that provide extensibility points, such as custom code generation templates or code analysis rules, which can be extended or customized by other developers as needed. This promotes collaboration and enables other teams or developers to extend the functionality of your codebase.

- **Innovation**: Reusing Roslyn extensions can foster innovation by sharing new ideas, techniques, or approaches with the community. If you have developed a novel or innovative Roslyn extension, sharing it with the community can encourage others to build upon your work, leading to new discoveries, solutions, or techniques. This contributes to the growth and advancement of the Roslyn ecosystem, benefiting the entire community.

By sharing and reusing Roslyn extensions, you can improve code quality, enhance productivity, and foster collaboration, contributing to a more robust and vibrant Roslyn ecosystem.

Roslyn extensions can be a powerful tool for metaprogramming, which involves writing code that generates or manipulates other code. By creating and packaging Roslyn extensions, you can leverage metaprogramming techniques to automate repetitive tasks, enforce coding standards, or apply compliance rules such as **General Data Protection Regulation (GDPR)** across different projects and solutions.

For example, consider a scenario where you have multiple projects that need to comply with GDPR by ensuring that certain data handling practices are followed consistently. Instead of manually checking and updating each project's codebase, you can create a Roslyn extension that encapsulates the compliance rules and distributes them across the projects. This way, you can ensure that the same compliance rules are applied uniformly in all projects, saving time and effort and reducing the risk of human error.

Furthermore, Roslyn extensions can also provide powerful metaprogramming capabilities to generate code or refactor existing code based on specific requirements. For instance, you can create a Roslyn extension that generates code snippets for common patterns or templates, such as implementing design patterns, handling common scenarios, or generating boilerplate code. By packaging and sharing this extension across projects, you can ensure that the generated code adheres to your organization's coding standards or follows specific patterns, promoting consistency and maintainability.

Common package properties

All NuGet packages can have additional metadata. This metadata is very useful when published to a NuGet package repository such as the official one at `https://nuget.org`. This metadata is typically then displayed on the information page of a package. The metadata you add contains information about the authors, copyright notices, where the project is located, and more.

Let's add all the properties for the metadata. Open the `Roslyn.Extensions.csproj` file and add the following code, typically after the first `<PropertyGroup>` instance within the `<Project>` tag:

```
<PropertyGroup>
  <Copyright>Packt Publishing</Copyright>
  <Authors>all contributors</Authors>
  <RepositoryUrl>https://github.com/PacktPublishing/Metaprogramming-
     in-C-Sharp</RepositoryUrl>
  <RepositoryType>git</RepositoryType>
  <PublishRepositoryUrl>true</PublishRepositoryUrl>
  <PackageLicenseExpression>MIT</PackageLicenseExpression>
  <PackageProjectUrl>https://github.com/PacktPublishing/
     Metaprogramming-in-C-Sharp</PackageProjectUrl>
  <PackageIcon>logo.png</PackageIcon>
  <PackageReadmeFile>README.md</PackageReadmeFile>
</PropertyGroup>
```

Obviously, you can set all these properties to what is right for your project. It includes also `logo.png` and a `README.md` file. If you don't have these, you can just take these out. Having a `README.md` file is, however, recommended when publishing to a package repository. Putting information into this file about how to use the package and what it is for would then be very helpful for the consumer of the package.

The metadata only points to the `logo.png` file and `README.md` file, but they have to be explicitly added for them to be part of the package. Add the following `ItemGroup` text after the `PropertyGroup` metadata:

```
<ItemGroup>
    <None Include="$(MSBuildThisFileDirectory)logo.png"
      Pack="true" Visible="false" PackagePath="" />
    <Content Include="$(MSBuildThisFileDirectory)README.md"
      PackagePath="/" />
</ItemGroup>
```

> **Important note**
>
> Notice the use of the `PackagePath` attribute. This instructs the NuGet packager which target path to put the file into. For the README.md file, it will be put at the root of the package.

For the common code properties, code analysis, and code style rules you added to the project earlier, they also need to be explicitly added to the package for them to work. Add another `ItemGroup` block for these files:

```
<ItemGroup>
    <Content Include=".globalconfig" PackagePath="build\" />
    <Content Include="stylecop.json" PackagePath="build\" />
    <Content Include="Roslyn.Extensions.props"
      PackagePath="build\" />
</ItemGroup>
```

For the `Roslyn.Extensions.props` file to work when used as a package reference, it needs to sit inside a folder called `build` within the package. Since we referred to the common files with a path prefixed with the `MSBuildThisFileDirectory` MSBuild variable, it means that the common files also have to be in the `build` path within the package.

Analyzer

The last piece of the puzzle is for the analyzer itself. For it to work, it needs to be within a specific part of the NuGet package, in a directory called `analyzers/dotnet/cs`.

Add another `ItemGroup` block to the `Roslyn.Extensions.csproj` file:

```
<ItemGroup>
    <None Include="$(OutputPath)\$(AssemblyName).dll"
            Pack="true"
            PackagePath="analyzers/dotnet/cs"
            Visible="false" />
</ItemGroup>
```

`ItemGroup` adds the DLL file of the project based on `OutputPath`, which will vary depending on whether you're building a debug or release version. Typically, for a release version, it would be `bin/Release/netstandard2.0` and then the `AssemblyName` variable reflects the output assembly name, which, in our case, would be `Roslyn.Extensions`.

Running `dotnet pack -c release` in a terminal from the root of the `Roslyn.Extensions` project should now create a package with all the artifacts in place.

The package will be output to the `bin/release` folder and called `Roslyn.Extensions.1.0.0.nupkg`.

We can investigate the content of the package to see that everything we wanted it to include is included and in the correct locations. The NuGet package is nothing more than a compressed ZIP file. That means we can open it with your favorite ZIP utility and see whether the content is as expected.

The content should be something like the following:

Figure 15.1 – Checking package content

This package would now be ready to be published to a centralized package manager such as NuGet. You can read more about how to package NuGet packages at Microsoft's official documentation for this (`https://learn.microsoft.com/en-us/nuget/nuget-org/publish-a-package`).

That is pretty much it. You've now configured everything for a Roslyn extension and also put in common properties you want for every project referencing the package you have just created.

Summary

In this chapter, we explored the technical setup of a Roslyn compiler extension project, covering the key moving parts of a Roslyn compiler extension. We discussed the various ways in which a Roslyn compiler extension can modify C# code.

We also delved into the process of packaging a Roslyn compiler extension for reuse, exploring the different packaging options available and discussing best practices for making your extension easy to consume by other developers.

In the next chapter, we will focus on generating code with Roslyn compiler extensions. We'll explore techniques for generating new code based on existing code, and we'll discuss best practices for ensuring that the generated code is of high quality and conforms to established conventions and standards. With the knowledge gained in this chapter and the next, you'll be well on your way to building powerful and flexible Roslyn compiler extensions that can significantly enhance the functionality of the C# compiler.

16
Generating Code

So far in the book, we've looked at how powerful metaprogramming can be in .NET at runtime. Doing everything at runtime has the benefit of the flexibility to adapt to things that occur at runtime. The downside of doing this at runtime is that it has a performance impact. This is where the C# Roslyn compiler really shines. We had the capability to generate code in the past with commercial products such as PostSharp (https://www.postsharp.net/) or **Intermediate Language** (**IL**) weaving, using projects such as Fody (https://github.com/Fody/Fody) But with Roslyn, code generation has truly been democratized and made easy for anyone to do.

Personally, I've worked with all the techniques throughout the years, and finally, with Roslyn, I can realize a lot of the metaprogramming I like to do without sacrificing performance. And I can do so in a more consistent way than before.

The C# Roslyn compiler enables this by allowing developers to be part of its compilation pipeline through a set of APIs. With the APIs, we can investigate the code that's there and reason about it and then generate new code, which will then be compiled and incorporated into the final binary.

In this chapter, we'll explore how to leverage Roslyn compiler extensions for generating code, taking a deep dive into the specifics of generating code at compile time. We'll learn how to examine syntax trees and generate additional code, and even look at how to use Roslyn to generate text reports from your code via metadata.

We will cover the following topics:

- Generating additional code for the Roslyn compiler
- (Ab)using the compiler to generate not just C# code
- Improving the developer experience

By the end of this chapter, you'll have a strong grasp of how to use Roslyn to generate code at compile time, and you'll have a toolkit of techniques and best practices for implementing metaprogramming techniques in C# that leverage the power of the Roslyn compiler platform. So, let's dive in!

Technical requirements

The source code specific to this chapter can be found on GitHub (`https://github.com/PacktPublishing/Metaprogramming-in-C-Sharp/tree/main/Chapter16`) and builds on top of the `Fundamentals` code, which can also be found on GitHub (`https://github.com/PacktPublishing/Metaprogramming-in-C-Sharp/tree/main/Fundamentals`).

Generating additional code for the Roslyn compiler

One of the most powerful capabilities of the Roslyn compiler platform is the ability to generate additional code at compile time. This means that we can create new C# code during the compilation process and have it compiled alongside the rest of our code.

We will look into how you can leverage Roslyn to generate additional code for the compiler. This is super helpful and can help increase your and your team's productivity by removing the need for repetitive tasks. Since you're working inside the compiler, you'll have to work with the language the compiler understands and how it represents code – **Abstract Syntax Trees (ASTs)**.

ASTs

An **AST** is a data structure used to represent the structure of source code. You can compare it to what you already find in the .NET Expression APIs, as we saw in *Chapter 7, Reasoning about Expressions*. It is a hierarchy consisting of nodes that represent the code elements found in the language, such as classes, methods, fields, and properties. The outcome from the compiler from the AST is in its final stage of the binary IL code. While Expressions do this at runtime and are mutable at runtime, ASTs are static when entering the final stage of the compiler pipeline. However, until the final stage, the AST can be reasoned about and changed.

The AST is constructed by parsing the source code, interpreting all the keywords and variables, and breaking it down into nodes, which then sit together in a tree-like structure. ASTs are used as an intermediate representation of code within compilers or code analysis tools. Once the source code has been converted into an AST, it becomes much easier to analyze and manipulate the code. For example, a tool might use an AST to identify potential bugs or transform the code in some way.

One of the key benefits of Roslyn is its extensibility. Because Roslyn is open source and provides a rich set of APIs for working with the AST, developers can easily create their own code analysis tools that leverage the compiler's AST. For example, a developer might create a tool that analyzes code for security vulnerabilities, or a tool that automatically generates documentation for a code base.

To make it easy for developers to extend Roslyn, the platform provides a number of extensibility points, such as the following:

- **Syntax trees**: Developers can create their own syntax trees to represent code, and use them with the Roslyn APIs

- **Syntax rewriters**: Developers can create syntax rewriters that transform the AST in various ways, such as renaming variables or extracting methods

- **Diagnostics**: Developers can create their own diagnostics that identify issues with code, such as potential bugs or style violations

- **Code fix providers**: Developers can create code fix providers that automatically fix any issues identified by diagnostics

With these extensibility points, Roslyn makes it easy for developers to create extensions that can improve the quality of the code written or improve productivity by automatically generating plumbing code.

Compiler theory and how ASTs work is a big topic on its own, something that is outside the scope of this book. Instead, let's get our hands dirty and get a glimpse of what can be done.

Application metrics

An important aspect of running systems in production is observability. By observability, I mean the ability to observe important aspects of an application. Logging is one of these aspects, where you instrument your code with log messages that get written and captured by a log search indexer. Logging can be very verbose, so it is not ideal for simple measurement values, such as counters, gauges, or histograms.

With the release of .NET 6, Microsoft introduced a namespace called `System.Diagnostics.Metrics`. The classes in this new namespace are perfect for when you want to observe values that change over time. In addition to this, there are packages out there that support **OpenTelemetry** (`https://opentelemetry.io`), enabling you to capture the different values in popular collectors such as Prometheus, Azure AppInsight, and more. For our sample, we will just be using the console viewer.

With how Microsoft has built support for metrics, it's very easy to use while it lacks the nice and structured approach Microsoft built for logging. To see the issue, we'll start by using the metrics as intended from the out-of-the-box experience and then improve on it. Let's get started!

1. Let's start by creating a new project for the chapter. You should create this new project next to the `Fundamentals` project you have been using throughout the book and also the `Roslyn.Extensions` project that was established in *Chapter 15, Roslyn Compiler Extensions*.

    Create a folder called `Chapter16`, change into this folder on your command line, and create a new web project:

    ```
    dotnet new web
    ```

2. You should know the basics of a web project. Let's change it so that we can use controllers. Change the `Program.cs` file to look like the following:

    ```
    var builder = WebApplication.CreateBuilder(args);
    builder.Services.AddControllers();

    var app = builder.Build();
    ```

```
app.UseRouting();
app.MapControllers();
app.Run();
```

This code adds the controllers to `builder.Services` and then maps all the controllers in your application before running the app.

3. Since the goal is to capture metrics, you're going to need what is called a `Meter`, which is used for the values you want to track. You can have multiple `Meter` classes for different areas of your system if you want, but it is common to have one per application. Add a file called `Metrics.cs` and make it look like the following:

```
using System.Diagnostics.Metrics;

namespace Chapter16;

public static class Metrics
{
    public static readonly Meter Meter =
        new("Chapter16");
}
```

The code pulls in the `System.Diagnostics.Metrics` namespace and then exposes a global `Meter` called `Chapter16`. This can then be used by any code in the application.

4. You now want to add something that creates values within the meter. Add a file called `EmployeesController.cs` and make it look like the following:

```
using Microsoft.AspNetCore.Mvc;

namespace Chapter16;

[Route("/api/employees")]
public class EmployeesController : Controller
{
    [HttpGet]
    public IActionResult Register()
    {
        return Ok();
    }
}
```

The code introduces a web API controller with a single action that lives in the `/api/employees` route. The action only returns `Ok()` – an HTTP 200 status.

> **Important note**
>
> For this chapter, we're not focused on the functionality of what we're building but rather focused on the technical problem we're trying to solve. For this reason, we also make it accept an HTTP GET. Normally, it would be an HTTP POST and also include a payload with details about the employee to register.

5. Let's instrument the code with a counter for counting the number of registered employees. To do this, you'll need to add a couple of using statements at the top of the EmployeeController. cs file:

```
using System.Diagnostics;
using System.Diagnostics.Metrics;
```

6. Now you can add a counter in the EmployeesController class. Add the following at the top of the class:

```
static Counter<int> _registeredEmployees =
    Metrics.Meter.CreateCounter<int>("Registered
    Employees", "# of registered employees");
```

This code introduces a counter that is created using the global meter. It is created statically so that we don't create multiple instances of the same counter in the same application.

7. To use the counter, change the Register() method to look like the following:

```
[HttpGet]
public IActionResult Register()
{
    var now = DateTimeOffset.UtcNow;
    var tags = new TagList(new ReadOnlySpan
        <KeyValuePair<string, object?>>(new
            KeyValuePair<string, object?>[]
    {
        new("Year", now.Year),
        new("Month", now.Month),
        new("Day", now.Day),
    }));

    _registeredEmployees.Add(1, tags);

    return Ok();
}
```

The code uses the _registeredEmployees counter by calling the Add() method on it. It also passes along tags, which it sets up before calling Add(). Tags are a way to group values being added. The counter, from a top level, will then aggregate all values tagged, while you can monitor each individual tagged value on its own. This is super helpful for breaking down the metrics you want to monitor. The `Register()` method breaks down the values by year, month, and day.

> **Important note**
>
> Tag values are `object`. You could pass it a `DateOnly` instance instead, but this illustrates the use of multiple tags.

8. With the first counter in place, it is time to see what this actually looks like. To do so, you need to install a tool called `dotnet-counters`. This is done by running the following in your terminal:

    ```
    dotnet tool install --global dotnet-counters
    ```

9. Then. you can start your application by running this:

    ```
    dotnet run
    ```

    You should see an output similar to the following:

    ```
    Building...
    info: Microsoft.Hosting.Lifetime[14]
          Now listening on: http://localhost:5000
    info: Microsoft.Hosting.Lifetime[0]
          Application started. Press Ctrl+C to shut down.
    info: Microsoft.Hosting.Lifetime[0]
          Hosting environment: Development
    info: Microsoft.Hosting.Lifetime[0]
          Content root path: /Users/einari/Projects/Metaprogramming-
    in-C/Chapter16
    ```

10. In another terminal, you can start the metrics monitor by running the following:

    ```
    dotnet counters monitor --name Chapter16 --counters
    Chapter16
    ```

    You should then see something like the following:

    ```
    Press p to pause, r to resume, q to quit.
        Status: Running
    ```

    Since there haven't been any requests yet to the API endpoint, the value won't show up yet. Keep the monitor running and open a browser and navigate to the endpoint (for example, `http://localhost:5000/api/employees`); you should then see something like the following:

    ```
    Press p to pause, r to resume, q to quit.
        Status: Running

    [Chapter16]
    ```

```
RegisteredEmployees (# of registered employees / 1
   sec)
      Day=1,Month=5,Year=2023    0
```

The value will be sampled once per second. If you hit your browser multiple times, you should see 0 at the end of the line increase and then fall back to 0. This is expected as it just shows the current measurements and not an aggregate over time.

Even though the metrics API in .NET is simple and easy to use, it can quite easily become very verbose, especially when you have tags you want to associate.

Improving the developer experience

In your business code, it looks strange to have the setup code for metrics on every method. It is also very verbose and cumbersome. Imagine an evolved application with a lot of metrics you want to collect; it kinda becomes messy. You can obviously clean this up by encapsulating the metrics, either with methods in the classes that need metrics or pulled out into their own classes.

However, I quite like the approach Microsoft has to logs, as we saw in *Chapter 14, Aspect-Oriented Programming*. For its approach to logging, it relies on a code generator that runs at compile time and puts in code that gets included in the finished binary.

Let's mimic this and create an improved developer experience:

1. Within the Fundamentals project, create a folder called Metrics. In this folder, add a file called CounterAttribute.cs and make it look like the following:

```
namespace Fundamentals.Metrics;

[AttributeUsage(AttributeTargets.Method)]
public sealed class CounterAttribute<T> : Attribute
{
    public CounterAttribute(string name, string
        description)
    {
        Name = name;
        Description = description;
    }

    public string Name { get; }

    public string Description { get; }
}
```

This code introduces an attribute that represents a counter. Counters can have a name and description associated with them. It is a generic attribute, allowing you to specify the type used for the counter.

2.   In the `Metrics` folder in the `Fundamentals` project, add a file called `GlobalMetrics.`
     `cs` and make it look like the following:

```
using System.Diagnostics.Metrics;

namespace Fundamentals.Metrics;

public static class GlobalMetrics
{
    public static Meter Meter = new("Global");
}
```

3.   This introduces a globally accessible `Meter` instance, which will make it predictable for the
     code generator you'll be building, as it will need access to this. However, it defaults to a meter
     called `Global`, which we want to override. Open the `Program.cs` file within `Chapter16`
     and add the following at the top of the file after the `using` statements:

```
GlobalMetrics.Meter = new Meter("Chapter16");
```

The goal of this chapter is to provide a simpler way of doing metrics. This will be done through
the technique of creating a partial class providing method signatures without implementations.
The source code generator will create an implementation of the partial class and provide
implementations for each of the methods.

4.   Let's add the metrics file for `EmployeesController`. Add a file called `Employees`
     `ControllerMetrics.cs` and add the following to it:

```
using System.Diagnostics.Metrics;
using Fundamentals.Metrics;

namespace Chapter16;

public static partial class EmployeesControllerMetrics
{
    [Counter<int>("RegisteredEmployees", "# of
        registered employees")]
    public static partial void
        RegisteredEmployees(DateOnly date);
}
```

The code sets up a static partial class, which is important as this will be a criterion for finding
which classes to generate source code for. All counters are then represented as methods with
a given name and a `[Counter]` attribute with details. Every parameter on the method will
be used as a tag.

You've now prepared the basics needed for the source code generator to be able to work.

Setting up the code template

The code generator will generate the code that will implement partial classes. To do this, you'll use a template file that represents the source code to generate. As a template language, you're going to be using something called **Handlebars** (https://handlebarsjs.com). There is a .NET implementation of this.

Open the `Roslyn.Extensions.csproj` file in the `Roslyn.Extensions` folder and add the following package reference in an `ItemGroup` with the other package references:

```
<PackageReference Include="handlebars.net" Version="2.1.4"
  GeneratePathProperty="true" PrivateAssets="all" />
```

The `PrivateAssets="all"` attribute instructs it to be a reference only for this project and only be used with the extension itself, meaning that any assemblies from `Handlebars` will not be included in any projects referencing this project. In addition, you have to set `GeneratePathProperty="true"`. This will create a variable specific to the package and allow us to instruct which specific assembly of `Handlebars` to use; otherwise, the compiler will say `FileNotFoundError`.

To specify the correct assembly, add the following to `Roslyn.Extensions.csproj` in the `Roslyn.Extensions` folder at the end of the file, within the `Project` tag:

```
<PropertyGroup>
    <GetTargetPathDependsOn>$(GetTargetPathDependsOn);
        GetDependencyTargetPaths</GetTargetPathDependsOn>
</PropertyGroup>

<Target Name="GetDependencyTargetPaths">
    <ItemGroup>
        <TargetPathWithTargetPlatformMoniker
        Include="$(PKGHandlebars_Net)\lib\netstandard2.0\
        Handlebars.dll" IncludeRuntimeDependency="false" />
    </ItemGroup>
</Target>
```

With `Handlebars` properly installed, you're ready to create the template you need for generating the code. Before you create the template, you'll need to set up all the types of data you'll pass to the template.

In the `Roslyn.Extensions` folder, create a folder called `Metrics`. Add a file called `MetricsTemplateData.cs` and add the following to it:

```
namespace Roslyn.Extensions.Metrics;

public class MetricsTemplateData
{
    public string Namespace { get; set; } = string.Empty;
```

```
    public string ClassName { get; set; } = string.Empty;

    public IEnumerable<CounterTemplateData> Counters { get;
        set; } = Enumerable.Empty<CounterTemplateData>();
}
```

`MetricsTemplateData` will be the root object being passed to the template. It contains the namespace for the generated code and then the class name for the class that will be generated. It then goes on to hold a collection of all the counters it will generate for.

For the counter definitions, add a file called `CounterTemplateData.cs` and add the following to it:

```
namespace Roslyn.Extensions.Metrics;

public class CounterTemplateData
{
    public string Type { get; set; } = string.Empty;

    public string MethodName { get; set; } = string.Empty;

    public string Name { get; set; } = string.Empty;

    public string Description { get; set; } = string.Empty;

    public IEnumerable<CounterTagTemplateData> Tags { get;
        set; } = Enumerable.Empty<CounterTagTemplateData>();
}
```

The `CounterTemplateData` type holds information about the type of counter, the method name representing it, the name of the counter, and a description to be used with the counter. Lastly, it holds all the tags associated with the counter when called.

For the tag definition, add a file called `CounterTagTemplateData.cs` and make it look like the following:

```
namespace Roslyn.Extensions.Metrics;

public class CounterTagTemplateData
{
    public string Type { get; set; } = string.Empty;

    public string Name { get; set; } = string.Empty;
}
```

The tag contains a type, which will be reflected in the signature of the method being called and then the name.

With the object definitions for the parameters for the template, it's time to add the template.

In the `Roslyn.Extensions` folder, create a folder called `Templates`, and within the `Templates` folder, add a file called `Metrics.hbs` and make it look like the following:

```
using System.Diagnostics;
using System.Diagnostics.Metrics;
using Fundamentals.Metrics;

namespace {{Namespace}};

#nullable enable

public static partial class {{ClassName}}
{
    {{#Counters}}
    static readonly Counter<{{Type}}> {{MethodName}}Metric
        = GlobalMetrics.Meter.CreateCounter<{{Type}}>
            ("{{Name}}", "{{Description}}");
    {{/Counters}}

    {{#Counters}}
    public static partial void {{MethodName}}({{#Tags}}
        {{Type}} {{Name}}{{#unless @last}}, {{/unless}}
            {{/Tags}})
    {
        var tags = new TagList(new ReadOnlySpan
            <KeyValuePair<string, object?>>(new KeyValuePair
                <string, object?>[]
        {
            {{#Tags}}
            new("{{Name}}", {{name}}){{#unless @last}},
                {{/unless}}
            {{/Tags}}
        }));

        {{MethodName}}Metric.Add(1, tags);
    }
    {{/Counters}}
}
```

Within the template, there is data context. The top-level item will be the `MetricsTemplateData` instance. This is where the `{{Namespace}}` and `{{ClassName}}` values are inserted. The use of

{ { } } with text represents values that can be replaced, and the text itself is then a property that exists in the current context it's in. When the value in the quotes starts with a # symbol, it uses a function to resolve it. Handlebars have some automatic magic and recognize enumerables, such as Counters. Handlebars will loop through these and anything within its scope will be output for each instance. The template uses these techniques throughout to replace all the values found in the objects passed to it.

The end result for EmployeesControllerMetrics will end up rendered like the following:

```
using System.Diagnostics;
using System.Diagnostics.Metrics;
using Fundamentals.Metrics;

namespace Chapter16;

#nullable enable

public static partial class EmployeesControllerMetrics
{
    static readonly Counter<int> RegisteredEmployeesMetric
      = GlobalMetrics.Meter.CreateCounter<int>
      ("RegisteredEmployees", "# of registered employees");

    public static partial void RegisteredEmployees(DateOnly
      date)
    {
        var tags = new TagList(new ReadOnlySpan
        <KeyValuePair<string, object?>>(new KeyValuePair
        <string, object?>[]
        {
            new("date", date)
        }));

        RegisteredEmployeesMetric.Add(1, tags);
    }
}
```

With the template in place, we need a way to programmatically access it in the code generator. To enable that, you want to embed any template files into the assembly at compile time.

Open Roslyn.Extensions.csproj and add an ItemGroup within the Project tag that looks like the following:

```
<ItemGroup>
    <EmbeddedResource Include="$(MSBuildThisFileDirectory)
    /Templates/**/*.hbs" />
</ItemGroup>
```

The `EmbeddedResource` tag instructs the compiler to include all `hbs` files within the `Templates` folder and make them embedded resources of the assembly.

Embedded resources are part of the assembly and are referred to as resources. They can be accessed directly on the assembly they belong to.

Let's create a helper class to get access to the template and future templates you'll be adding. In the `Templates` folder of the `Roslyn.Extensions` project, add a file called `TemplateTypes.cs`. Make it look like the following:

```
using HandlebarsDotNet;

namespace Roslyn.Extensions.Templates;

public static class TemplateTypes
{
    public static readonly HandlebarsTemplate<object,
      object> Metrics = Handlebars.Compile
        (GetTemplate("Metrics"));

    static string GetTemplate(string name)
    {
        var rootType = typeof(TemplateTypes);
        var stream = rootType.Assembly.GetManifest
        ResourceStream($"{rootType.Namespace}.{name}.hbs");
        if (stream != default)
        {
            using var reader = new StreamReader(stream);
            return reader.ReadToEnd();
        }

        return string.Empty;
    }
}
```

The code introduces a private method called `GetTemplate()` on the `TemplateTypes` class. It leverages `GetManifestResourceStream()` on the assembly instance. The compiler will by convention make namespaces of the folder and any subfolder of the embedded resource. Accessing the resources will then be like accessing types in it. Since the template sits in the `Templates` folder, it will be in the same folder and then the same namespace as the `TemplateTypes` class. This is therefore used as the prefix for the name of the template before the name of the template. The code then uses a `StreamReader` to read the resource stream to the end, giving you a string holding the template.

At the top of the `TemplateTypes` class sits a property representing the `Metrics` template.

Now we have the template and code for accessing it, you can move on to creating the code generator.

Building the source code generator

In order for the code generator to generate code only for classes that match the criteria, you need a syntax receiver that gets called on every node from the source code being compiled.

Add a file called `MetricsSyntaxReceiver.cs` in the `Metrics` folder within the `Roslyn.Extensions` project. Add the following code to it:

```
using Microsoft.CodeAnalysis;
using Microsoft.CodeAnalysis.CSharp;
using Microsoft.CodeAnalysis.CSharp.Syntax;

namespace Roslyn.Extensions.Metrics;

public class MetricsSyntaxReceiver : ISyntaxReceiver
{
    readonly List<ClassDeclarationSyntax> _candidates =
      new();

    internal IEnumerable<ClassDeclarationSyntax> Candidates
      => _candidates;

    public void OnVisitSyntaxNode(SyntaxNode syntaxNode)
    {
        if (syntaxNode is not ClassDeclarationSyntax
          classSyntax) return;

        if (classSyntax.Modifiers.Any(modifier =>
          modifier.IsKind(SyntaxKind.PartialKeyword)) &&
            classSyntax.Modifiers.Any(modifier =>
              modifier.IsKind(SyntaxKind.StaticKeyword)))
        {
            if (classSyntax.Members.Any(member =>
              member.IsKind(SyntaxKind.MethodDeclaration) &&
                member.Modifiers.Any(modifier =>
                  modifier.IsKind
                    (SyntaxKind.PartialKeyword)) &&
                member.Modifiers.Any(modifier => modifier
                  .IsKind(SyntaxKind.StaticKeyword))))
            {
                _candidates.Add(classSyntax);
            }
        }
    }
}
```

The code implements the ISyntaxReceiver interface with the OnVisitSyntaxNode() method, which will be called on every AST node from the compiler. The purpose of MetricsSyntaxReceiver is to narrow down what classes are of interest for code generation. First, it filters down by requiring it to be a class, then it looks as if the class is partial and static. The last filter is to look for any members of the class, looking for static partial methods. If all of the criteria are met, it will add the class to a candidate list.

With the receiver filtering down, it's time for the generator itself to be set up. Next to the MetricsSyntaxReceiver.cs file, add a file called MetricsSourceGenerator.cs. Add the following code to it:

```
using Microsoft.CodeAnalysis;
using Microsoft.CodeAnalysis.CSharp.Syntax;
using Roslyn.Extensions.Templates;

namespace Roslyn.Extensions.Metrics;

[Generator]
public class MetricsSourceGenerator : ISourceGenerator
{
    public void Execute(GeneratorExecutionContext context)
    {
    }

    public void Initialize(GeneratorInitializationContext
      context)
    {
        context.RegisterForSyntaxNotifications(() => new
          MetricsSyntaxReceiver());
    }
}
```

The code creates a class called MetricsSourceGenerator, which implements the ISourceGenerator interface with its Execute() and Initialize() methods. For the generator to work, you also have to add the [Generator] attribute. In the Initialize() method, the code registers the syntax receiver you put in.

In the Execute() method is where all the magic will happen. Let's start by adding the following to the body of the Execute() method:

```
if (context.SyntaxReceiver is not MetricsSyntaxReceiver
  receiver) return;

var counterAttribute = context.Compilation
    .GetTypeByMetadataName("Fundamentals
      .Metrics.CounterAttribute`1");
```

```
foreach (var candidate in receiver.Candidates)
{
    var templateData = new MetricsTemplateData
    {
        Namespace = (candidate.Parent as
          BaseNamespaceDeclarationSyntax)!.Name.ToString(),
        ClassName = candidate.Identifier.ValueText
    };
    var semanticModel = context.Compilation
      .GetSemanticModel(candidate.SyntaxTree);
    foreach (var member in candidate.Members)
    {
        if (member is not MethodDeclarationSyntax method)
          continue;

        var methodSymbol = semanticModel
          .GetDeclaredSymbol(method);
        if (methodSymbol is not null)
        {
            var attributes = methodSymbol.GetAttributes();
            var attribute = attributes.FirstOrDefault(_ =>
            SymbolEqualityComparer.Default.Equals
              (_.AttributeClass?.OriginalDefinition,
              counterAttribute));
            if (attribute is not null)
            {
                // Generate
            }
        }
    }

    if (templateData.Counters.Count > 0)
    {
        var source = TemplateTypes.Metrics(templateData);
        context.AddSource($"{candidate.Identifier
          .ValueText}.g.cs", source);
    }
}
```

The code is expecting `SyntaxReceiver` to be `MetricsSyntaxReceiver`; if it's not, it's just returned. Then, it goes on to get an instance of the type definition for the `CounterAttribute` type. Notice the name is a little strange; `CounterAttribute'1`. This is because the type is a generic type and internally in .NET, the type will get the postfix with a number of saying the number of generic arguments it has.

For all the candidates `MetricsSyntaxReceiver` has found, the code loops through and sets up a `MetricsTemplateData` instance for the class. It then gets what is known as the semantic model based on the syntax tree of the class. The semantic model in Roslyn provides a deeper understanding of the meaning of code beyond its syntax. It can be used for tasks such as name binding, type checking, error checking, and automated refactoring.

Classes have members and the code walks through all the members and filters and skips those that are not methods. From the semantic model, it gets the declared symbol of the method, which lets us nicely access the attributes on it. It then looks for `CounterAttribute`.

At the very end, it generates the source code from the template, but only if there are any counters to generate for. It provides the source code by using the `AddSource()` method provided by `GeneratorExecutionContext`. The convention for generated files is to include the type name and then postfix it with `.g.cs`.

For the generator to kick in, it needs the counters. Add the following code to the `Execute()` method, replacing the `// Generate` comment:

```
var tags = method.ParameterList.Parameters.Select(parameter
  => new CounterTagTemplateData
{
    Name = parameter.Identifier.ValueText,
    Type = parameter.Type!.ToString()
});

var type = attribute.AttributeClass!.TypeArguments[0]
      .ToString();
var name = attribute.ConstructorArguments[0].Value!
      .ToString();
var description = attribute.ConstructorArguments[1].Value!
      .ToString();

templateData.Counters.Add(
        new CounterTemplateData
        {
            Name = name,
            Description = description,
            Type = type,
            MethodName = method.Identifier.ValueText,
            Tags = tags
        });
```

The code gathers the information from the attribute and method information to provide the data the template needs.

That is pretty much it for the generator to work. Since we're leaning on the setup done in *Chapter 15, Roslyn Compiler Extensions*, all we now need to do is start using it.

Test driving the source generator

To get the Chapter16 code compiled and working, follow these steps:

1. First, you need to add a reference to the Fundamentals project:

    ```
    dotnet add reference ../Fundamentals/Fundamentals.csproj
    ```

2. Then, you need a reference to the Roslyn.Extensions project. This needs to be a little bit different since you want it to automatically use the generator. Add a ProjectReference in the Chapter16.csproj file next to the reference to the Fundamentals project, looking like the following:

    ```
    <ProjectReference Include="..\Roslyn.Extensions\
      Roslyn.Extensions.csproj" OutputItemType="Analyzer"
        ReferenceOutputAssembly="false" />
    ```

    This instructs the reference to use the analyzer and not include any of its assemblies in the output of Chapter16.

3. To start using the new way of doing metrics, you'll need to change the EmployeeController class. Open the EmployeeController.cs file in the Chapter16 folder and change the Register() method to look like the following:

    ```
    [HttpGet]
    public IActionResult Register()
    {
        EmployeesControllerMetrics.RegisteredEmployees
            (DateOnly.FromDateTime(DateTime.UtcNow));

        return Ok();
    }
    ```

    The code now uses the new partial class instead of dealing with the counter and tags itself.

4. Perform a build on the Chapter16 project:

    ```
    dotnet build
    ```

Within the `obj` folder, you can now see the result of the source generator:

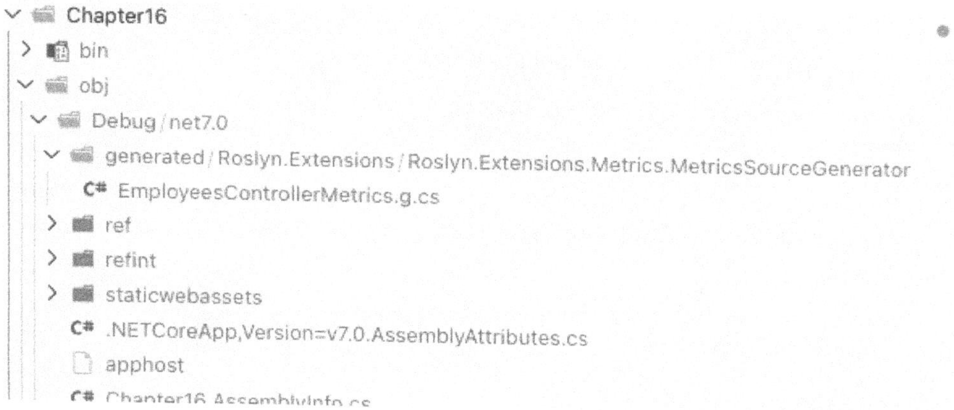

```
∨  📁 Chapter16
  >  📁 bin
  ∨  📁 obj
    ∨  📁 Debug / net7.0
      ∨  📁 generated / Roslyn.Extensions / Roslyn.Extensions.Metrics.MetricsSourceGenerator
          C# EmployeesControllerMetrics.g.cs
      >  📁 ref
      >  📁 refint
      >  📁 staticwebassets
          C# .NETCoreApp,Version=v7.0.AssemblyAttributes.cs
          📄 apphost
          C# Chapter16.AssemblyInfo.cs
```

Figure 16.1 – Generated file in the filesystem

5. Open `EmployeesControllerMetrics.g.cs` and confirm you have the expected result:

```csharp
using System.Diagnostics;
using System.Diagnostics.Metrics;
using Fundamentals.Metrics;

namespace Chapter16;

#nullable enable

public static partial class EmployeesControllerMetrics
{
    static readonly Counter<int> RegisteredEmployees
  Metric = GlobalMetrics.Meter.CreateCounter
    <int>("RegisteredEmployees", "# of registered
      employees");

    public static partial void RegisteredEmployees
      (DateOnly date)
    {
        var tags = new TagList(new ReadOnlySpan
          <KeyValuePair<string, object?>>(new
            KeyValuePair<string, object?>[]
        {
            new("date", date)
        }));

        RegisteredEmployeesMetric.Add(1, tags);
```

```
        }
    }
```

6. Run your project and then start the monitor by running this:

    ```
    dotnet counters monitor -n Chapter16 --counters
    Chapter16
    ```

7. And then trigger the API by using a browser and navigating to the endpoint (for example, `http://localhost:5000/api/employees`). You should see an output similar to the following:

    ```
    Press p to pause, r to resume, q to quit.
        Status: Running

    [Chapter16]
        RegisteredEmployees (# of registered employees / 1
          sec)
            date=5/1/2023                    0
    ```

This technique can be very powerful. More types of metrics can be supported and extended, giving you a more intuitive and simple way of working with metric values.

Adding source code that gets compiled is very powerful and you are not limited to adding just partial classes; you can in fact add anything you want, which can be super useful. That being said, you're not just limited to outputting source files for the compiler. You can produce other artifacts as well.

(Ab)using the compiler to generate not just C# code

Since you can basically do anything within the code generator, you could go and generate anything else. One of the things we use it for in my day-to-day work is to generate TypeScript files from our C# code. This is super useful and we save a lot of time and gain consistency in the TypeScript, in line with the REST APIs in C#.

Let's go and do something that doesn't end up in a C# file. Based on the `Fundamentals` project in the GitHub repository and what you have built so far in the book, you should have a namespace called `Fundamentals.Compliance.GDPR` and an attribute called `PersonalIdentifiableInformation`, which was introduced in *Chapter 5, Leveraging Attributes*.

This attribute is great for marking types that collect **Personally Identifiable Information** (**PII**) as well as the reason for collecting PII. In *Chapter 5, Leveraging Attributes*, we used it at runtime to create a runtime report. What we could instead do is create this report at compile time.

Add a file in the `Chapter16` folder called `Employee` and make it look like the following:

```
using Fundamentals.Compliance.GDPR;
```

```
namespace Chapter16;

public record Employee(
    [PersonalIdentifiableInformation("Needed for
      registration")]
    string FirstName,

    [PersonalIdentifiableInformation("Needed for
      registration")]
    string LastName,

    [PersonalIdentifiableInformation("Needed for uniquely
      identifying an employee")]
    string SocialSecurityNumber);
```

The Employee type has its properties annotated with the [PersonalIdentifiableInformation] attribute, declaring the specific reason for collecting the information. This is what we want to output in a GDPR report saying which types have members that hold PII.

Building the generator

In order for our generator to know where to output the resulting file, it will need a configurable property. The current directory when running in the context of the compiler will be the path where the compiler sits and typically a place you don't have write access to write to. Besides, it is not very useful to write files at a random location.

Generators can have properties that get configured in the .csproj files. For them to be visible to the generator, you need to tell the compiler that the property should be visible. To do this, open the Roslyn.Extensions.props file, which you should have in the Roslyn.Extensions folder, and add an ItemGroup within the Project tag that looks like the following:

```
<ItemGroup>
    <CompilerVisibleProperty Include="GDPRReport"/>
</ItemGroup>
```

Then, in the Chapter16.csproj file in the Chapter16 folder, you will need to add a reference to the props file. Add the following at the top of the file within the Project tag:

```
<Import Project="$(MSBuildThisFileDirectory)../
  Roslyn.Extensions/Roslyn.Extensions.props"/>
```

Then, within PropertyGroup, you need to add the following:

```
<GDPRReport>$(MSBuildThisFileDirectory)GDPRReport.txt</GDPR
  Report>
```

This configures the GDPRReport variable to point to the folder of the Chapter16.csproj file and then adds GDPRReport.txt to the path.

As you did with the metrics source generator, you'll need a syntax receiver for filtering the candidates.

Create a folder called GDPR in the Roslyn.Extensions project and add a file called GDPRSyntaxReceiver.cs. Make the file look like the following:

```
using Microsoft.CodeAnalysis;
using Microsoft.CodeAnalysis.CSharp.Syntax;

namespace Roslyn.Extensions.GDPR;

public class GDPRSyntaxReceiver : ISyntaxReceiver
{
    readonly List<TypeDeclarationSyntax> _candidates =
      new();

    internal IEnumerable<TypeDeclarationSyntax> Candidates
      => _candidates;

    public void OnVisitSyntaxNode(SyntaxNode syntaxNode)
    {
        if (syntaxNode is not TypeDeclarationSyntax
          typeSyntax) return;
        _candidates.Add(typeSyntax);
    }
}
```

The filter for this syntax receiver is a simple one. It's interested in syntax nodes that are types. This would include classes and records.

Now you need the source generator. Add a file called GDPRSourceGenerator.cs alongside the GDPRSyntaxReceiver.cs file and add the following to it:

```
using Microsoft.CodeAnalysis;
using Microsoft.CodeAnalysis.CSharp.Syntax;

namespace Roslyn.Extensions.GDPR;

[Generator]
public class GDPRSourceGenerator : ISourceGenerator
{
    public void Execute(GeneratorExecutionContext context)
    {
        if (context.SyntaxReceiver is not
```

```
        GDPRSyntaxReceiver receiver) return;

    context.AnalyzerConfigOptions.GlobalOptions
      .TryGetValue("build_property.GDPRReport", out var
        filename);

    var writer = File.CreateText(filename);
    writer.AutoFlush = true;

    var piiAttribute = context.Compilation
    .GetTypeByMetadataName("Fundamentals.Compliance
    .GDPR.PersonalIdentifiableInformationAttribute");
}

public void Initialize(GeneratorInitializationContext
  context)
{
    context.RegisterForSyntaxNotifications(() => new
      GDPRSyntaxReceiver());
}
}
```

The code sets up the basics for the source generator and also sets up the initials for the `Execute()` method. It will only perform the job if `SyntaxReceiver` is `GDPRSyntaxReceiver`. Next, it goes and gets the `GDPRReport` variable from config. All values are prefixed with `build_ property` for the ones coming from the build. It then goes on to create the report file before it gets the `PersonalIdentifiableInformationAttribute` type for filtering later.

Continue the `Execute()` method with the following code:

```
foreach (var candidate in receiver.Candidates)
{
    var semanticModel = context.Compilation
      .GetSemanticModel(candidate.SyntaxTree);

    var symbols = new List<ISymbol>();

    if (candidate is RecordDeclarationSyntax record)
    {
        foreach (var parameter in record.ParameterList!
          .Parameters)
        {
            var parameterSymbol = semanticModel
              .GetDeclaredSymbol(parameter);
            if (parameterSymbol is not null)
            {
```

```
                    symbols.Add(parameterSymbol);
                }
            }
        }

        foreach (var member in candidate.Members)
        {
            if (member is not PropertyDeclarationSyntax
                property) continue;

            var propertySymbol = semanticModel
                .GetDeclaredSymbol(property);
            if (propertySymbol is not null)
            {
                symbols.Add(propertySymbol);
            }
        }
    }
}
```

The code looks at the candidates from the syntax receiver. If the candidate is a record, it enumerates the parameters of it and adds them as a symbol of interest. It then goes on to walk through the members of the candidate, adding them as a symbol of interest.

Now that you've collected all symbols of interest, it's time to filter down only the symbols that are annotated with the PersonalIdentifiableInformation attribute.

Within the candidates foreach loop, add the following at the end:

```
var memberNamesAndReasons = new List<(string MemberName, string
Reason)>();

foreach (var symbol in symbols)
{
    var attributes = symbol.GetAttributes();
    var attribute = attributes.FirstOrDefault(_ =>
        SymbolEqualityComparer.Default.Equals(
            _.AttributeClass?.OriginalDefinition,
            piiAttribute));
    if (attribute is not null)
    {
        memberNamesAndReasons.Add((symbol.Name,
            attribute.ConstructorArguments[0].Value!
            .ToString()));
    }
}
```

```
if (memberNamesAndReasons.Count > 0)
{
    var @namespace = (candidate.Parent as
      BaseNamespaceDeclarationSyntax)!.Name.ToString();
    writer.WriteLine($"Type: {@namespace}
      .{candidate.Identifier.ValueText}");
    writer.WriteLine("Members:");
    foreach (var (memberName, reason) in
      memberNamesAndReasons)
    {
        var reasonText = string.IsNullOrEmpty(reason) ? "No
          reason provided" : reason;
        writer.WriteLine($"   {memberName}: {reasonText}");
    }

    writer.WriteLine(string.Empty);
}
```

The code iterates the symbols by looking at any attributes. If the symbol has the [Personal
IdentifiableInformation] attribute, it's added to the memberNamesAndReason list.

If there are members in the memberNamesAndReason list, it outputs the type and the members
with the reason.

Now, you can build your application (in the Chapter16 folder):

dotnet build

You should now see a file called GDPRReport.txt in your project folder. Open it and confirm that
you're seeing something similar to the following:

```
Type: Chapter16.Employee
Members:
  FirstName: Needed for registration
  LastName: Needed for registration
  SocialSecurityNumber: Needed for uniquely identifying an
    employee
```

Having this level of transparency in your code and the ability to show it to official auditors is great. It
shows you have control over compliance and this will ultimately help you in the long run. You could
also version this file by simply adding it to your source code repository and then during release builds,
you could commit any changes to it.

It is different to work with extending the compiler itself, it is a somewhat different runtime environment from what you'd expect in normal application development. You've probably already started asking how to debug and might have experienced your code not working even though it should have.

Improving the developer experience

Working with the Roslyn compiler can be hard. After all, it's running inside the context of the compiler. One way to ease the pain is to do unit testing and actually test all your code from tests, something we will look into more in *Chapter 17, Static Code Analysis*.

Debugging

However, sometimes, you just simply need to see things with your bare eyes through the debugger. The technique I use for this is to add the following code into my Roslyn extension code:

```
while (!System.Diagnostics.Debugger.IsAttached)
    Thread.Sleep(10);
```

Then, I can put breakpoints for the places at which I want to break and then attach the debugger. You want to attach it to the compiler and it typically shows up like the following:

```
dotnet 5608
VBCSCompiler.dll -pipename:Lun2X+71zJcK+oOxL0zg8291WixFLGXxWR0Hju6iJgU
```

Figure 16.2 – Compiler process to attach to caching

Another thing that can be painful is if you're doing changes in the extension and these are not reflected. There are a couple of reasons why this might be the case. One is that it doesn't see any changes during an incremental build in the project using the extension. You can clean the build output by doing the following:

```
dotnet clean
```

Otherwise, you can run the build telling it to not perform an incremental build as follows:

```
dotnet build --no-incremental
```

Another condition that could occur is that compiler holds a build server in memory that caches things and optimizes the developer experience. Sometimes, you need to shut it down. You do that by issuing the following:

```
dotnet build-server shutdown
```

Optimization

A form of optimization that can be applied to source generators is to use the incremental source generator approach. It combines the syntax receiver and generator and runs consistently while the build server is running, providing code generation as you type in the editor (for editors that support it).

Working with the compiler can be a bit tedious, but is totally worth it when you get everything working.

Summary

In this chapter, we explored how to leverage Roslyn compiler extensions for generating code at compile time. We looked at the basics of generating additional code for the compiler. We also looked at how you can leverage the Roslyn source generators to generate files other than C#, which is a powerful technique that can increase productivity and also provide true business value.

You should now have an understanding of what C# code generators are and how you can implement one. And hopefully, you also have a few ideas brewing of what you can use it for.

As I mentioned in the chapter, we use the compiler's extensibility and ability to generate code to actually generate TypeScript code. This has proven to be a major productivity boost for our developers. There are some code generators already out there that take OpenAPI definitions and convert them into JavaScript or TypeScript, but they're then limited to what this standard supports. And if you want it to be in a certain shape, or support a specific frontend framework, that might not be enough. We had these requirements and then decided on building an extension that supports our needs.

In the next chapter, we'll take things a step further and explore how to use Roslyn compiler extensions for static code analysis. As you might have picked up thus far, I tend to focus on code quality. Coming up, we'll explore how to build custom code analyzers and code fixes, and we'll see how these tools can be used to automatically detect and correct coding issues.

17

Static Code Analysis

In today's software development world, I believe it's more important than ever to write clean and maintainable code. The increasing complexity of software, lower retention in the workforce, and increased competition should lead us to standardize our way of writing software more and put the next developer in the pit of success coming into the codebase. Catching errors early is super important when the developers have it in their mind, preferably. One of the ways to achieve this is through the use of static code analysis, which allows developers to identify potential issues and bugs in their code before it is even executed. With the Roslyn compiler extensions in C#, developers have the ability to create custom analyzers and code fixes that can help automate this process.

In this chapter, we'll explore the basics of static code analysis and how to use Roslyn compiler extensions to write your own analyzers and code fixes. We'll cover everything from the fundamentals of writing an analyzer to create automated tests to ensure that your code is working as intended.

Whether you're a seasoned developer looking to improve your code quality or a newcomer to the world of static code analysis, this chapter will provide you with the tools and knowledge you need to get started with Roslyn compiler extensions and take your code analysis to the next level.

- What is static code analysis?
- How to write an analyzer
- How to write a code fix for an analyzer
- How to write automated tests

By the end of this chapter, you should have a solid understanding of how to use Roslyn compiler extensions to implement static code analysis in C#. You should be able to write your own custom analyzers and code fixes and know how to create automated tests to ensure the correctness of their implementation. Additionally, you should have a good understanding of the benefits of static code analysis and how it can improve the overall quality and maintainability of their code. With this knowledge, you will be well equipped to apply static code analysis techniques in your own development projects, leading to more efficient and effective software development.

Technical requirements

The source code specific to the chapter can be found on GitHub (`https://github.com/PacktPublishing/Metaprogramming-in-C-Sharp/tree/main/Chapter17`), and it builds on top of the `Fundamentals` code that is found on GitHub (`https://github.com/PacktPublishing/Metaprogramming-in-C-Sharp/tree/main/Fundamentals`). It also leverages the `Roslyn.Extensions` code that is found in the GitHub repository (`https://github.com/PacktPublishing/Metaprogramming-in-C-Sharp/tree/main/Roslyn.Extensions`).

What is static code analysis?

Static code analysis is a powerful technique for detecting issues and bugs in your code before it's even executed. While it may seem like a relatively new development, the truth is that static code analysis has been around for decades and has been used in languages such as C/C++ through tools such as linters.

Linters are essentially static code analysis tools that analyze source code to flag suspicious constructs or style inconsistencies. They have been around for several decades and are widely used in languages such as C/C++ to improve code quality and maintainability.

In recent years, static code analysis has gained more popularity with the rise of languages such as JavaScript and TypeScript. Tools such as ESLint have been developed to provide similar benefits to JavaScript and TypeScript developers by analyzing code for potential issues and providing feedback on best practices.

The .NET Compiler **Software Development Kit** (**SDK**) from Microsoft takes a comprehensive approach to extending the compiler. Rather than just focusing on expanding its functionality, the SDK also enables the code to identify potential issues within your code editor or **Integrated Development Environment** (**IDE**). This feature is supported by popular editors, including **Visual Studio Code** (**VSCode**), Rider, and Visual Studio. As you work with files, the editors run analyzers in the background, highlighting potential issues with squiggly underlines. These analyzers can flag code that is incorrect or could be improved, providing real-time feedback to help you catch and correct mistakes more efficiently.

Alongside analyzers, Microsoft has introduced code fixers, a feature that enables analyzer vendors to provide code that can automatically fix flagged code issues. These code fixes are represented by light bulbs within the editor, and you can click on them to execute the code fix. With this feature, you can quickly and easily apply fixes to your code and improve its overall quality.

In the following sections, we will provide an overview of static code analysis and code fixes in the context of the C# compiler and how they work. Although we won't delve into the subject in great depth, we'll provide you with the necessary information to get started. It's important to note that the C# compiler APIs are extensive and offer great possibilities, and this introduction will serve as a starting point for exploring these features.

Let's dive into writing an analyzer.

How to write an analyzer

Writing an analyzer that gets automatically run as part of the compile process has been made very simple by Microsoft. It follows the same principles as source generators, as we saw in *Chapter 16, Generating Code*. Once you have the project set up, as we did back in *Chapter 15, Roslyn Compiler Extensions*, it's all about dropping in a class that represents the analyzer.

In this chapter, all code assumes you have the `Roslyn.Extensions` project that we established in *Chapter 15, Roslyn Compiler Extensions*.

The analyzer we're going to make is a highly opinionated one that affects the naming of exception types. One of the things we tend to do is to suffix our types with what they technically represent; for instance, exceptions are often suffixed with `Exception`. Looking at exceptions found in the .NET base class libraries, you'll see things such as `NotImplementedException`, `ArgumentException`, or `ArgumentNullException`. This is something I personally don't like, and I believe that it is not important information to communicate, and we should instead put effort into properly naming the types for what they do.

Take `ArgumentException` as an example. Its name does not convey its purpose. By simply changing it to be called `InvalidArgument`, it communicates that there is a violation – *the argument is invalid*.

You might not agree with this type of rule in your code base. But let's set aside that for a minute and just use this as an example.

Fleshing out an analyzer

Let's start by creating a home for the analyzer. In the `Roslyn.Extensions` project, add a folder called `CodeAnalysis`. I like to have folders for every analyzer type since we might be providing code fixes for the analyzer, and we might want to have more than just the analyzer class to create the analyzer. With that as a principle, add a folder within the `CodeAnalysis` folder called `ExceptionShouldNotBeSuffixed`; this will be the name of the analyzer.

In `ExceptionShouldNotBeSuffixed`, you can now add a file called `Analyzer.cs`. Put the following into the file:

```
using System.Collections.Immutable;
using Microsoft.CodeAnalysis;
using Microsoft.CodeAnalysis.CSharp;
using Microsoft.CodeAnalysis.CSharp.Syntax;
using Microsoft.CodeAnalysis.Diagnostics;

namespace Roslyn.Extensions.CodeAnalysis
  .ExceptionShouldNotBeSuffixed;

[DiagnosticAnalyzer(LanguageNames.CSharp)]
```

```
public class Analyzer : DiagnosticAnalyzer
{
}
```

The code sets up the basics for an analyzer by inheriting the `DiagnosticAnalyzer` type from the **.NET Compiler SDK**. In addition to this, it adorns the class with an `[DiagnosticAnalyzer]` attribute, instructing it that the supported language is C#. All the `using` statements are for the code to come.

> **Important note**
> Analyzers can support multiple languages by specifying the additional languages it supports. It can, however, affect the complexity of your analyzer as there are differences in how the **abstract syntax tree (AST)** is represented.

For the analyzer to work and be hooked up, it needs to be configured properly and register any actions that should be called.

Add the following method to the `Analyzer` class:

```
public override void Initialize(AnalysisContext context)
{
    context.EnableConcurrentExecution();
    context.ConfigureGeneratedCodeAnalysis
        (GeneratedCodeAnalysisFlags.None);
    context.RegisterSyntaxNodeAction(
        HandleClassDeclaration,
        ImmutableArray.Create(
            SyntaxKind.ClassDeclaration));
}
```

The code calls `EnableConcurrentExecution()` on the `AnalysisContext` passed, which informs the compiler that your analyzer can be executed concurrently with other analyzers in an asynchronous manner. If your analyzer does not support concurrent execution, you can simply omit this call. If your analyzer does support concurrent execution, it can help to speed up your builds, making your development process more efficient. Next, it configures whether or not your analyzer should be run on generated code. The analyzer you're building now should not care about generated code; it is therefore configured to ignore it.

Lastly, the code registers an action to be run on syntax nodes. A **syntax node** is a fundamental unit of the AST, as we looked at in *Chapter 16, Generating Code*, and corresponds to a specific syntactic construct, such as a method call, a loop statement, or a class declaration. Syntax nodes are represented as objects in memory and are linked together in a tree-like structure that mirrors the structure of the source code.

In our case, we're only interested in class declarations; it therefore registers a `HandleClassDeclaration` callback with `SyntaxKind.ClassDeclaration`.

When an analyzer encounters a problem, it needs to produce a response to the compiler that tells there is an issue, and it should be reported back to the developer. The representation of the issue is formalized into something called `DiagnosticDescriptor`. You need to create specific ones of these for every specific broken rule you get.

Add the following to the top of the `Analyzer` class:

```
public const string DiagnosticId = "PP0001";

public static readonly DiagnosticDescriptor BrokenRule =
  new(
        id: DiagnosticId,
        title: "ExceptionShouldNotBeSuffixed",
        messageFormat: "The use of the word 'Exception'
        should not be added as a suffix - create a well
        understood and self explanatory name for the
        exception",
        category: "Naming",
        defaultSeverity: DiagnosticSeverity.Error,
        isEnabledByDefault: true,
        description: null,
        helpLinkUri: string.Empty,
        customTags: Array.Empty<string>());

public override ImmutableArray<DiagnosticDescriptor>
  SupportedDiagnostics => ImmutableArray.Create
    (BrokenRule);
```

The code establishes a custom `DiagnosticDescriptor` that holds a reference to a unique diagnostic identifier (`PP0001`), a title, and a message to display to the developer. It also puts the broken rule into a category (`Naming`). Since the category is a string, this could be anything, but there are a few well-known ones used by other analyzers, such as **Naming**, **Design**, **Correctness**, **Performance**, and **Documentation**. The categories are used by tools to let developers group warnings or errors in a codebase. In the descriptor, you also put the severity level for the broken rule. The levels are shown in this table:

Level	Description
Hidden	Not surfaced through normal means
Info	Information that does not indicate a problem
Warning	Suspicious but allowed; the developer should just know about it
Error	Not allowed; the build will be broken

> **Important note**
>
> If the developer using your analyzer decides to use the `TreatWarningsAsErrors` option in the `.csproj` file, the warnings will be treated as errors and break the build. The `Roslyn.Extension.props` file that is included in projects using this extension has that option turned on.

The last few properties of `DiagnosticDescriptor` are further details to help the developers understand the compiler error or warning you want to communicate. You could, for instance, include a link to a web page describing in detail the analyzer or the specific rule you have implemented.

Handling the syntax nodes

For the analyzer to work, you're going to need an implementation of the `HandleClassDeclaration` callback that was given during the `Initialize` method. Add the following private method to the `Analyzer` class:

```
void HandleClassDeclaration(SyntaxNodeAnalysisContext
  context)
{
    var classDeclaration = context.Node as
      ClassDeclarationSyntax;
    if (classDeclaration?.BaseList == null ||
      classDeclaration?.BaseList?.Types == null)
        return;

    var classSymbol = context.SemanticModel
      .GetDeclaredSymbol(classDeclaration);
    if (classSymbol?.BaseType is null) return;

    var exceptionType = context.Compilation
      .GetTypeByMetadataName("System.Exception");
    if (SymbolEqualityComparer.Default.Equals
      (classSymbol?.BaseType, exceptionType) &&
        classDeclaration.Identifier.Text
          .EndsWith("Exception", StringComparison
          .InvariantCulture))
    {
        var diagnostic = Diagnostic.Create(BrokenRule,
          classDeclaration.Identifier.GetLocation());
        context.ReportDiagnostic(diagnostic);
    }
}
```

The code starts by looking at the syntax node being analyzed. The syntax node would typically be things such as a method declaration, a class definition, or a variable declaration. Syntax nodes are used to represent the structure of the code but do not convey information about the meaning or semantics of the code.

The code assumes the syntax node is a `ClassDeclarationSyntax` node, as that was what was configured as a filter in the `Initialize()` method. It then looks at the `BaseList` property to see whether the class declaration inherits from another type. If it doesn't, the analyzer is not interested in the node, as it only wants to analyze types that inherit from `Exception`.

For the analyzer to understand the semantic meaning of the node being passed, it has to use `SemanticModel` to do so. From the declared symbol, it makes sure it has a base type; if not, it just returns.

Next, the code asks for a representation of the `System.Exception` type, which is then used to check if `BaseType` is, in fact, an exception. If it is an exception, it then checks the class identifier to see whether it is suffixed with the `Exception` text. If it is suffixed, it then reports back with an instance of the broken rule that holds the location of the class declaration identifier that was wrong.

That is pretty much it for creating a simple analyzer.

Release tracking

Suppose you go and build the `Roslyn.Extensions` project, you will get a warning that looks something like the following:

```
MSBuild version 17.5.1+f6fdcf537 for .NET
  Determining projects to restore...
  All projects are up-to-date for restore.
/Users/einari/Projects/Metaprogramming-in-C/
Roslyn.Extensions/CodeAnalysis/ExceptionShouldNotBeSuffixed
/Analyzer.cs(15,10): warning RS2008: Enable analyzer
release tracking for the analyzer project containing rule
'PP0001' [/Users/einari/Projects/Metaprogramming-in-C/
Roslyn.Extensions/Roslyn.Extensions.csproj]
  Roslyn.Extensions -> /Users/einari/Projects/
Metaprogramming-in-C/Roslyn.Extensions/bin/
Debug/netstandard2.0/Roslyn.Extensions.dll

Build succeeded.

/Users/einari/Projects/Metaprogramming-in-C/
Roslyn.Extensions/CodeAnalysis/ExceptionShouldNotBeSuffixed
/Analyzer.cs(15,10): warning RS2008: Enable analyzer
release tracking for the analyzer project containing rule
'PP0001' [/Users/einari/Projects/Metaprogramming-in-
```

```
C/Roslyn.Extensions/Roslyn.Extensions.csproj]
    1 Warning(s)
    0 Error(s)

Time Elapsed 00:00:00.52
```

The RS2008 warning tells you that we could add information to our project that would make it easier to track releases of your packaged analyzers and the rules it provides. If this is not important to you, you can ignore this warning and move on.

To satisfy the warning, we need to provide two files. One that contains the shipped rules and one that contains the unshipped rules. For an initial release, the unshipped rules file would typically be empty, while you might be putting in unshipped rules as part of releases for rules that are upcoming. When the rules are shipped, you typically move these from unshipped to shipped.

You can read more detail about the purpose of these files on GitHub (https://github. com/dotnet/roslyn-analyzers/blob/main/src/Microsoft.CodeAnalysis. Analyzers/ReleaseTrackingAnalyzers.Help.md).

Let's add a file in the root of the Roslyn.Extensions project called AnalyzerReleases. Shipped.md and add the following content to it:

```
## Release 1.0

### New Rules

Rule ID | Category | Severity | Notes
--------|----------|----------|--------------------
PP0001  | Naming   | Error    |
```

The content indicates a release version of 1.0 and provides a table of rules. In your case, you only have one rule. The Notes column could hold the name of the analyzer and, if you'd like, a link to a description of the broken rule.

With the shipped file in place, you'll need a file for unshipped. Add a file called AnalyzerReleases. Unshipped.md. This file can be empty at this point, so just leave it as is.

When packaging your Roslyn extension as a NuGet package, you want the files to be included. Open the Roslyn.Extensions.csproj file and add the following at the bottom of the file, within the Project tag:

```
<ItemGroup>
    <AdditionalFiles Include="AnalyzerReleases.Shipped.md" />
    <AdditionalFiles Include="
    AnalyzerReleases.Unshipped.md" />
</ItemGroup>
```

That's it! Your analyzer is now ready to be put into the real world and used.

Trying out the analyzer

To test the analyzer and see that it works and performs the way we expect it to, you'll need a project that has code that violates the rule put into the analyzer:

1. Create a new folder, next to the `Roslyn.Extensions` folder called `Chapter17`. Within the `Chapter17` folder in a terminal, create a new project:

    ```
    dotnet new console
    ```

2. Then you need a reference to the `Roslyn.Extensions` project. The project reference can not be a standard project reference; it needs to be slightly different. Add the following within the `Project` tag of the `Chapter17.csproj` file:

    ```
    <ItemGroup>
        <ProjectReference Include="..\Roslyn.Extensions\
          Roslyn.Extensions.csproj" OutputItemType=
            "Analyzer" ReferenceOutputAssembly="false" />
    </ItemGroup>
    ```

    By telling it that `OutputItemType` is `Analyzer`, it will automatically hook up the assembly output from the `Roslyn.Extensions` project to the compiler. `ReferenceOutputAssembly` set to `false` tells it that the compiled output of the project will not reference the output assembly of the `Roslyn.Extensions` project.

3. Since your `Roslyn.Extensions` project should, at this point in time, be holding the **General Data Protection Regulation** (**GDPR**) solution built in *Chapter 16*, *Generating Code*, and it has a requirement of a configuration property to be present, you'll need to add the following within a `PropertyGroup` tag in the `Chapter17.csproj` file:

    ```
    <GDPRReport>$(MSBuildThisFileDirectory)GDPRReport.txt
      </GDPRReport>
    ```

4. Then, in the `Chapter17.csproj` file in the `Chapter17` folder, you will need to add a reference to the props file from the `Roslyn.Extensions` project. Add the following at the top of the file within the `Project` tag:

    ```
    <Import Project="$(MSBuildThisFileDirectory)
      ../Roslyn.Extensions/Roslyn.Extensions.props"/>
    ```

5. In the `Chapter17` folder, add a file called `MyException.cs` and add the following to it:

    ```
    namespace Chapter17;

    public class MyException : Exception
    ```

```
    {
    }
```

6. Open your terminal and do a build, you should see something like the following:

```
MSBuild version 17.5.1+f6fdcf537 for .NET
  Determining projects to restore...
  All projects are up-to-date for restore.
  Roslyn.Extensions -> /Users/einari/Projects/
Metaprogramming-in-C/Roslyn.Extensions/bin/Debug/
netstandard2.0/Roslyn.Extensions.dll
/Users/einari/Projects/Metaprogramming-in-C/
Chapter17/MyException.cs(3,14): error PP0001: The use
of the word 'Exception' should not be added as a
suffix - create a well understood and self explanatory
name for the exception [/Users/einari/Projects/
Metaprogramming-in-C/Chapter17/Chapter17.csproj]

Build FAILED.

/Users/einari/Projects/Metaprogramming-in-C/
Chapter17/MyException.cs(3,14): error PP0001: The use
of the word 'Exception' should not be added as a
suffix - create a well understood and self explanatory
name for the exception [/Users/einari/Projects/
Metaprogramming-in-C/Chapter17/Chapter17.csproj]
      0 Warning(s)
      1 Error(s)

Time Elapsed 00:00:01.81
```

The output clearly says that you have a PP0001 error, and the text describes the actual problem.

This is pretty cool, but what's even cooler is that in your editor, you should get a clear indication that you have an error by getting a squiggly line underlining the MyException class name. In **Visual Studio Code** (**VS Code**), this would look like the following:

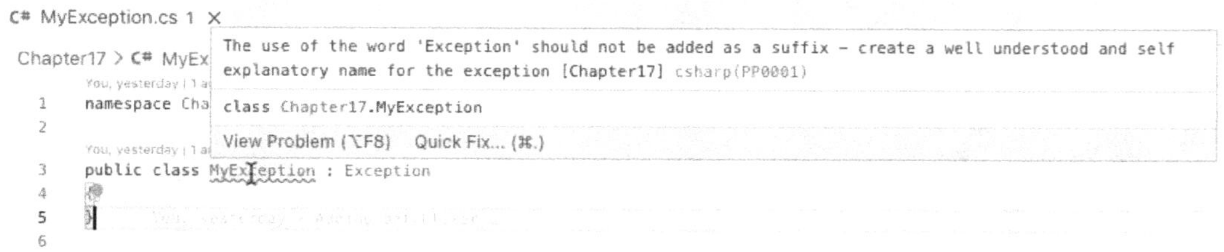

Figure 17.1 – VS Code analysis error

> **Important note**
>
> If you're having trouble getting your editor to show the analyzer error, you might need to restart it, or if it has a language server, just restart that. For VS Code, you can simply bring up the command palette (*F1*) and type OmniSharp and then select **OmniSharp: Restart OmniSharp**.

With an analyzer in place, it's time to look into making your developers more productive so that they can fix errors quite easily.

How to write a code fix for an analyzer

As discussed earlier, the .NET Compiler SDK supports more than just writing analyzers that analyze your code. You can also provide code that quickly fixes any errors that occur. These are understood by most editors and IDEs and will automatically be loaded and presented when applicable.

You'll be reusing the `Roslyn.Extensions` project for the code fix as well. The code fix needs to tap into specific APIs and needs another package reference. Add a reference to `Microsoft.CodeAnalysis.CSharp.Workspaces` by running the following in your terminal within the `Roslyn.Extensions` folder:

```
dotnet add package Microsoft.CodeAnalysis.CSharp.Workspaces
```

With the package reference in place, it's time for the implementation of the code fix:

1. Start by adding a file called `CodeFix.cs` within the `CodeAnalysis/ExceptionShouldNotBeSuffixed` folder in the `Roslyn.Extensions` project folder. Add the following to it:

    ```
    using System.Collections.Immutable;
    using System.Composition;
    using Microsoft.CodeAnalysis;
    using Microsoft.CodeAnalysis.CodeActions;
    using Microsoft.CodeAnalysis.CodeFixes;
    using Microsoft.CodeAnalysis.CSharp;
    using Microsoft.CodeAnalysis.CSharp.Syntax;

    namespace Roslyn.Extensions.CodeAnalysis
      .ExceptionShouldNotBeSuffixed;

    [ExportCodeFixProvider(LanguageNames.CSharp, Name =
      nameof(CodeFix))]
    [Shared]
    public class CodeFix : CodeFixProvider
    {
    }
    ```

The code sets up a code fix by inheriting from the `CodeFixProvider` and adding the `[ExportCodeFixProvider]` attribute. It specifies the language it supports and the name of the code fix. As with the analyzer, you can support multiple languages by specifying that on the attribute. If you want, you can narrow down the document types you want to support and also file extensions by setting the `DocumentKinds` or `DocumentExtensions` properties of `ExportCodeFixProvider`. We leave these as default, as we trust the editor to call us correctly.

2. For the code fix to be invoked, it needs to specify what broken rule it can fix. This is done by providing an array of the rule diagnostic identifier. Add the following within the `CodeFix` class:

```
public override ImmutableArray<string>
  FixableDiagnosticIds => ImmutableArray.Create
    (Analyzer.DiagnosticId);
```

3. With the broken rule association in place, the next thing you'll need is a method that registers the code fix and the code to be called when the code fix is invoked. Add the following method to the `CodeFix` class:

```
public override Task RegisterCodeFixesAsync
  (CodeFixContext context)
{
    var diagnostic = context.Diagnostics[0];
    context.RegisterCodeFix(
        CodeAction.Create(
            title: "Remove Exception suffix",
            createChangedDocument: c =>
                RemoveSuffix(context.Document,
                    diagnostic, c)),
        diagnostic);

    return Task.CompletedTask;
}
```

The code assumes there is only one `Diagnostic` that can be errored. This is because there is only one in the analyzer. If you have more, you'd need to find the correct diagnostic and match the appropriate code fix to it. However, for maintainability, I would recommend having one file per code fix linked to one broken rule.

4. Next, the code registers a code fix for the diagnostic; it does so by creating a `CodeAction` that holds a title to display the code fix and the callback to be called when the code fix is invoked by the developer.

All code fix providers can fix single problems, but they can also fix multiple by providing `FixAllProvider`. This is something you can choose to implement yourself if it needs special handling or use the default `BatchFixer`. Add the following method to provide

FixAllProvider. This is completely optional; by default, it does not provide any:

```
public override FixAllProvider?
  GetFixAllProvider() => WellKnownFixAllProviders
    .BatchFixer;
```

5. The last thing you'll need is the code that performs the code fix. The only fix you can really do is to provide code that removes the suffix. Add the following code to the CodeFix class:

```
async Task<Document> RemoveSuffix(Document document,
  Diagnostic diagnostic, CancellationToken c)
{
    var root = await document.GetSyntaxRootAsync(c);

    if (!(root!.FindNode(diagnostic.Location
      .SourceSpan) is ClassDeclarationSyntax node))
        return document;
    var newName = node.Identifier.Text.Replace
      ("Exception", string.Empty);
    var newRoot = root.ReplaceNode(node,
      node.WithIdentifier(SyntaxFactory.Identifier
        (newName)));
    return document.WithSyntaxRoot(newRoot);
}
```

The code navigates the document and finds the ClassDeclarationSyntax node. If it can't find it, the code fix does not do anything. It then replaces the Exception text in the Identifier of the node with string.Empty and then replaces the node. It then returns a modified version of the document with the modified node.

Important note

Since this code fix is a very simple one, it does not leverage much of the APIs available for code fixes. An important aspect of code fixes is to be aware of formatting and make sure the result is formatted correctly. This is done by adding .WithAdditionalAnnotations(Formatter.Annotation) on the node when altering it.

This is all you need to do for a simple code fix to work. All you now need to do is compile it and open a file that violates the rule. In your case, that would be the MyException.cs file within the Chapter17 folder.

Editors do this slightly differently, but within VS Code, the code fix capability would show up as a lightbulb, and clicking the lightbulb would then show the Remove Exception suffix code fix:

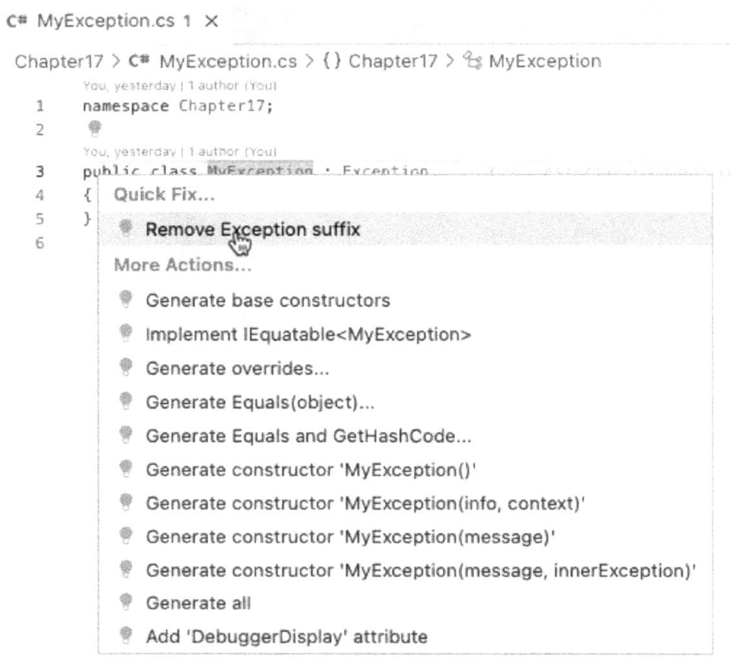

Figure 17.2 – VS Code code fix

Important note

If you're having trouble getting your editor to show the code fix, you might need to restart it, or if it has a language server, just restart that. For VS Code, you can simply bring up the command palette (*F1*) and type `OmniSharp` and then select **OmniSharp: Restart OmniSharp**.

Testing your analyzer and code fix with the compiler and an editor does not give you the best feedback loop, and as with any code you write, it would be hard to catch regression bugs.

How to write automated tests

Writing automated tests for all your code gives you the confidence to change your code and know whether you broke anything. This applies to all code, including analyzers and code fixes. For anything that extends the compiler or provides editors or IDEs with new capabilities, it's also harder to test whether or not your implementation works. It can be frustrating at times to get things working and can hamper your productivity by building these.

Luckily, Microsoft has provided an easy way to test your analyzers and code fixes:

1. Next to the `Roslyn.Extensions` folder, create a folder called `Roslyn.Extensions.`
    `Tests`. In a terminal, navigate to the `Roslyn.Extensions.Tests` folder and run
    the following:

    ```
    dotnet new xunit
    ```

    The command will set up a test project using the xUnit (`https://xunit.net`) testing library.

> **Important note**
> You can use other testing frameworks as well, such as MSTest or NUnit.

We will not cover unit testing or the specifics of xUnit. You can read more about xUnit on its site.

2. The next thing you'll need is a project reference to the `Roslyn.Extensions` project. Run
    the following command within the `Roslyn.Extensions.Tests` folder:

    ```
    dotnet add reference ../Roslyn.Extensions
    ```

    This adds a project reference to the `Roslyn.Extensions` project, and you may notice that
    you did this differently than with the `Chapter17` project. The reason is that in the context of
    testing, you need the `Roslyn.Extensions` assembly to be referenced by the test assembly
    and be present at the runtime of the tests.

Analyzer tests

With the test project in place and the reference to the extension project itself, we can start filling it with
the tests we want. The first thing you want to write a test for is the analyzer. The purpose of the tests
for the analyzer is to verify that the analyzer will give an error when the code contains an exception
that is suffixed and not give an error when exception types do not have a suffix.

Add a folder called `ExceptionShouldNotBeSuffixed` within the `Roslyn.Extensions.`
`Tests` folder. Then add a file called `AnalyzerTests`. Put the following content into it:

```
namespace Roslyn.Extensions.CodeAnalysis
  .ExceptionShouldNotBeSuffixed;

using Xunit;
using Verify = Microsoft.CodeAnalysis.CSharp.Testing
  .XUnit.AnalyzerVerifier<Analyzer>;

public class AnalyzerTests
{
}
```

This sets up the basics needed for writing the tests. You're probably asking yourself why the namespace
declaration comes before the `using` statements. We're doing that to avoid having to use the fully qualified
name in `Verify` using an alias. The `Verify` alias creates an alias for the `AnalyzerVerifier<>`

generic type and gives it the analyzer under test as a generic parameter. The aliasing is just for convenience, making your tests easier to read and write.

Also, another slightly different thing is the word `Tests`, which the `Roslyn.Extensions.Tests` project name is suffixed with, which is normally something you would also reflect in the namespace. Personally, I prefer not to, as test projects are not something you're deploying, and it generally makes things simpler if you omit this from your namespace. But that is entirely a personal preference.

The first thing you want to test is whether the analyzer is analyzing the correct code. Add the following method to the `AnalyzerTests` class:

```
[Fact]
public async Task WithoutSuffix()
{
    const string content = @"
            using System;

            namespace MyNamespace;
            public class SomethingWentWrong : Exception
            {
            }
        ";

    await Verify.VerifyAnalyzerAsync(content);
}
```

The test sets up a valid C# program and calls the `VerifyAnalyzerAsync()` method for that program.

Then you need a test for testing the violation of the rule. Add the following method to the `AnalyzerTests` class:

```
[Fact]
public async Task WithSuffix()
{
    const string content = @"
            using System;

            namespace MyNamespace;
            public class MyException : Exception
            {
            }
        ";

    var expected = Verify.Diagnostic().WithLocation(5,
      30).WithArguments("MyException");
    await Verify.VerifyAnalyzerAsync(content, expected);
}
```

The test sets up an invalid C# program and sets up an expectation of a failure at line 5 and column 30. Since you're putting in the content of the file this way, the first line will be empty, and the column is also then the column you see in the editor, which should be 30 with the method indented. You could improve this by embedding files as embedded resources that you could then maintain separately and have a more predictable setup for. The `VerifyAnalyzerAsync()` method is then called with the content and the expectations.

That's the tests we want to perform for the analyzer at this point. But we do also have a code fix for the analyzer.

Code fix tests

As with the analyzer, you can create tests specific to code fixes. It uses a different verifier than the analyzer: `CodeFixVerifier`. Let's get started:

1. Add a file called `CodeFixTests` within the `ExceptionShouldNotBeSuffixed` folder in the `Roslyn.Extensions.Test` project folder. Then add a file called `CodeFixTests.cs` and add the following content to it:

```
namespace Roslyn.Extensions.CodeAnalysis
  .ExceptionShouldNotBeSuffixed;

using Xunit;
using Verify = Microsoft.CodeAnalysis.Csharp
  .Testing.XUnit.CodeFixVerifier<Analyzer, CodeFix>;

public class CodeFixTests
{
}
```

As you did with the analyzer tests, you used a verifier. For code fixes, it is a different type of verifier: `CodeFixVerifier`.

The `CodeFixVerifier` verifier needs two generic arguments, the first one representing the analyzer and the second representing the code fix being tested.

2. Add the following test method to the `CodeFixTests` class:

```
[Fact]
public async Task WithoutSuffix()
{
    const string content = @"
        using System;

        namespace MyNamespace;
        public class SomethingWentWrong :
          Exception
```

```
                {
                }
        ";

        await Verify.VerifyCodeFixAsync(content, content);
}
```

The code verifies that the code fix does not perform any actions when the C# program is a valid program that doesn't break the rule.

3. Next, you need a test that verifies the code fix actually performs what is expected. Add the following method to the `CodeFixTests` class:

```
[Fact]
public async Task WithSuffix()
{
    const string content = @"
            using System;

            namespace MyNamespace;
            public class MyException : Exception
            {
            }
        ";

    var expected = Verify.Diagnostic().WithLocation(5,
      30).WithArguments("MyException");
    await Verify.VerifyCodeFixAsync(content, expected,
      content.Replace("MyException", "My"));
}
```

As with the analyzer test for the broken rule scenario, it sets up an expectation that there should be a compiler error at a specific location. Additionally, it then verifies that the code fix actually replaces the `MyException` text by removing the suffix.

4. With tests for both the analyzer and the code fix in place, you can run these by running the following in your terminal within the `Roslyn.Extensions.Tests` folder:

```
dotnet test
```

You should then see something like the following:

```
Microsoft (R) Test Execution Command Line Tool Version
17.5.0 (arm64)
Copyright (c) Microsoft Corporation. All rights
reserved.

Starting test execution, please wait...
```

```
A total of 1 test files matched the specified pattern.

Passed!  - Failed:      0, Passed:      4, Skipped:
0, Total:      4, Duration: 522 ms - Roslyn.Extensions
.Tests.dll (net7.0)
```

If you are using an editor that supports xUnit tests, chances are they are already visible in the test explorer of your editor, and you can run them from there as well.

For a full overview of the `Microsoft.CodeAnalysis.Testing` project, I recommend heading over to GitHub (`https://github.com/dotnet/roslyn-sdk/blob/main/src/Microsoft.CodeAnalysis.Testing/README.md`).

Summary

In this chapter, we've covered the use of Roslyn compiler extensions for performing static code analysis in C#. We began by explaining what static code analysis is and how it differs from dynamic analysis, as well as its benefits and limitations. We then covered how to write custom analyzers using Roslyn, using diagnostics to report issues, and implementing code fixes to automatically correct issues.

We also discussed best practices for testing and maintaining code analysis tools, as well as how to build rules that are specific to your team and domain. Catching errors fast is crucial for minimizing development time and cost, and static code analysis is a powerful tool for achieving this. By detecting issues and bugs in your code before it's even executed, you can avoid costly mistakes and improve overall code quality and maintainability.

You should now have a solid understanding of how to use Roslyn for static code analysis in C#, as well as the benefits and challenges of this approach. You should also understand how to write effective analyzers and code fixes and how to build custom rules for their specific team and domain.

Static code analysis is a powerful technique for catching errors quickly and improving overall code quality and maintainability. By building custom rules that are specific to your team and domain, you can ensure that your code is not only error-free but also conforms to your team's standards and practices. This can save time and resources that would otherwise be spent on debugging and testing, allowing you to deliver higher-quality software faster.

This chapter concludes the practical sides of the book, and the next and final chapter will cover general caveats and some final words about everything discussed in the book.

18
Caveats and Final Words

Congratulations, you've made it to the last chapter of this book on metaprogramming in C#! By now, you should have a solid understanding of the various techniques and tools that are available to you when it comes to doing metaprogramming with C#.

In this final chapter, we'll take a step back and look at some of the bigger-picture implications of metaprogramming in C#. We'll explore some of the performance implications of metaprogramming, and we'll discuss some best practices for handling the hidden magic that can come with these powerful techniques.

Finally, we'll wrap up the book with a summary of everything we've covered so far and some closing remarks, hoping to inspire you as you continue on your journey as a metaprogrammer in C#. So let's dive in and explore the exciting world of metaprogramming one last time!

Performance implications

One of the most important things to keep in mind when working with metaprogramming in C# is its potential impact on performance. When it comes to metaprogramming in C#, there are a few key performance implications to keep in mind:

1. **Additional runtime overhead**: Metaprogramming typically involves additional runtime overhead compared to traditional programming techniques. This is because it often involves dynamic code generation or manipulation, which can require extra processing time and memory usage. For example, if you use reflection to dynamically invoke methods or access properties, this can be slower than calling the method or property directly.

2. **Increased memory usage**: Metaprogramming can also lead to increased memory usage, especially if you're generating or manipulating objects dynamically. This can result in higher memory usage, or even memory leaks if you're not careful. For example, if you're using reflection to dynamically generate new types or objects, this can result in additional memory usage that may not be released until the garbage collector runs.

3. **Potential for suboptimal code**: Metaprogramming can also lead to suboptimal code in some cases, especially if you're not careful. For example, if you're using dynamic code generation to generate code on the fly, this can lead to suboptimal code that is hard to optimize at compile time. This can result in slower execution times and increased runtime overhead.

To mitigate these performance implications, it's important to keep a few best practices in mind:

1. **Use metaprogramming sparingly**: Metaprogramming should only be used when it provides clear benefits over traditional programming techniques. If the benefits are unclear or marginal, it may be better to avoid metaprogramming altogether.

2. **Test your metaprogramming code thoroughly**: Metaprogramming code can be harder to test than traditional code, so it's important to thoroughly test your metaprogramming code to ensure that it's working as expected.

3. **Optimize your metaprogramming code as needed**: If you find that your metaprogramming code is impacting performance, it may be necessary to optimize it as needed. For example, you may need to refactor your code to use more efficient algorithms or data structures, or you may need to avoid certain metaprogramming techniques that are known to be slow.

4. **Consider using caching**: If your metaprogramming code generates or manipulates objects frequently, you may want to consider using caching to reduce runtime overhead and memory usage. This can involve caching generated types or objects or using a tool such as Expression Trees to generate compiled code that can be cached for reuse.

By keeping these best practices in mind, you can minimize the performance implications of metaprogramming in C# and ensure that your code is both flexible and performant.

Hidden magic – handle with care

Metaprogramming in C# can be a powerful tool, but it also comes with some hidden risks. One of the biggest dangers of metaprogramming is its potential to make code hard to understand and maintain. Because metaprogramming often involves dynamic code generation or manipulation, it can be difficult to trace and debug and may lead to unexpected behavior if not used carefully. Additionally, metaprogramming code can be hard to read and comprehend, especially if it involves complex reflection or dynamic code generation. To avoid these issues, it is important to use metaprogramming judiciously and only when it provides clear benefits, such as increased flexibility or reduced boilerplate code.

When it comes to metaprogramming in C#, there are several techniques that can be considered *hidden magic*. These are techniques that can seem deceptively simple but can have complex and potentially unexpected behavior. Here are some examples of hidden magic in metaprogramming:

1. **Reflection**: Reflection is a powerful tool that allows you to inspect and manipulate objects at runtime. However, it can also be complex and error-prone if not used carefully. For example, if you use reflection to access private fields or methods, this can lead to unexpected behavior or even break your code if the underlying implementation changes.

2. **Dynamic**: The `dynamic` keyword in C# allows you to write code that defers binding until runtime, which can be useful for metaprogramming scenarios. However, it can also be difficult to reason about and can lead to subtle bugs if not used carefully. For example, if you use `dynamic` to call a method that doesn't exist, this can result in a runtime error that may be difficult to debug.

3. **Code generation**: Code generation is a powerful technique that allows you to generate C# code dynamically, either at runtime or at design time. However, it can also be error-prone and lead to subtle bugs if not used carefully. For example, if you generate code that contains syntax errors or is otherwise invalid, this can cause compilation errors that may be difficult to diagnose.

To handle hidden magic with care, it's important to keep a few best practices in mind:

1. **Understand the underlying mechanics**: Before using any metaprogramming technique, it's important to understand the underlying mechanics and potential pitfalls. This can involve reading documentation, studying sample code, or consulting with experts in the field.

2. **Test thoroughly**: Metaprogramming code can be difficult to test, but it's important to thoroughly test your code to ensure that it's working as expected. This can involve writing unit tests, integration tests, or other types of tests as needed.

3. **Use defensive coding techniques**: To guard against unexpected behavior, it's important to use defensive coding techniques such as input validation, error handling, and defensive programming practices.

4. **Document your code**: Finally, it's important to document your metaprogramming code carefully to ensure that other developers can understand how it works and use it effectively. This can involve writing clear and concise comments, providing examples and sample code, and maintaining up-to-date documentation as your code evolves.

By keeping these best practices in mind, you can handle hidden magic with care and ensure that your metaprogramming code is robust and maintainable.

When to use what

Knowing when to use which metaprogramming technique in C# is crucial for writing effective and maintainable code. Some common use cases for metaprogramming include the following:

1. **Reducing boilerplate code**: Metaprogramming can help reduce the amount of repetitive, boilerplate code you need to write by generating it dynamically at runtime.

2. **Enabling dynamic behavior**: Metaprogramming can make your code more dynamic and flexible, allowing you to modify behavior at runtime or add new functionality on the fly.

3. **Supporting code generation**: Metaprogramming can help you generate code dynamically based on input data or other factors, allowing you to create more complex and customized code structures.

However, there are also cases where metaprogramming should be avoided, such as the following:

1. **When performance is critical**: As discussed earlier, metaprogramming can introduce runtime overhead and impact performance. In cases where performance is critical, it may be better to avoid metaprogramming altogether or use it sparingly.

2. **When readability is important**: Metaprogramming can make code hard to read and understand, especially if it involves complex reflection or dynamic code generation. In cases where readability is important, it may be better to stick with more traditional code structures.

3. **When the benefits are unclear**: As mentioned earlier, metaprogramming should only be used when it provides clear benefits over traditional programming techniques. If the benefits are unclear or marginal, it may be better to avoid metaprogramming altogether.

Summary

In this book, we've explored the exciting world of metaprogramming in C#. We've seen how metaprogramming techniques can help us write more flexible, powerful, and maintainable code, and we've learned about the various tools and techniques that are available to us.

We've seen how reflection can be used to inspect and manipulate objects at runtime, how code generation can help us generate code dynamically, and how the `dynamic` keyword can be used to write code that defers binding until runtime. We've also explored some of the pitfalls and challenges associated with metaprogramming, and we've learned how to handle hidden magic with care by following best practices such as testing, defensive coding, and documentation.

As you finish this book, I hope that you're inspired by the power and potential of metaprogramming in C#. Metaprogramming can be a powerful tool in the hands of a skilled developer, allowing you to write code that is more flexible, more maintainable, and more powerful than you ever thought possible.

So, go forth and explore the exciting world of metaprogramming! Experiment with different techniques, try new things, and push the boundaries of what's possible. And remember, as with any powerful tool, with great power comes great responsibility. Always use metaprogramming with care, following best practices and taking the time to understand the underlying mechanics.

Thank you for reading this book. I hope that it has been a valuable resource on your journey to becoming a master of metaprogramming in C# and helps you remember to let your code work for you.

Index

Symbols

.NET Compiler Platform SDK
  reference link 255
.NET Compiler SDK 300
.NET runtime 14
.NET SDK
  prerequisites 26
  reference link 26

A

Abstract Syntax Trees (ASTs) 270, 271, 300
action filter 33
  reference link 33
analyzers 256, 299-302
  code fix, writing for 307-310
  releases, tracking 303, 304
  syntax nodes, handling 302, 303
  testing 305, 306
  writing 299
analyzer tests 311-313
API
  testing 141-143

aspect-oriented programming
  (AOP) 225, 226
  aspect 226
  join points 227, 228
  logging 228
  pointcuts 226
ASP.NET 7, 25
ASP.NET controllers 26, 27
  creating 29
  custom HTTP Get handler 27, 28
ASP.NET Core
  authorization, setting for controllers based
    on metadata or structure in 212-223
ASP.NET Core 6 26
ASP.NET MVC 25
ASP.NET pipeline
  CommandResult 203-212
  consistent result objects, building 201-203
  leveraging 201
ASP.NET validation 30-33
  model state handling 33, 34
Assembly
  discovery, in running process 40, 41
assembly language 6

attributes 18, 19, 55
  applying 55-57
  class, sealing 59
  usage, limiting 57-59
authentication 5
authorization 5, 245, 246
  pointcuts, using 246-252
  setting, for controllers in ASP.
    NET Core 218-223
  setting, for controllers in ASP.NET Core
    based on metadata or structure 212-217
automated tests
  writing 310, 311

B

backend code 5
behavior-driven design (BDD) style 22
Binary Expression 95
Binary JSON (BSON) objects 16
binders 121
bitwise OR construct 58

C

C# 3.0 90
C# 11 64
call site 121
Castle Project 229
  URL 229
Castle Windsor
  reference link 226
C/C++ 6
C# code
  generator, building 289-294
  Roslyn compiler, abusing to
    generate not just 288, 289
C# compiler 42, 255

code fix
  writing, for analyzer 307-310
code fix providers 256
code fix tests 313-315
code, reasoning 3, 4
  automation 5
  developer concerns 4, 5
  metaprogramming 5, 6
CommandResult 203-212
Common Language Runtime (CLR) 118, 238
  assembly management 119
  automatic memory management 118
  cross-language interoperability 118
  debugging 119
  exception, handling 118
  just-in-Time (JIT) compilation 118
  profiling 119
  reflection 119
  type safety 118
  versioning 119
consistent result objects
  building 201-203
C# parses 14
Cratis 10
  URL 182
Create, Read, Update, Delete (CRUD) 182
cross-cutting concerns 200, 201, 225
cURL 26
custom attributes
  creating 19-21
custom HTTP Get handler 27, 28

D

Dapper 16
data modeling 5
deferred execution 90
dependency inversion principle 149

developer experience, Roslyn compiler
  debugging 294
  improving 294
  optimization 295
DevOps 5
domain-specific language (DSL) 21, 22
  Gherkin 22, 23
dynamic assembly 68
  creating 68-73
Dynamic Language Runtime (DLR) 118
  binders 121
  blocks, building 119
  call site 121
  Common Language Runtime (CLR) 118
  dynamic code generation 119-121
  dynamic type, reasoning 121-124
  dynamic type system 119
  methods, dynamic dispatching 119
Dynamic Link Library (DLL) file 14
dynamic module
  creating 68-73
DynamicObject
  creating 124
dynamic type
  reasoning 121-124

E

ECMA-335 14
ESLint 6
evaluation stack 72
event store 182
expressions 90-94
  creating 104, 105
  creating, as delegates 105, 106
  executing 105, 106

  tree, traversing 95-98
  using, as descriptors of members
    on types 98-101

F

frontend code 5
functional programming (FP) 226

G

**General Data Protection Regulation
    (GDPR) 19, 51, 234, 263, 305**
  infrastructure, using 174
generator
  building 289-294
generic attributes 64-66
get operation 130
Gherkin 22, 23

H

Handlebars
  URL 277

I

ildasm 14
INotifyPropertyChanged interface
  implementing 78-80
instances discovery
  encapsulating 165, 166
**Integrated Development Environment
    (IDE) 242, 298**
interceptors 232-235
  testing 235-238

interface
  implementing 75, 77
  NotifyObjectWeaver class 77, 78
interface, NotifyObjectWeaver class
  initialization API 85, 86
  INotifyPropertyChanged interface,
    implementing 78-80
  OnPropertyChanged method 80-82
  properties, overriding 82-85
  public API 85, 86
  type, creating 78
  using 86-88
Intermediate Language code (IL-code) 14
Intermediate Language (IL) 40, 67, 68, 118
introspection 40
inversion of control container
    (IoC container) 149
Inversion of Control (IoC) 138, 229
  API, testing 141-143
  code, refactoring 143
  module, building for registering
    users 138-140
  role 138
Inversion of Control (IoC), code
  contract oriented 147-149
  controller, modifying 145-147
  services, creating 143-145

J

JavaScript 6
JetBrains dotPeek 14
JetBrains Rider
  reference link 26
join points 227

join points, examples
  exception handling 227
  field access 227
  method calls 227
JSON schema type
  building 125-127
  getting and setting properties,
    implementing 129-131
  properties, validating 127, 128
  schema infrastructure, using 131-133
Just-in-Time (JIT) compilation 118

L

lambda expression 94, 95, 114
Language-Integrated Query (LINQ) 46, 90
library metadata, leveraging to obtain
    referenced assemblies 41
  business app 45, 46
  reusable fundamentals 42-44
lint 6
linters 298
logging 228
  creating 229, 230
  Microsoft logger, adding 230-232

M

manual structure and process, code
  generating 8-10
  removing 7
  software, maintaining 8
  time safety, compiling 10, 11
metadata 6
  providing 124
metaprogramming 3-6

metaprogramming, C#
best practices, for handling
hidden magic 319
best practices, for mitigating
performance implications 318
code generation 319
dynamic 319
hidden magic 318
performance implications 317, 318
reflection 318
use cases 319
metaprogramming, concepts
attributes 18, 19
implicit 14, 15
power of reflection, leveraging 15-17
metaverse 3
method signature conventions 181-184
infrastructure 185-193
infrastructure, using 194-198
Microsoft logger
adding 230-232
Microsoft's Entity Framework 16
mixins 238, 239
benefits 245
implementing 239-245
model state handling 33, 34
module
building, for user registrations 138-140
MongoDB 107, 108
MongoDB C# Driver 16

N

NHibernate 16
NotifyObjectWeaver class 77, 78
NuGet 41
URL 264

O

object-oriented programming (OOP) 226
OnPropertyChanged method 80-82
op-code 68
open-closed principle 53
goal 162, 163
OpenTelemetry
URL 271
opt-out model 88

P

**Personal Identifiable Information
(PII) 19, 60-64**
**Personally Identifiable Information
(PII) 51, 168, 288**
pointcut expression 246
pointcut language 246
pointcuts 226, 246
using 246-252
Postman
reference link 26
**practical use case, open-closed
principle 167-169**
developer, helping with 170-172
GDPR infrastructure, using 174-177
providers, adding 178-180
supporting properties 172-174
providers
adding 178

Q

query engine
building 108-115
creating 106, 107
MongoDB 107, 108
query operation
distinct parts 90

R

recipe-driven development 7
Reflection Emit 67, 68
representational state transfer
(REST) API 200
Roslyn 252
Roslyn compiler
abusing, to generate not just
C# code 288, 289
additional code, generating 270
Roslyn compiler, additional code
application metrics 271-275
ASTs 270, 271
code template, setting up 277-281
developer experience, improving 275, 276
extensibility points 270
source code generator, building 282-286
source generator, test driving 286-288
Roslyn compiler, extensions 255, 256
analyzer 265, 266
common package properties 264, 265
common project settings 261, 262
common rules, adding 259-261
packaging, for reuse 263
setting up 257-259

Roslyn compiler extensions, for
metaprogramming
code analysis 256
code generation 256
Domain-Specific Language
(DSL), creating 257
experimentation and innovation 257
tooling and productivity 257

S

security 5
Seq
reference link 230
Serilog
reference link 230
service collection
hooking up 166, 167
ServiceCollection, by convention
code, composing 154-158
code, refactoring 150-154
service registrations, automating 149, 150
Sharplab 68
software development kit (SDK) 298
source generators 256
SpecFlow
URL 23
specific attributes
types, finding with 60
SQL injection 4
SQL statements 16
static code analysis 298
syntax node 300
handling 302, 303

T

test-driven development (TDD) style 22
types
  business sample 47-49
  cross-cutting concerns 51-53
  discovering 46, 47
  discovery, encapsulating 163-165
  domains 49-51
TypeScript 6

U

Universal Windows Platform (UWP) 8
user experience 5

V

virtual
  members 74, 75
  overrides 74, 75
Visual Studio
  reference link 26
Visual Studio Code (VS Code) 298, 306
  reference link 26

W

Wget 26
Windows Presentation Foundation (WPF) 8

X

xUnit
  reference link 311

Packtpub.com

Subscribe to our online digital library for full access to over 7,000 books and videos, as well as industry leading tools to help you plan your personal development and advance your career. For more information, please visit our website.

Why subscribe?

- Spend less time learning and more time coding with practical eBooks and Videos from over 4,000 industry professionals

- Improve your learning with Skill Plans built especially for you

- Get a free eBook or video every month

- Fully searchable for easy access to vital information

- Copy and paste, print, and bookmark content

Did you know that Packt offers eBook versions of every book published, with PDF and ePub files available? You can upgrade to the eBook version at packtpub.com and as a print book customer, you are entitled to a discount on the eBook copy. Get in touch with us at customercare@packtpub.com for more details.

At www.packtpub.com, you can also read a collection of free technical articles, sign up for a range of free newsletters, and receive exclusive discounts and offers on Packt books and eBooks.

Other Books You May Enjoy

If you enjoyed this book, you may be interested in these other books by Packt:

Real-World Implementation of C# Design Patterns

Bruce M. Van Horn II

ISBN: 9781803242736

- Get to grips with patterns, and discover how to conceive and document them
- Explore common patterns that may come up in your everyday work
- Recognize common anti-patterns early in the process
- Use creational patterns to create flexible and robust object structures
- Enhance class designs with structural patterns
- Simplify object interaction and behavior with behavioral patterns